A Bibliography of Negro Migration

Frank Alex Ro
and
Louise Venable Kennedy

ISBN: 978-1-63923-790-6

Printed: March 2023

Published and Distributed By:
Lushena Books
607 Country Club Drive, Unit E
Bensenville, IL 60106
www.lushenabks.com

ISBN: 978-1-63923-790-6

"But now I am hungry. Dost thou hunt with me this dawn?" said Kaa.

The Second Jungle Book

Kipling has pictured for us the quests of the jungle folk. In fashion similar to theirs we salute our fellow sojourners in the thickets of social research with the familiar "Good hunting, all!"

PREFACE

This bibliography is the fifth volume produced under the project Negro Migration, conducted in the Department of Sociology at Columbia University, under subsidy by the Social Science Research Council, and the Columbia University Council for Research in the Social Sciences. The previous volumes, in order of appearance, are:

Kennedy, Louise Venable, *The Negro Peasant Turns Cityward*

Dutcher, Dean, *The Negro in Modern Industrial Society*

Lewis, Edward E., *The Mobility of the Negro*

Kiser, Clyde Vernon, *Sea Island to City*

The present authors are most appreciative of the financial aid and encouragement given by the Social Science Research Council, and the Columbia University Council for Research in the Social Sciences. They also realize their debt to those who have presided over, and participated in, the building up of the splendid files of the National Urban League, the Russell Sage Foundation, and the Division of Negro Literature of the One Hundred and Thirty-fifth Street Branch of the New York Public Library. Without these collections the bibliography would have been far less complete than it now is. Access to them, and aid in their use, have greatly facilitated its preparation. Finally, invaluable criticism and suggestion have been afforded by many, colored and white, who are interested in this important topic. To all these, the authors extend their thanks.

COLUMBIA UNIVERSITY
November 1, 1933

FRANK A ROSS
LOUISE V. KENNEDY

CONTENTS

INTRODUCTION

Among the materials of research available to the social scientist, the most important body is that of previous investigations made by others. Yet of all the materials, these have been most frequently slighted or neglected, since they are the most difficult to locate and to handle. The present authors, approaching the subject, Negro Migration, as a project under the joint subsidy of the Social Science Research Council and the Columbia University Council for Research in the Social Sciences, realized that considerable work had been done on this subject, but at the inception of the study had not the least glimmering of the extensiveness of the material available in earlier studies.

More or less haphazard measures soon unearthed a formidable number of documents, presenting a mass of unorganized data. Attempts to utilize existing bibliographies merely added to the confusion of material already found. It early became apparent that an extensive list of documents must be established, that there was needed some sort of digest of each document as it was found, and that these must be placed in useful order.

It was soon discovered that, to he of any use, the digest reference file must be all-inclusive, for even after the early beginnings had developed into fairly sizeable dimensions, new works of vital importance continued to crop up, convincing the workers that other important documents had not been discovered. In consequence, the task was undertaken of making the file as nearly complete as possible, and of keeping it up-to-date as new material appeared. It was therefore decided to establish a comprehensive, well-organized and annotated bibliographic file.

The library and manuscript facilities available were the collections of the New York Public Library Central Branch at Fifth Avenue and Forty-second Street, and the Special Division on Negro Literature of the One Hundred and Thirty-fifth Street Branch; the files of the National Urban League; the Library of the Russell Sage Foundation; and libraries at Columbia University.

As to procedure, recourse was had, not only to the general catalogues of these collections, but also to the several cumulative indexes of periodicals, government lists of publications, and various other reference indexes.[1] To the list of prospective titles set up in this fashion, there were added large numbers derived from bibliographies in the various books consulted. These were further supplemented by textual and footnote references in the documents read. Finally, in certain of the libraries, the entire shelves devoted to the Negro were examined volume by volume. Needless to say, careful examination was made of the indexes of all periodicals, reports and proceedings which at any stage were found to have yielded results warranting such search.[2]

While much interesting material exists in newspapers, this field has had to be ignored, except as exploration of other sources has brought to light occasional newspaper citations.

There are many collections of valuable material.[3] Only those located in New York were consulted. These are so comprehensive that it was felt to be highly improbable that reference to libraries and files outside of that city would yield important new titles of published material. Limited time and funds, as well as the demands of other lines of exploration, precluded an exhaustive search for unpublished manuscripts.

It soon became apparent that, if the material in the file were to be

[1] In detail these were: *Agricultural Index; Annual Literary Index; Art Index; Book Review Digest; Catholic Periodical Index; Catalogue of Public Documents of the United States*, July 1, 1895, to June 30, 1896; *Check List of United States Public Documents; Comprehensive Index to the Publications of the United States Government, 1881-1893; Comprehensive Index to the Publications of the United States Government, 1896-1921; Education Index; Engineering Index; Faxon, The Magazine Subject Index*; House Documents, 1893 to 1895; *Industrial Arts Index; International Index to Periodicals; Loyola Educational Index; Poole's Index; Public Affairs Information Service; Readers' Guide; Review of Reviews* [London] *Index to Periodicals*; Select References, Library of Congress; Senate Miscellaneous Documents, 1774 to 1881; *Social Science Abstracts; Subject Index to Periodicals*; Tables of, and Index to, Congressional Series of Public Documents United States Catalogues of Books in Print at various dates; United States Index to the Subjects of Documents and Reports; *United States Monthly Catalogue of Public Documents; United States Monthly List of State Documents.*

[2] Among these the most important were: *Crisis, Journal of Negro History, National Conference of Social Work Proceedings, Opportunity*, reports of certain state departments of education and labor, *Southern Workman, Survey.*

[3] Important among these are those of the following institutions Carnegie Institute of Technology at Pittsburgh; University of Pittsburgh; Branches of the National Urban League, particularly in Pittsburgh and Philadelphia (Armstrong Association), Chicago and Baltimore Philadelphia Housing Association; University of Chicago; Congressional Library at Washington Association for the Study of Negro Life and History.

usable by others than those individuals building up the file, some basic system for classifying the material in each of the citations must be created. In consequence, both a temporal and a functional classification was evolved. Digests of the material were indexed under each category, and page references to each of the works cited were listed, as the various books, papers and manuscripts were read. Finally, since for certain studies material was needed by localities, a geographical classification was instituted.

The bibliography has proved indispensable to those engaged on the project, or concerned with collateral studies. It also appears that others working in kindred fields on other aspects of the Negro problem, or on other phases of the migration problem, will find it of material aid. Problems, both of race and of migration, are increasing in importance, and much research remains to be done in these fields. It is felt that the present bibliography is both timely and a definite stride in facilitating research.

Those engaged on various other phases of Negro research will find the work a real aid. While it is in no way the intention of the compilers to claim that it is inclusive on all topics pertaining to the Negro,[4] they do feel that its intelligent and judicious use should save many hours of arduous labor to those interested in topics other than migration. It should be borne in mind, however, that the categories used in Part D were selected from the point of view of Negro migration, and that they are different from those that would have been chosen, had the central theme been discrimination,[5] or a similar topic.

Many uses for the bibliography suggest themselves, in addition to the usual purposes of such a work. It is apparent that not only will those engaged in elaborate researches find it a material convenience, but that those concerned with the organization of courses on race relations, with the preparation of special articles, or with suggesting theses for the master's degree or subjects for term papers, will find great aid. Each of the ultimate categories points out a line of useful exploration. Anyone wishing to arrange a reading list for personal or for classroom use, will find it valuable.

[4] The most exhaustive general bibliography on this subject is Monroe N Work's *Bibliography of the Negro in Africa and America*, New York, H W Wilson, 1928, 698 pp.

See Introduction to Part D, p. 197. Category headings and footnotes in the body of this section are designed to aid those approaching the bibliography with other points of view

It is urged that utilization of the present work be supplemented by reference to the Bibliographic Appendix in *The Negro Peasant Turns Cityward*, by Louise Venable Kennedy (New York, 1930, pp. 239-63), which contains references to some of the works used herein, similarly classified, and has the added advantage of giving specific page references.

Scope and Organization

This bibliography attempts to cover all books and journal articles, published in the continental United States since 1865, bearing directly or indirectly on the subject, Negro migration. It also includes large numbers of pamphlets and some multigraphed and typewritten manuscripts. In all, over three thousand titles have been looked up and read by the authors. From these, nearly thirteen hundred, pertinent to the general subject, have been selected, as being either of use to the future student in the field, or so conspicuous and at the same time of so little use as to warrant warning him against wasting his time with them.

The remaining thousands, forming, with the abstracts, a large mass of notes, repose in the file of the present authors. This file comprises three types of documents: (1) those bearing on migration or on the Negro, but not concerned with Negro migration; (2) those bearing on Negro migration, but of little value to the student of the subject and, at the same time, sufficiently obscure and unavailable to present little probability of the student's discovering them; and (3) those titles offering some promise of yielding worth-while material, which, on reading, proved of value neither in the general fields nor in the special subject.

Some users of the present bibliography will feel dissatisfied because of seeming omissions. Such must bear in mind that the authors have been forced to limit the number of titles included in the printed document, as well as its scope. In most cases where such apparent incompleteness exists, the document has probably been located, read and assigned to the residual file, because it seemed to belong in one of the three categories of that file, rather than in the printed bibliography itself.

The twelve hundred titles selected for printing in the bibliography, together with abstracts of their contents, are presented in Parts A, B, and C of this volume. The more accessible, primarily those that have been printed, supplemented by a few widely distributed mimeographed documents, are set forth alphabetically [6] by author and title, or by title

[6] Some users will be disappointed in not being able to locate all documents

alone, in Part A. United States Government Documents have been collected under "U3," and are in turn listed by author and / or title. A limited amount of cross-referencing has been resorted to. It is by no means complete, but experience has indicated that it is sufficiently so for the needs of the average trained research worker. Most of the references should be found in any large university or metropolitan public library.

Part B presents, in similar arrangement, unpublished material, *i.e.*, mimeographed, typewritten, and, in a very few instances, penned manuscripts, which have been located in New York City.[7] This list consists primarily of reports of original investigations, a few copies of which have been struck off, either for administrative or similar purposes, on the part of the surveying agencies; as masters' theses; or as doctoral dissertations. No attempt has been made to compile an exhaustive list. Neither funds nor time warranted such an attempt. However, both the National Urban League and the Russell Sage Foundation have tried to make their files complete, and it is felt that Part B contains the bulk of the significant documents extant, particularly since the most important have been published, either in whole or in part.

Part C contains significant bibliographies, published as such. It does not include any lists incorporated in books. It is expected that the reader of such books will find these himself.

Part D presents a classification of both Part A and Part B, for four periods, 1865-75, 1875-1900, 1900-15, and 1915 to date, and also according to a functional arrangement. It is probable that many readers will find the classification inadequate to their purposes. The system adopted is the one found convenient by those engaged on the project. It has the merit of subdividing the two lists into a usable number of

by title The presentation of an already large and intricate mass of material would have been greatly complicated had this been provided for. The users must know, for other than unsigned documents the name of the author of the work This can usually be obtained from library card indexes in the case of books from periodical guides in the case of articles or by intelligent though laborious use of the bibliography itself

[7] The files of the National Urban League contain the fullest collection of these Other accumulations are to be found at the Library of the Russell Sage Foundation; the New York Public Library Central Branch, and the One Hundred and Thirty Fifth Street Branch (Special Division on Negro Literture) · at Columbia University; and at the headquarters of the New York Urban League.

categories, specific enough to guide the user, yet sufficiently vague to assure comprehensiveness.

Part E contains the geographic classification of such items of Part A and Part B as contain original material of geographic significance. Mere mention of a locality has not seemed sufficient warrant for classification under this part. It consists, first, of a general class, dealing with the country as a whole, or with several states, or many cities; and second, of specific categories, either for states or for localities. No functional or temporal arrangement has been attempted in this part of the bibliography. Experience has shown that the use of Part E in conjunction with Part D is sufficient.

In addition to the above classifications of material, a general index listing authors, associations, and learned institutions mentioned as making studies of, or concerning themselves with, the Negro, has been added. In it are grouped all the works of any one author, or institution, together with references to them, throughout the text. In the latter, the reference may be by symbol only.

The Purposes of the Several Parts

Part A and Part B enable the research worker quickly to refer to all pertinent works of a single author,[8] or to any specific document, and afford a basis for judging the bearing of any particular work on various phases of the problem. Part D permits immediate reference to all the important material on any one of a variety of significant topics, and for each of the several periods. Part E collects for the research worker, all the material available for any definite locality. Each part has a definite organization within itself. Such organization is fully discussed in an introduction to each part. To this is added, where necessary, an exemplification of the way in which each part may be utilized.

Wherever the words "to date" are used, they should be taken to mean, in general, January 1, 1932. The bibliography includes all material published or, in the case of manuscripts, filed, by that date. The task of keeping the bibliography up-to-date has been most trying, particularly since, in many instances, works have been promised for publication, but have not yet been released. In consequence, the latest months may be

[8] Part A and Part B are distinct entities, and there is but limited cross-referencing between them. For works of a given author, see each part. See also introduction to Part A, p. 13, and introduction to Part B, p. 177.

incomplete. Furthermore, some important documents appearing in 1932 have been included. The authors do not feel, however, that this period has been adequately covered.

A "late list" has been added as Appendix I. It includes documents discovered after the manuscript was prepared for the printer, and after the inflexible numbering system needed for Part D and Part E had been finally set up. It also contains some items listed by title early in the study, but the location of which has eluded the most careful search.

With the exception of the last items mentioned, none has been included in this bibliography that has not been located and read. No hearsay title has been used. Many authors who cite documents in text or reading lists, have done so in slovenly fashion. In most instances, the citation has been traced and the correct reference established. In some instances, it has been impossible to identify the article, book or manuscript. The brief list of these — they number about fifty — is being kept as a separate part of the residual file.

Astonishing difficulties, too numerous to enumerate here, face the conscientious bibliographer. They not only involve locating the final elusive publication, but persist throughout the entire handling of any citation. A given reference may be designated in several different ways. It may take any one of many positions in an alphabetical list. It may merit classification under many or few of the categories. Many arbitrary decisions must be made, regarding nearly every document. Its very inclusion or elimination is arbitrary; its evaluation is arbitrary. Even the selection of the categories themselves is a personal matter, and subject to personal predilection. Finally, it is extremely difficult to be sure that a citation, after it has passed through the several stages of procedure and appears in print, is a true description.

This bibliography undoubtedly contains much of personal bias. There are sins of omission, as well as of commission, though every effort has been made to perfect it. One step should have been taken that could not be. Every citation should have been checked in galley proof to the original sources. This for many reasons has been impossible. However, the authors feel that only a minimum of blunders exists. They hope to receive criticisms and suggestions from users of the bibliography, and will appreciate having their attention called to errors.

BRIEF SELECTED READING LIST[9]

The following is offered as a general reading list for all students of the problem of Negro migration. It contains some indispensable background material, as well as the most necessary works within the field itself. It requires wide supplementation from the body of the bibliography.

American Academy of Political and Social Science, *The American Negro, Annals*, Vol. CXL.

Chicago Commission on Race Relations, *The Negro in Chicago.*

Johnson, Charles S., *The Negro in American Civilization.*

Kennedy, Louise V., *The Negro Peasant Turns Cityward*

Moton, Robert R., *What the Negro Thinks.*

Reuter, Edward B., *The American Race Problem.*

Scott, Emmett J., *Negro Migration During the War.*

Spero, Sterling D., and Abram L. Harris, *The Black Worker.*

Wesley, Charles H., *Negro Labor in the United States.*

Woodson, Carter G., *A Century of Negro Migration.*

——— *The Rural Negro.*

Woofter, Thomas J., Jr., *The Basis of Racial Adjustment.*

[9] For full citations see body of bibliography

Part A

PRINTED MATERIAL AND READILY ACCESSIBLE MIMEOGRAPHS

Part A

PRINTED MATERIAL AND READILY ACCESSIBLE MIMEOGRAPHS

Alphabetical List by Author and / or Title

The content of this portion of the bibliography is made up of all printed material of importance to the student of Negro migration and allied subjects. There are also included a few widely distributed and important mimeographed documents. Most items should be available in any large university or metropolitan public library.

The material is listed alphabetically, usually by author and title, or by title alone. In some instances, however, a document is entered in the alphabetical arrangement according to presidmg or publishing agency. This is done only where the authorship is not given, or where there is such multiple authorship as to make other types of entry confusing. In certain cases, the entry has been listed by the most generally used designation. United States Government Documents have been collected in a single place, and there alphabetized, as in the rest of the list.

All titles, except those for works issued by the United States Government, are preceded by a capital letter, a number, and a lower case letter in parentheses. The first of these is the initial of the name or word under which the document is listed. The number is the order of author or title in the subsequent alphabetization. The parenthetical letter is the distinguishing mark of the particular work in an alphabetization under author or publishing agency.

Thus, F21(h) is the specific designation for "The Negro Family" by E. Franklin Frazier: "F" being the initial letter of the author's name, there having been twenty other authors, or single titles without authors, preceding him in the alphabetical list under that initial, and this particular work being the eighth in an alphabetization of pertinent works by this author.

An exception is to be found in the case of United States Government Documents. The designation for each of these is "U3" followed in parentheses by a number as well as a letter. The number indicates author, agency or title-order; and the letter, alphabetical rank under such authorship.

A limited amount of cross referencing has been resorted to. It applies particularly where there is joint authorship, where there are reprintings of original publications in whole or in part, or where there is intimate relationship between documents to which attention should be called

The method of using this Part requires little explanation. Every pertinent work by a given author will be found in one of two places— in the general list or under United States Government Documents, and these latter are cross referenced in the general part. If the book or article were published over an author's name, or in the name of an agency, it is listed under such authorship; and the author's name must be known in order to locate the document. The exact title of all unsigned articles or reports must be known or lengthy search must be pursued. Books by joint authors are listed under the first signatory and are segregated from and follow the alphabetization of his independent productions.

In the interest of space conservation semipopular abbreviations of full titles of some publications have been used, such as *Annals*, for *Annals of the American Academy of Political and Social Science.* It is felt that all of these are sufficiently obvious to require no key.

A1 Abell, John B.

(a) "The Negro in Industry," *Trade Winds* (March, 1924), pp. 17-20.

A general discussion of the characteristics of migrants and their success in northern industry as shown by a résumé of the experience of manufacturing concerns in Cleveland Ohio. *See also* S45(a).

(b) "Southern Negro in Northern Industry," *Economic World*, XXVII, 620-22 (May 3, 1924).

Another printing of A1 (a).

A2 Adams, Faith

(a) "A Question to Democracy," *Nation*, CXI, 524-26 (November 10, 1920).

A personal narrative of one southern colored family in a northern town showing the constant discriminations to which they are subjected

A3(a) "Adaptation of Negroes to Northern Industrial Conditions," *Monthly Labor Review*, XXIII, 29-30 (July, 1926).

Excellent summary of the article listed as J4(f).

A4 Albany City Club

(a) *Survey of Albany's Negro Population.* Albany, New York, Albany City Club Bulletin, Vol. IX, No. 5 (March, 1929), 15 pp.

A detailed study made during November, 1928, by the National Urban League, Ira de A Reid Director. The survey covered 255 families and studied problems of housing, health, employment, earnings and occupations, business education delinquency and relationship to the welfare of the city A complete report in typewritten form exists in the files of the National Urban League [see R12(a), Z35(g)].

A5 Alexander, Raymond P.

(a) "The Negro Lawyer" *Opportunity*, IX, 268-71 (September, 1931).

A thoughtful presentation of the duty of colored lawyers to work for the impartial enforcement of laws and so to break down the discriminations constantly practised against Negroes

A6 Alexander, Sadie T M.

(a) "Negro Women in Our Economic Life," *Opportunity*, VIII 201-3 (July, 1930).

Describes the entrance of colored women into industry and their general economic status, so far as the nature of occupations and wages is concerned

A7 Alexander, Will W.

(a) "Helping Workers Get and Keep Jobs," *Southern Workman*, LIX, 497-500 (November, 1930).

An account of organizations in Atlanta which have tried to help incoming white and colored workers find jobs and to train them to hold jobs

(b) "The Negro in the New South," *Annals*, CXL, 14562 (November, 1928).

Brief consideration of the present status of the Negro in the agricultural, industrial and business life of the South, and of developments in the problem of race relations

(c) "Negroes and Organized Labor in the South," *Opportunity*, VIII 109-11 (April, 1930).

An article on the difficulty of organizing labor in the South because of the southern white worker's prejudice against the Negroes

(d) "Negroes and the Economic Structure," *Southern Workman*, LX, 269-77 (June, 1931).

A survey of the present economic status of the Negro in Americ n economic life dealing with unemployment, competition of whites and blacks for jobs, and probable outcome of this period of competition and depression. Holds that the race line in jobs has broken down which makes it difficult for Negroes now but will eventually better their lot.

A8 Allen, Floyd P.

(a) "Cardio-Vascular Impairment among 1,000 Negro Factory Workers," *Journal of Industrial Hygiene*, XIII, 164-68 (May, 1931).

A discussion of the physical condition of 1,032 factory workers who were examined and studied. *See also* P18(a).

(b) "Physical Impairment among 1,000 Negro Factory Workers," *Journal of Industrial Hygiene*, XIII, 157-63 (May, 1931).

A discussion of the high mortality rates among Negroes in Cincinnati mentioning the effect of migration on health with particular reference to the physical condition of 1,032 industrial workers. *See also* P18(a).

A9 Allen, Nimrod B.

(a) "Interracial Relations in Columbus, Ohio," *Southern Workman*, LV, 161-69 (April, 1926).

The secretary of the Columbus Urban League discusses the attitude of the churches and courts toward Negroes, the Negro's place in industry, conditions of housing, problems in schools, and the relation of Negroes to social agencies Mentions migration and its effect upon the attitude of northern Negroes, educational problems and crime.

A10 American Academy of Political and Social Science

(a) *The American Negro, Annals*, CXL, 1-359 (November, 1928).

A very important collection of articles by various authors on many phases of Negro life in America. Articles dealing with migration are listed under individual authors: A7(b), B58(a), C3(a), D17(c), F21(h), F25(a), H19(a), J4(d), J10(a), J16(j), L3(a), M57(d), N93(a), N95(a), P3(a), S18(a), T20(a), W9(g).

(b) *The Coming of Industry to the South, Annals*, CLIII, 1-296 (January, 1931).

A fur her collection of articles dealing with the industrial development of the South as a whole, and of certain specific states their industrial resources and labor problems, and problems of social and economic adjust ment to industrial changes The entire volume is important as showing present-day conditions The article of specific value for this bibliography is listed separately as H29(g).

(c) *Industrial Condition of the Negro in the North, Annals*, XXVII 543609, Part III (May, 1906).

An early collection of articles by various authors. Those concerned with migration are listed under B55(a), M39(d), O6(c), W49(c).

(d) *The Negro's Progress in Fifty Years, Annals*, XLIX, 1-266 (September, 1913).

Another collection of short discussions of various phases of the economic political, educational and social life of Negroes Gives a general background of the Negro's status prior to the World War. Articles concerned with migration are listed under individual authors: C19(a), E9(a), E17(a), H19(c), J18(a), O2(a), W44(c), W49(j).

A11 American Federation of Labor

(a) *Proceedings of Annual Conventions* (1915-28, inclusive).

The only mention of migration in this set of *Proceedings* is on pp. 223 and 255 of the report for 1916. These present the resolution favoring the organization of Negroes in the South because of their migration to northern cities and entrance into industry Shows the slight notice taken of the problem of migration by the American Federation of Labor.

A12 American Management Association

(a) *The Negro in Industry*. New York, American Management Association, Survey Report No. 5 (1923), 28 pp.

A preliminary survey summarizing some of the causes and results of Negro migration. Also sets forth the industrial status of the Negro and probable future trends

A13 American Negro Academy

(a) *The Negro and the Elective Franchise*. Washington, D.C., The Academy (1905), 85 pp.

Chap. v, by Kelly Miller is chiefly a comparison of the voting power of the Negro in the North and in the South

A14 Andrews, W. T

(a) "Address at Race Conference," *Crisis*, XIV, 78-79 (June, 1917).

Quotations from an address delivered at a Race Conference in South Carolina, presenting the colored man's view of the causes of the Negro's unrest and migration. Also printed as pamphlet *Causes of Migration from the South*, which is inaccessible

A15 *Annual Cyclopedia*. New York, D. Appleton and Co. (1866-1902).

(a) *1866:* p. 765. A quotation from a Richmond, Virginia, paper on the exodus of Negroes from V rginia to more southerly states.

(b) *1879*: pp. 354-58, 537, 634-35. An excellent contemporary account of the 1879 migration, consisting of several articles giving both points of view, North and South.

(c) *1880*: pp. 394, 417, 481. Brief reports of the condition of Negroes in Indiana, Kansas and Louisiana after the migration.

(d) *1881*: p. 812. A short discussion of causes of Negro migration in 1881 from South Carolina.

(e) *1886*: pp. 571-72. A good account of the migration of Negroes from the hill counties in Mississippi to the Yazoo Basin.

A16(a) "Another Negro Exodus to the North," *Literary Digest*, LXXVI, 18 (February 17, 1923).
A summary of editorial comment on the migration of 1923, giving causes and the press attitudes in various parts of the country

A17 Arkansas Department of Education

(a) *Four Years with the Public Schools in Arkansas*, 1923-27. Little Rock, State Department (1927), 747 pp.
A series of bulletins describing the growth of the Arkansas system of schools and educational conditions at the time of the survey

Armstrong, B. K., *see* G13(a).

A18 Arnold, Benjamin W.

(a) *Concerning the Negroes of the City of Lynchburg, Virginia.* Washington, D.C., Southern History Association Publications, X 19-30 (1906).
A very general, impressionistic account of the criminal, educational, moral and economic status of the Negroes in Lynchburg. Mentions movement of Negroes from the city (pp. 20-21) giving population figures and causes of leaving.

A19 Aronovici, Carol

(a) *Housing Conditions in New Haven.* New Haven, Civic Federation of New Haven, Document No. 12 (October, 1913), 48 pp.
A first-hand survey of housing conditions among three districts composed largely of Jews, Italians and Negroes, showing the ethnic composition of each district, and housing conditions

A20 Atlanta University Studies of the American Negro

(a) *Social and Physical Condition of Negroes in Cities*, Atlanta University Press (1897), 86 pp. Atlanta University Publications No. 2.
Report of an investigation of environmental and social conditions among Negroes in cities, particularly in the South, and a report of the second annual Atlanta University conference Deals with health conditions in Atlanta and Memphis, Charleston and Richmond, giving death rates and causes of death.

An appendix contains tables from U3(8a). *See also* B45(a), D18(b), D18(g), D18(m), D18(n), D19(a), D20(a).

A21 Attwell, Ernest T

(a) "Recreation for Colored America," *American City*, XXXV, 162-65 (August, 1926).

Tells of recreation centers for Negroes that have been established in Rich mond, Memphis, and Greenville, South Carolina.

B1 Bagnall, Robert W.

(a) "The Labor Problem and Negro Migration," *Southern Workman*, XLIX, 518-23 (November, 1920).

A somewhat emotional but generally reliable comparison of recent migrations with that of 1879 in regard to characteristics, causes and the attitude of the South

(b) "Michigan — The Land of Many Waters," *Messenger*, VII 101-2 (April, 1926).

A brief history of the Negro in Michigan and of the prejudice and race antagonisms resulting from the recent migration.

(c) "Two Decades of Negro Life," *New Republic*, LIX, 304-6 (August 7, 1929).

Somewhat over-optimistic inventory of the progress made by Negroes during the l st twenty years, in economic status, education, increased self-confidence and in obtaining a higher place in the estimate of whites Migration is incidentally discussed

B2 Baker, Ray Stannard

(a) *Following the Color Line*: An Account of Negro Citizenship in the American Democracy. New York, Doubleday, Page and Co. (1908), 307 pp.

A popularly written description of an extensive trip through the South by an experienced observer Deals with the political, economic and social status of the Negro in the South Mentions the movement to cities the nature of the migration to the North and the results of this movement both in the North and in the South See particularly pp. 101-47.)

Many chapters were printed in *The American Magazine* March-August, 1907; March, 1908), LXIII, 517-21, 563-79; LXIV, 3-18, 135-48, 297-311, 381-95; LXV, 473-85.

(b) "The Negro Goes North," *World's Work*, XXXIV, 314-19 (July, 1917).

A popular account of causes and results of the early war-time movement

B3 Baker-Crothers, Hayes, and Mrs. R. A. Baker-Crothers.

(a) *Problems of Citizenship.* New York, Henry Holt and Co. (1924), 514 pp.

The section on the Negro, Chaps. viii xi gives a general discussion of the social, political and economic status of the Negro in present-day society, and some suggestions for improving race relations Good synthesis of several of the best documents

Baker-Crothers, Mrs. R. A., *see* B3(a).

B4 Baldwin, George J.

(a) "The Migration: A Southern View," *Opportunity*, II, 183 June, 1924).

A brief statement of the need for better economic treatment of the Negro in order to keep him in the South Its main value is its expression of the southern point of view

B5 Baldwin, W. H.

(a) "Negroes in the Cities," *Standard*, XIII 174-81 (February, 1927).

A general picture of the war-time migration its extent and direction; such causes as economic opportunity and letters of migrants; and the results in the North with particular reference to Harlem.

B6 Baltimore Urban League

(a) *Keeping Tab on the Grim Reaper.* Baltimore, Baltimore Urban League (1926), 23 pp.

A statistical study of the death r tes among the colored population of Baltimore

B7 Banks, Enoch Marvin

(a) *The Economics of Land Tenure in Georgia.* New York, Columbia University Press (1905), 143 pp. Columbia University Studies in History, Economics and Public Law, No. 158.

An early analysis of the extent and nature of land ownership in Georgia among whites and Negroes Contains a description of the credit system and share tenancy, and a discussion of the economic soundness and efficiency of production of the various systems of land tenure

B8 Barnett, Claude A.

(a) "We Win A Place in Industry," *Opportunity*, VII, 82-6 (March, 1929)

Pictures the migration to Chicago as a response to the demand for labor there and gives a good discussion of the nature of occupations in which Negroes are found in that city the effect of migration upon occupational distribution and the work of the Urban League in increasing economic opportunities

B9 Barton, J. W.

(a) "Negro Migration," *Methodist Quarterly Review*, LXXIV, 84-101 (January, 1925).

A summary of the history of Negro migration, causes of movements at various periods, and suggestions for improvement of conditions among Negroes in the South. Especially valuable for earlier migrations and for an introduction to the whole subject

Beahan, Willard, *see* H39(a).

B10 Beales, Le Verne

(a) "Negro Enumeration of 1920," *Scientific Monthly*, XIV, 352-60 (April, 1922).

A reply to M39(f), endeavoring to disprove Miller's assertion that the 1920 census figures are unreliable Mentions the ef ect of migration on birth rates and census returns

B11 Beckham, Albert S

(a) "Juvenile Delinquency and the Negro," *Opportunity*, IX, 300-2 (October, 1931).

A general discussion of the problem of juvenile delinquency among Negroes and its underlying factors, particularly low mentality Gives the laws of various states for methods of handling cases of delinquency

B12 Benner, Thomas E.

(a) *A Comparative Study of the Elementary Schools White and Colored of the 67 Counties in Alabama.* Pamphlet reprint from *Alabama School Progress* (February, 1921), 14 pp.

A statistical comparison of size length of term, enrollment etc., of white and colored schools.

B13 Bennett, Hugh H.

(a) *The Soils and Agriculture of the Southern States.* New York, Macmillan Co. (1921), 399 pp.

A discussion of the chief crops and an exhaustive analysis by sections, of types of soil in the South.

B14 Benson, William E.

(a) "Kowaliga: A Community with a Purpose," *Charities*, XV, 22-24 (October 7, 1905).

An attempt of one community through education, to prevent migration.

B15 Bergman, Ruth G.

(a) "The Negro's Livelihood," *Survey*, LXV, 80-82 October 15, 1930).
An excellent summary of W41(k), the original of which is not easily available

B16 Berry, Theodore M.

(a) "The Negro in Cincinnati Industries," *Opportunity*, VIII, 361-63 (December, 1930).
Findings of a survey sponsored by the Cincinnati Chamber of Commerce and Department of Public Welfare to obtain information concerning the occupations of Negroes, their success in industry wages, opportunities available, relations with white workers and to make suggestions for stabilizing and improving economic conditions

Best, Ethel L., *see* U3(2a).

B17 Bethune, Mary M.

(a) "The Problems of the City Dweller," *Opportunity*, III, 54-55 (February, 1925).
A general discussion of the reasons why both whites and Negroes migrate to northern and southern cities

Bickford, Mabel E., *see* C14(a).

B18 Binder, Carroll

(a) *Chicago and the New Negro.* Chicago Daily News (1927), 24 pp.
A reprint of articles which appeared in the *Chicago Daily News*, describing the migration of Negroes to Chicago and the resulting social and economic conditions.

B19 Bishop, S. H.

(a) "Industrial Condition of Negro Women in New York" *Southern Workman*, XXXIX, 525-28 (September, 1910).
Report of an investigation of Negro women workers Maintains that southern Negroes who migrate North are not used to competition and so consider it prejudice

B20 Bitting, Samuel Tilden

(a) *Rural Land Ownership among the Negroes of Virginia with Special Reference to Albermarle County.* Charlottesville, The Michie Co. (1915), 110 pp. Phelps-Stokes Fellowship Papers, No. 2.
An intelligent discussion of the agricultural situation in Virginia, Negro land ownership, and economic and social conditions among the Negroes

B21 Bizzell, William B.

(a) *Farm Tenantry in the United States.* Texas Agricultural Experiment Station, Bulletin No. 278 (April, 1921), 408 pp.

An exhaustive analysis of the system of farm tenancy in the United States, including a discussion of the Negro tenant

B22(a) "Black and White Ratios for Eleven Decades," *Nation*, LXXIII, 391-92 (November 21, 1901).

General statistical recapitulation of the increase or decrease of Negro population by geographical divisions for the several Federal Censuses

B23(a) "Black Harlem Dramatized," *Literary Digest*, C, 21-22 (March 16, 1929).

A summary of reviews of the play Harlem," which portrays characters who have migrated to Harlem from South Carolina, and the problems connected with heir adjustment to city life

B24(a) "Black Metropolis," *Opportunity*, IX, 235 (August, 1931).

An editorial on the increase of the Negro population in New York City

B25 Blackman, W. F.

(a) "Movement of Negro Population in the Last Decade," *Yale Review*, X, 428-30 (February, 1902).

A summary of the points brought out in U3(27a) showing the southwestward and northern trends of Negro population before 1900.

B26 Blascoer, Frances

(a) *Colored School Children in New York.* New York, Public Educational Association of the City of New York, Reports (1915), 176 pp.

A study occasioned by the need of aiding colored school children obviously unadjusted to their environment Gives a general survey of school conditions and agencies working with colored children, and a detailed study of 500 elementary children their homes families school records etc

Blose, David T., *see* U3(4a).

Bludworth, G. T., *see* M15(a).

Boeger, E. A., *see* U3(5a).

B27 Boie, Maurine

(a) "An Analysis of Negro Crime Statistics for Minneapolis for 1923, 1924 and 1925," *Opportunity*, VI 171-73 (June, 1928).

An analysis of Negro crimes in this city on the basis of police records Corrects previously published erroneous figures of the annual official reports and arrives at conclusions regarding the actual situation.

B28(a) "Bolshevizing the American Negroes," *Independent*, CXV, 631 (December 5, 1925).

An unsigned article on the activities of Communists among Negro laborers

B29 Bond, Horace M.

(a) "Survey of Negro Education in Oklahoma," *Crisis*, XXXV, 113-16, 228 (April and July, 1928).

Discusses the administration, control, financing, enrollment and attendance types of schools, per capita expenditure by counties, and salaries of teachers Mentions the decrease of Negroes in Oklahoma, owing to migration.

B30 Bowen, Louise De Koven

(a) *The Colored People of Chicago.* Chicago, Juvenile Protective Association (1913), 32 pp.

A report of an investigation of the social and economic condition of the Negro in Chicago. Very brief mention of the migration to Chicago. For summary, see B30(b).

(b) "The Colored People of Chicago *Survey*, XXXI 117-20 (November 1, 1913).

Same material as B30(a), B30(c).

(c) *Safeguards for City Youth at Work and at Play.* New York, Macmillan Co. (1914), 241 pp.

The section on Negroes (pp. 170-201) contains the same material and practically the same wording as B30(a), B30(b).

B31 Bowers, George B.

(a) "Will Imperial Valley Become a Land of Opportunity for Negro Citizens?" *Southern Workman*, LIX, 305-13 (July, 1930).

A picture of the Imperial Valley as a land of opportunity for Negroes, with accounts of individuals who have succeeded there

B32 Brackett, Jeffrey R.

(a) *Notes on the Progress of the Colored People of Maryland since the War.* Baltimore, Johns Hopkins University Press (1890), 96 pp. Johns Hopkins University Studies in Historical and Political Science, Series 8, Vols. VII-IX

Discusses the progress made by Negroes in politics wealth, economic standing, business education and social organizations Pages 25-26 mention the movement to Baltimore after the Civil War and the migration to Maryland from Virginia.

B33 Brandt, Lilian

(a) "The Make-up of Negro City Groups," *Charities*, XV, 7-11 (October 7, 1905).

A good discussion of the composition of Negro groups in cities especially in the North, and how this composition indicates a migrant group. *See also* N73(a).

(b) "Negroes of St. Louis," *Journal of the American Statistical Association*, VIII, 203-68 (March, 1903).
A statistical discussion of the growth, composition, vital statistics industrial and social conditions of the Negro in St. Louis at the opening of the century Slight reference is made to migration. *See also* B33(c).

(c) "Negroes of St. Louis," *Southern Workman*, XXXIII, 223-28 (April, 1904).
A brief rewriting of material contained in

B34 Brannen, C. O

(a) *Relation of Land Tenure to Plantation Organization with Developments since 1920.* Fayetteville, Arkansas (1928), 85 pp.
An analysis and description of the plantation system in the South its organ ization and management the nature of plantation labor, systems of tenancy single crop, credit system, wages, etc Scattered references are made to Negro migration, especially on pages 44 *et seq.*, in which are mentioned the characteristics of recent movements and such causes as the boll weevil and desire for economic advancement Contains second part in addition to United States Department of Agriculture Bulletin 1269, for which see U3(6a).

B35 Brawley, Benjamin Griffith

(a) *A Short History of the American Negro.* New York, Macmillan Co. (1919), 280 pp.
A biographic economic and social picture of the Negro in American life including a clear, brief summary of the causes and characteristics of the exodus (pp. 129-32) and of the 1915-19 migration (pp. 171-74).

(b) *A Social History of the American Negro.* New York, Macmillan Co. (1921), 420 pp.
Another history of the Negroes since their coming to America, with emphasis on social conditions in the South and the Negro's social progress Contains brief references to various Negro movements, emphasizing as a cause of migration the social conditions and oppression of the Negro in the South The exodus of 1879 is referred to in Chap. xiii Sec the movement of in Chap. xv Sec. 7; and the migrations 1910-20 in Chap. xvi

B36 Brearley, H. C.

(a) "The Negro and Homicide," *Social Forces*, IX, 247-53 (December, 1930).
A discussion of homicide rates among Negroes as compared with those of whites in various states and in the country as a whole

B37 Breckenridge, Sophonisba P.

(a) "The Color Line in the Housing Problem," *Survey*, XXIX, 575-76 (February 1, 1913).
Summary of C28(a).

B38 Brooklyn Urban League

(a) *First Annual Report*. Brooklyn Urban League Bulletin, Vol. I, No. 2 (December, 1917), 7 pp.
A brief account of the founding of the League and its accomplishments during 1917. States that it was organized to cope with the problems aroused by the migration.

B39 Brooks, Robert P.

(a) *The Agrarian Revolution in Georgia, 1865-1912*. Madison (1914), 129 pp. University of Wisconsin History Series, Vol. III, No. 3.
An excellent discussion of the changes in the agricultural systems in Georgia; considers the economic history and land tenure movements in various sections of the state. Casual references to migration.

(b) "Local Study of the Race Problem in Georgia," *Political Science Quarterly*, XXVI, 193-221 (June, 1911).
A statistical study and comparison of conditions of Negroes in Georgia, based on census figures. Mentions intra-state and city migration.

B40(a) "Brothers, Come North," *Crisis*, XIV, 105 January, 1920).
An editorial urging Negroes to come North and denouncing the attitude of white people and conditions in the South Illustrates the influence of Negro leadership in stimulating migration.

B41 Brown, Frederick John

(a) "Migration of Colored Population," *Journal of the American Statistical Association*, VI, 46-48 (March, 1898).
A letter correcting some misstatements in a previously published review of his book, *Northward Movement of the Colored Population*. *See also* B41(b). Gives some statistics on the early movement of Negroes to the North Usable where the original volume is not available. For the review see W28(c).

(b) *Northward Movement of the Colored Population*: A Statistical Study. Baltimore, Cushing and Co. (1897), 50 pp.
Probably the best early discussion of the northward migration from 1870 to 1890, showing from census sources the percentage of Negro population in the various sections of the country Contains a good discussion of the causes of migration and an analysis of the statistics of state of birth Relatively inaccessible because out of print. *See also* B41(a), W28(c).

B42 Brown, Hugh V

(a) "The Pro and Con of Negro Migration in America," *Southern Workman*, LIII, 348-52 (August, 1924).

A discussion of the causes of recent migrations and of the growing opportunities for Negroes in the United States, particularly in the South, giving reasons against migrating.

B43 Brown, Jean Collier

(a) "The Economic Status of Negro Women," *Southern Workman*, LX, 428-37 (October, 1931).

A study of the occupations of Negro women and the changes that have occurred since the War, with mere mention of migration.

B44 Brown, Phil H.

(a) "Negro Labor Moves Northward," *Opportunity*, I, 5-6 (May, 1923).

A sane and sympathetic discussion of the general nature of the migration, comparing it with that of 1917-19.

B45 Brown, T I

(a) *Economic Coöperation among the Negroes of Georgia.* Atlanta University Press (1917), 56 pp. Atlanta University Publications, No. 19.

A report of an investigation of the economic condition of the Negro and ways in which it can be improved Mentions causes of and remedies for migration (pp. 27-31) in brief quotations from southern newspapers

B46 Brown, W. O

(a) "The Negro Problem: A Sociological Interpretation," *Opportunity*, VIII, 330-33 (November, 1930).

Presents what seem to the author the basic factors in the problem.

B47 Brown, William Henry

(a) *The Education and Economic Development of the Negro in Virginia.* Charlottesville, Virginia, Surber-Arundale-Co. (1923), 150 pp. Phelps-Stokes Fellowship Papers, No. 6.

Gives the history and development of Negro education in Virginia and shows the effect of this education on the Negro's social and economic progress and on the part which he has played in the economic life of the state.

B48 Bruce, Philip

(a) *The Plantation Negro as a Freeman*: Observations on His Character, Condition and Prospects in Virginia. New York, G. P. Putnam's Sons (1889), 262 pp.

An impressionistic picture of the characteris ics and status of the Negro in religion, politics, morals, education, etc Contends that education of Negroes is useless because of their improvident and immoral natures and low mentality Pictures lax parental authority, lax marital relations, inefficiency as agricultural laborers etc

B49 Bruce, Roscoe Conkling

(a) "The Dunbar Apartment House," *Southern Workman*, LX, 417-28 (October, 1931).

An account of some of the housing problems that developed out of the migration and how the Dunbar Apartments try to solve them.

(b) "Good Homes for Negroes," *Housing*, XIX, 15-21 (March, 1930).

Another description of the housing problem in Harlem.

(c) "Towards a Solution of a National Housing Problem" *Southern Workman*, LVII, 291-97 (August, 1928).

A further discussion of the housing problems in the North resulting from recent migrations, particularly in New York City

B50 Bruère, Martha B.

(a) "The Black Folk Are Coming On," *Survey*, L, 432-35 (July 15, 1923).

Deals with both war-time migration and that of 1922-23, emphasizing mainly the causes of the movement and the problems resulting therefrom in the North

B51 Buckner, George W.

(a) "St. Louis Revives the Segregation Issue," *Opportunity*, I, 238-39 (August, 1923).

Effect of migration on the housing situation and, through that, on race relations

B52 Buckner, Jenny C.

(a) "Problems of Women Workers: General Statement of Women's Employment Department of St. Louis Urban League," *Chronicle*, III, 81-82 (April, 1930).

A report of the work of the Womens Department of the St. Louis Urban League, showing the difficulties encountered in trying to find positions for colored women

B53 Buffalo Federation of Churches

(a) *Religious and Social Surveys: Foreign and Negro Sections of Buffalo*. Buffalo, Federation of Churches (1922), 30 pp.

Pages 15-30 by Harold Husted discuss the religious conditions recreation employment education, interracial relations, etc., of the Negro.

B54 Buffalo Foundation Forum

(a) "The Negro in Buffalo," *Buffalo Foundation Bulletin* No. 66, 20-40 (1928).

A study of the Negro population of Buffalo as shown by records of deaths Mentions migration casually and gives birthplace of those dying, 1925-27.

B55 Bulkley, W. L.

(a) "Industrial Condition of the Negro in New York City," *Annals*, XXVII, 590-96 (May, 1906).

A brief discussion of industrial conditions of Negroes in New York Ci y opportunities and kinds of employment open, race prejudice etc. Says adult Negroes learned skilled trades in the South

——— For other works by this author, *see* N7(a).

B56 Bunche, Ralph J.

(a) "The American City as a Negro Political Laboratory," *Governmental Research Association Proceedings* (1928), 53-64.

A description of the historical part Negroes have played in politics and the part they are now playing in northern cities showing how migration to the North has increased their political influence

(b) "The Negro in Chicago Politics," *National Municipal Review*, XVII, 261-64 (May, 1928).

An account of the Negroes increasing political influence in Chicago.

(c) "Negro Political Laboratories," *Opportunity*, VI, 370-73 (December, 1928).

Describes the participation of Negroes in municipal and state governments Mentions migration as affecting this increased activity

(d) "The Thompson-Negro Alliance," *Opportunity*, VII 78-80 (March, 1929).

An account of the Negro's political activities in Chicago, particularly of his support of Mayor Thompson, showing the effect of migration on the politics of that city

B57 Bundesen, Herman N.

(a) "The Negro Health Survey," *Chicago's Health*, XXI, 270-76 (November 1, 1927).

A full summary of the findings of the survey made by Dr H L Harris in 1927 regarding the status of Negro health in Chicago. *See also* H11(a), H11(b). Original report not accessible

B58 Burgess, Ernest W.

(a) "Residential Segregation in American Cities," *Annals*, CXL, 105-15 (November, 1928).

A general discussion of urban zoning, mentioning segregation of Negroes in Chicago.

B59 Burton, Charles Wesley

(a) *Living Conditions among Negroes in the Ninth Ward, New Haven, Connecticut.* Civic Federation of New Haven Document No. 14 (December, 1913), 31 pp.

A first-hand investigation of social and economic conditions among Negroes in New Haven discussing their birthplace, marital and age status, occupations, housing, crime, education, etc

C1(a) "C. I. Resolution on Negro Question in the United States," *Communist*, IX, 48-55 (January, 1930).

A resolution of the Communist Party in regard to the necessity of including Negroes and what must be done by the Party to improve conditions among them.

C2 Caffey, Francis G.

(a) "Suffrage Limitations in the South," *Political Science Quarterly*, XX, 53-67 (March, 1905).

An account of political practices and constitutional provisions in the South which restrict suffrage

C3 Carpenter, Niles

(a) "Feebleminded and Pauper Negroes in Public Institutions," *Annals*, CXL, 65-76 (November, 1928).

An analysis and comparison of statistics of feebleminded and pauper Negroes and whites for the country as a whole and by states

(b) *Nationality, Color, and Economic Opportunity in the City of Buffalo.* University of Buffalo Studies, Vol. V, No. 4 (June, 1927), pp. 95-194.

Chap. vii of this original survey contains a discussion of the economic situation of the Negro worker in Buffalo, including brief mention of migration and a map showing the trend of the movement A d study of a particular city. *See also* C4(a). Also published separately New York, *The Inquiry* (1927), 100 pp.

(c) "The Negro in Industry," *Southern Workman*, LVIII, 195-202 (May, 1929).

A general discussion of the recent entrance of the Negro into the industrial field the nature of his occupations and his success Mentions migration briefly Similar to J4(h), pp. 385-94.

C4 ——— and M. E. Wagner

(a) "Hope on the Job," *Survey*, LVIII, 403-5 (July 15, 1927).
A popular summary of information contained in C3(b), including a map showing sources of migration to Buffalo and emphasizing the lack of economic opportunities for Negroes there Is mainly a collection of stories of individual cases illustrating economic handicaps.

C5 Carroll, Charles E.

(a) "Waiting at the Church," *World Outlook*, V, 16-17 October, 1919).
A description of conditions in colored churches in northern cities showing the effect of migration on religious activities

C6 Carter, Elmer A.

(a) "Organization of Negro Labor: A Challenge to the A. F. of L.," *Labor Age*, XIX, 9-11 (February, 1930).
Deals with the part Negroes play in the industrial life of the South and summarizes the attitude of the A F. of L. toward colored workers in the face of this challenge to include them.

C7 Caudill, Rebecca

(a) "Plight of the Negro Intellectual," *Christian Century*, XLVII 1012-14 (August 20, 1930).
An article on the problem of the young educated Negro who is faced with discrimination in the South with particular reference to conditions in Nashville

C8(a) "Census of 1930," *Opportunity*, IX, 169 (June, 1931).
An editorial comment on the phenomenal increase of Negroes in northern and southern cities during the decade 1920-30, showing that migration has continued

Channing, Alice, *see* U3(7a).

C9 Chapman, Paul W.

(a) "Problems and Progress in Negro Education," *Southern Workman*, LX, 325-29 (July, 1931).
An address on the necessity and problem of keeping the Negro child in school. Mentions the effect of migration on educational problems in Georgia.

C10 Cheyney, Alice S

(a) "Negro Woman in Industry," *Survey*, XLVI, 119 (April 23, 1921).
Summary of P8(a).

C11 Chicago Commission on Race Relations

(a) *The Negro in Chicago*: A Study of Race Relations and a Race Riot. University of Chicago Press (1922), 672 pp.

A thorough, careful and impartial survey of the status of the Negro in Chicago made by a commission composed of leading Negro and white citizens Discusses the Chicago Riot, causes of racial antagonism, causes and effects of Negro migration (*see* pp. 79-105 particularly) character of Negro neighborhoods and housing problems, racial contacts, crime, the Negro in industry, and how public opinion on race relations is developed One of the most valuable investigations because of the breadth of the study and particularly because of its accent on the formation and influence of public opinion. *See also* T4(b), T4(c).

— — *Negro in Industry in 1922.*

An occasional designation of the industrial section of the above.

C12(a) *Chicago Daily News Almanac and Year Book.* Chicago Daily News Company.

See index of each year for references on Negro migration, particularly in the 1923 volume and those following.

C13 Childs, Benjamin G.

(a) *The Negroes of Lynchburg, Virginia.* University of Virginia (1923), 57 pp. Phelps-Stokes Fellowship Papers, No. 5.

A history of the development and progress of the Negroes in Lynchburg and an account of their social and economic status at the time of the survey Casual reference to migration

C14 Chivers, Walter R., and Mabel E. Bickford

(a) "Over-Age Negro Children," *Opportunity*, II 149-51 (May, 1924).

An investigation of the physical, social and psychological situation of a group of northern Negro children who had been given psychological tests and made a poor showing. Merely mentions the fact that many of the misfits had come from the South

C15(a) *Chronicle*: The Official Organ of the Federated Colored Catholics of the United States. Vols. I-IV (1928-31).

The issues of this magazine contain numerous articles religious in tone, on the Negro's status in modern society

C16 Citizens Protective League of New York

(a) *Story of the Riot.* New York, Published by the League, 79 pp. (no date).

A story of the persecution of Negroes and of the riot of August, 1900, in

New York City. Includes public statements of Negroes as to the brutality of policemen

C17 Clark, H. L.

(a) "Growth of Negro Population in the United States and Trend of Migration from the South since 1860," *Manufacturers Record*, LXXXIII, 61-63 (January 25, 1923).

A brief study of the relative growth of Negro and white population in the country as a whole and in the various states showing from census sources that whites are increasing in numbers more rapidly than Negroes in the South Discusses the extent of migration and emphasizes its economic causes

Clark, Jessie, *see* N84(a).

C18 Clark, John T

(a) "The Migrant in Pittsburgh: A Story of the Pittsburgh Urban League," *Opportunity*, I, 303-7 (October, 1923).

A description of the work of the local Urban League among the migrants, containing a comparison of the 1923 migration with those of former years.

(b) "Negro in Steel," *Opportunity*, II, 299-301 October, 1924).

A discussion of the number of Negroes in the steel industry in 1923 and the type of jobs they held

(c) "Negro in Steel," *Opportunity*, IV, 87-88 (March, 1926).

A general discussion of how the Negro has fared since he entered the steel industry and of his success and retention in that field

C19 Clarke, James B.

(a) "The Negro and the Immigrant in the Two Americas," *Annals*, XLIX, 32-37 (September, 1913).

Deals with relations of foreign-born immigrants to Negroes and their economic competition.

C20 Clayton, Powell

(a) *The Aftermath of the Civil War, in Arkansas.* New York, Neale Publishing Co. (1915), 378 pp.

An autobiographical account of Reconstruction Days in Arkansas by the governor who held office at that time. Outrages of the Ku Klux are described in Chap. viii

C21 Cleveland Health Council, Bureau of Statistics and Research

(a) *A Study of the Movement of the Negro Population of Cleveland, 1924.* Cleveland Bureau of Statistics, Howard W. Green, Director. Mimeographed, 15 pp.

A statistical and graphic presentation of the trend of the colored population within the city of Cleveland, as shown by the number of Negroes in various wards according to the 1910 and 1920 census figures, and by the 1921 and 1923 school census figures

Coad, B. R., *see* U3(21a).

C22(a) "Color and Crime," *Nation*, LXXVI, 24-25 (January 8, 1903).

An editorial concerning crime rates among Negroes, showing conditions of criminal justice and giving some 1890 figures on crime.

C23(a) "Colored Women in Industry in Philadelphia," *Monthly Labor Review*, XII, 1046-48 (May 8, 1921).

Summary of P8(a), which is not easily available

C24 Coman, Katharine

(a) "The Negro as a Peasant Farmer," *Journal of the American Statistical Association*, IX, 39-54 (June, 1904).

Tests the conclusions of various writers as to the progress and future of the Negroes, using statistics of the twelfth Census

C25 Commission on Interracial Coöperation

(a) *Annual Reports* of Progress of the Work of the Commission. Atlanta, The Commission.

Reports of the program and accomplishments of the Commission for each year are published annually

(b) *Black Spots on the Map*. Atlanta, Commission on Interracial Coöperation, 16 pp. (no date).

A report of the number of lynchings by states in the South from 1900 to 1922.

——— For other works by the Commission, *see* E11(a), M18(a), M43(a), M43(b), P33(a), W42(a), Z14(a).

C26(a) "Communism and the Negro Tenant Farmer," *Opportunity*, IX, 234-35 (August, 1931).

An editorial on a race clash in Alabama when the sheriff broke up a meeting of the Share Croppers Union

C27(a) "Communist Propaganda," *Commonweal*, XIII, 508 (March 11, 1931).

An editorial paragraph on the party trial of a Communist janitor in Harlem for discriminations against Negroes showing it to be Communistic propaganda to win the colored laborers

C28 Comstock, Alzada P.

(a) "Chicago Housing Conditions: The Problem of the Negro,"

American Journal of Sociology, XVIII, 241-57 (September, 1912).
A careful study of housing conditions among Negroes in Chicago. Covers conditions, congestion, rents, lodgers, etc. For summary, see B37(a).
Also published in an inaccessible pamphlet under title *Housing Conditions in Chicago*, edited by S. P. Breckinridge and Edith Abbott.

C29 Connelly, William E., and E. M. Coulter

(a) *History of Kentucky.* Chicago and New York, The American Historical Society (1922), 5 vols.
A detailed account of Kentucky s history Contains a description of Reconstruction Days, political and economic conditions. There is little on the Negro.

C30 Cook, Myrtle

(a) "Housing Conditions among Negroes in Kansas City, Missouri," *Missouri Negro Industrial Commission: Semi Annual Report, January 1-July 1, 1921*, 18-33.
Report of a valuable first-hand investigation of living conditions in that city. [Part 2 of M46(e).]

C31 Cooke, Dennis H.

(a) "The Negro Rural School Problem" *Southern Workman*, LX, 156-60 (April, 1931).
A survey of the availability of schools in rural districts in North Carolina.

(b) *The White Superintendent and the Negro Schools in North Carolina.* Nashville, Tenn., George Peabody College for Teachers (1930), 176 pp.
An exhaustive analysis of the present status of education for Negroes in North Carolina with a history of its course Deals with the organization, administration and supervision of colored schools.

Cooper, Herman, *see* C32(a).

C32 Cooper, Richard W., and Herman Cooper

(a) *Negro School Attendance in Delaware.* Newark University of Delaware Press (1923), 389 pp.
An exhaustive statistical analysis of the attendance of colored school children in Delaware during 1920-21, with an investigation of the causes of absences relation of attendance to promotions, effect upon attendance of age, sex, occupation of parents distance from schools, etc

Corson, John J., *see* G4(a).

C33 Coulter, E. Merton

(a) *The Civil War and Readjustment in Kentucky.* Chapel Hill, University of North Carolina Press (1926), 468 pp.

Chap. xvi deals with conditions among the Negroes after the Civil War and mentions influx to towns in 1865 and the work of the Freedmen's Bureau.

——— For other works by this author, *see* C29(a).

C34(a) "'Crisis' on the Southern Exodus," *Nation*, CXVII, 227 (September 5, 1923). An editorial paragraph quoting E27(a).

C35 Crossland, W. A.

(a) *Industrial Conditions among the Negroes in St. Louis.* St. Louis, Washington University School of Social Economy (1914), 123 pp.

A discussion, mainly statistical, of wages, hours, types of work and indus trial opportunities of Negroes in St. Louis before the War.

Croxton, F. C., and F. E. Croxton, *see* N91(a).

C36 Cutler, James Elbert

(a) *Lynch Law*: An Investigation into the History of Lynching in the United States. New York, Longmans, Green and Co. (1905), 287 pp.

An impartial and thorough study of the development and significance of the lynching practice

D1 Dabney, Thomas L.

(a) "The Conquest of Bread," *Southern Workman*, LVII, 418-22 (October, 1928).

A thoughtful discussion of the increasing seriousness of the unemployment situation among Negroes in the South, owing to whites entering fields hitherto reserved for Negroes

(b) "Local Leadership among V rginia Negroes," *Southern Workman*, LIX, 31-35 (January, 1930).

Pictures the need for leadership among Negroes in the small towns and cities, and the dearth of such leaders, owing to migration.

(c) "Negro Workers at the Crossroads," *Labor Age*, XVI 8-10 (February, 1927).

A discussion of increasing race friction in industry since the migration brought Negroes into industrial work, and of the relation of Negroes to trade unions

(d) "Organized Labor's Attitude towards Negro Workers," *Southern Workman*, LVII, 323-30 (August, 1928).

A concise report of a questionnaire study of the present attitude of organized labor.

(e) "Southern Labor and the Negro," *Opportunity*, VII, 345-46 (November, 1929).

A general discussion of increased race feeling in the South due to growing economic competition

D2 Daniels, John

(a) *In Freedom's Birthplace.* Boston, Houghton, Mifflin Co. (1914), 496 pp.

A thorough study of the history and the social, economic and political condition of the Negro in Boston before the War. Contains a few casual references to the migration of Negroes

(b) "Industrial Conditions among Negro Men in Boston," *Charities*, XV, 35-39 (October 7, 1905).

A description of the nature of occupations and business enterprises of Negro men in Boston.

D3 Daves, J. J.

(a) *A Social Study of the Colored Population of Knoxville, Tennessee.* Knoxville Free Colored Library (1926), 27 pp.

A report of a social study of the Negroes of Knoxville, made in the summer of 1925, covering housing, industry education, religion, economic and social conditions, and health

D4 Davis, J. R.

(a) "Reconstruction in Cleveland County," Duke University, *Trinity College Historical Society Papers*, Series 10, 5-31.

An account of the economic, social and political conditions in Cleveland County North Carolina, during Reconstruction.

D5 Davis, Katharine B.

(a) "The Philadelphia Negro, Du Bois and Eaton's," *Journal of Political Economy*, VIII, 248-60 (March, 1900).

A comprehensive review and discussion of D18(i).

D6 Davis, P. O

(a) "Negro Exodus and Southern Agriculture," *American Review of Reviews*, LXVIII, 401-7 (October, 1923).

A good discussion of the economic causes of migration, giving suggestions for the improvement of farming conditions in the South

D7 Davis, William W.

(a) *The Civil War and Reconstruction in Florida.* New York, Columbia University Press (1913), 418 pp. Columbia University Studies in History, Economics and Public Law No. 131.

Books 1 and 2 are concerned with conditions before and during the Civil War. Books 3 and 4 deal with political reconstruction and the troubles and mob violence incident to the attempt of southern whites to regain control of the government

D8 Detroit Bureau of Governmental Research

(a) *The Negro in Detroit.* Prepared for the Mayor s Interracial Committee by a Special Survey Staff, 12 sections, 2 vols. (1926). (Mimeographed.)

Full report of the special survey made for the Mayor's Interracial Committee. An impartial and statistical investigation of the Negro's place in the industrial and social life of Detroit, showing the growth of the colored population in the city the effect of migration on northern Negroes, the nature of colored workers' occupations, conditions of housing, crime, business and thrift health recreation, political, religious and social activities One of the valuable original investigations of Negro life in a northern city since the war-time migration Limited in edition but available in most large libraries. For printed summaries see D9(a), D23(a), G5(a), L6(a), N26(a), R2(a).

D9 Detroit: Mayor's Committee on Race Relations

(a) *Report of the Mayor's Committee.* Detroit Bureau of Governmental Research, Public Business No. 108, Vol. IV, No. 3 (March 10, 1927), 16 pp.

A concise summary of findings and recommendations based upon the survey of race conditions made during 1926 by the Detroit Bureau of Governmental Research. For full account of this survey see D8(a).

D10 Detweiler, Frederick Gorman

(a) *The Negro Press in the United States.* University of Chicago Press (1922), 274 pp.

A careful analysis of the n ture influence and policies of the Negro news papers showing the influence of these papers on migration.

D11 Devison, L. C.

(a) "Effect of Negro Migration on Advertisers' Markets," *Printers Ink*, CIV, 25-28 (August 1, 1918).

A practical discussion of one of the results of migration, showing how it has influenced the sale of labor-saving devices in the South

D12 Dickson, Harris

(a) "The Negro in Politics," *Hampton's Magazine*, XXIII, 225-36 (August, 1909).

A discussion of the political turmoil of Reconstruction in the South and why and how the South has disfranchised the Negroes Mentions influx to Washington, D C., after the Civil War and contends this was the reason for the passage of the bill abolishing enfranchisement for all residents of Washington.

Dill, A. G., *see* D19(a).

D13 Donald, H. H.

(a) "Negro Migration of 1916-1918," *Journal of Negro History*, VI 383-498 (October, 1921).

A graduate thesis on Negro migration, based largely on surveys by the United States Labor Department Scott, Epstein Woofter Woodson and others, and presenting a thoughtful, general analysis of the phenomenon of migration.

D14 Douglass, Frederick

(a) "Negro Exodus from the Gulf States," *American Journal of Social Science*, XI, 1-22 (May, 1880).

An emotional expression of opinion by a contemporary Negro leader concerning the causes and advisability of the 1879 movement. *See also* G21(a).

(b) "Remarks on the Exodus (1879)," *Journal of Negro History*, IV, 56 (January, 1919).

Extract from a letter written during the early eighties, opposing the migration of 1879 and giving reasons for the opposition of the author.

D15 Dowd, Jerome

(a) *The Negro in American Life*. New York, Century Co. (1926), 611 pp.

A presentation of many phases of the Negro's status in American life, among them a brief but important discussion of past and present migrations of Negroes (pp. 243-63). Uses the 1920 census figures in dealing with recent movements and emphasizes a comparison of migrations of whites and Negroes.

D16 Drucker, A. P., and Others

(a) *Colored People of Chicago*. Chicago Juvenile Protective Association Publications (1913). (Unpaged pamphlet.)

A general survey of the economic and social status of Negroes in Chicago, constituting a good summary of conditions before 1915.

D17 Dublin, Louis I.

(a) "Effect of Health Education on Negro Mortality," *Opportunity*, II, 232-34 (August, 1924).

A general discussion of the status of health among Negroes. Mentions very briefly migration and its effect on health problems in northern cities Also in *National Conference of Social Work Proceedings* 1924, 274-79.

(b) *Health and Wealth.* New York, Harper and Bros. (1928), 361 pp.

A collection of addresses and articles on various subjects connected with public health Chap. xii on "Life Death and the Negro" is a reprint of D17(e).

(c) "The Health of the Negro," *Annals*, CXL, 77-85 (November, 1928).

A statistical discussion of the death rate among Negroes, deaths from various diseases, and general status of the health of colored people

(d) "The Health of the Negro: The Outlook for the Future," *Opportunity*, VI, 198-200 (July, 1928).

A very general description of the progress made in the Negro's health status and the part the colored physician should play in improving it Mentions the movement to cities and the effect on the birth rate

(e) "Life, Death and the Negro," *American Mercury*, XII, 37-45 (September, 1927).

An account of the birth and death rates among Negroes before and since emancipation, and trends in specific diseases Discusses recent northern migrations in accounting both for the increase in mortality since 1921 and for lowered birth rates. Same as Chap. xii of D17(b).

(f) *Recent Changes in Negro Mortality.* New York, Metropolitan Life Insurance Co. (1924), 10 pp.

Reprint of an address before the National Conference of Social Work in 1924. *See also* D17(a).

(g) "Recent Improvement in the Negroes' Mortality," *Opportunity*, I, 5-8 (April, 1923).

Discusses causes of mortality and the changes which occurred in Negro death rates, 1911-22.

(h) *The Reduction in Mortality among Colored Policy Holders.* New York, Metropolitan Life Insurance Co. (1920), 7 pp.

Report of an address delivered to the annual conference of the National Urban League on death rates among Negroes.

(i) "Some Observations on the Mortality of Negroes in America," *Economic World*, n.s., XXVIII, 384-86 (September 13, 1924).

Same as D17(a).

(j) "Suicide among Negroes in the United States," *American Journal of Public Health*, XX, 1347-48 (December, 1930).

Discussion of suicide rates among Negroes. Mentions effect of migration to cities, and especially to the North, on the increase in suicides. Same material as M25(b).

D18 Du Bois, W. E. Burghardt

(a) "The Black Vote of Philadelphia," *Charities*, XV, 31-35 (October 7, 1905).
Indicates how the corrupt political clubs of Philadelphia influence the migrants

(b) *Economic Coöperation among Negro Americans*. Atlanta University Press (1907), 184 pp. Atlanta University Publications No. 12.
A discussion of the efforts of Negroes to better their own condition. Section 8 contains extracts from reports of conferences on the 1879 migration of Negroes

(c) "Economic Future of the Negro," *American Economic Association Publications*, Third Series, Vol. VII, No. 1: 219-42, Macmillan Co. (1906).
An intelligent discussion of the historical rise of various economic classes among Negroes, their present condition and probable future

(d) "Georgia Negroes and Their Fifty Millions of Savings," *World's Work*, XVIII, 11550-54 (May, 1909).
Discussion of the increase of land and property ownership among Negroes since the Civil War.

(e) "Hosts of Black Labor," *Nation*, CXVI, 539-41 (May 9, 1923).
Discusses the effect of migration upon the relations of the southern Negro to white labor, to capitalists North and South, and to northern Negroes.

(f) "Migration of Negroes," *Crisis*, XIV, 63-66 (June, 1917).
An excellent account of the extent and causes of war-time migration. An interesting map shows the approximate trend and volume of migration. *See also* R8(a).

(g) *The Negro American Family*. Atlanta University Press (1908), 156 pp. Atlanta University Publications No. 13.
A survey of the size of family, sexual morals types of homes economics of the family including rent budgets and incomes, and descriptions of specific family groups. Includes city and rur l homes

(h) "Passing of Jim Crow," *Independent*, XCI, 53-54 (July 14, 1917).
A sane account of the causes of migration writ en from the Negro viewpoint.

(i) *The Philadelphia Negro*: Together with a special report on domestic service by Isabel Eaton. Philadelphia, University of Pennsylvania (1899), 520 pp.
An unusually careful original survey of the social, economic and moral

conditions of Negroes in a northern city before 1900. Brief discussion (pp. 73-82) of the sources of the Negro population, showing migration from the South. *See also* D5(a).

(j) "The Problem of Amusement," *Southern Workman*, XXVII 181-84 (September, 1897).

A discussion of the problem of adequate recreation for young people among the colored population, as an important cause of migration, mentioning other causes as well

(k) "Republicans and the Black Vote," *Nation*, CX, 757-58 June 5, 1920).

A description of the growing Negro power in politics due to migration and of the Negro's trend toward independent voting.

(l) "The Segregated Negro World," *World Tomorrow*, VI, 136-38 (May, 1923).

Considers the growing tendency among Negroes to develop a closed economic circle within their own race, owing to economic handicaps; and the increase of this tendency due to migration.

(m) *Some Notes on Negro Crime, Particularly in Georgia.* Atlanta University Press (1904), 68 pp. Atlanta University Publications No. 9.

A discussion of crime among Negroes, both North and South Deals with the extent and causes of crime, and with criminal rates among urban Negroes. Mentions the effect of migration upon crime, p. 15.

(n) *Some Notes on the Negroes in New York City.* Atlanta University Press (1903), 5 pp.

A brief statistical survey of the increase of population and distribution with in New York City, 1704-1900, the character of the population, occupations, vital statistics etc., in 1900.

For other works by this author, *see* A20(a), D19(a), D20(a), U3(12a), U3(12b), U3(12c), U3(44a), W8(a).

D19 ——— and A. G. Dill

(a) *The Common School and the American Negro.* Atlanta University Press (1911), 140 pp. Atlanta University Publications No. 16.

A careful analysis of educational facilities for Negroes in the South Covers equipment, attendance expenditures etc., for each southern state

D20 ——— and Others

(a) *The Negro American Artisan.* Atlanta University Press (1912), 114 pp. Atlanta University Publications No. 17.

A survey of the status of the Negro artisan in Africa, in the ante bellum

South and during Reconstruction, and an analysis of the occupations of Negroes in 1900 in the country as a whole and by states. For each state there is a summary of answers to questionnaires dealing with number and occupations of Negro skilled laborers

D21 Duke, Charles S

(a) *The Housing Situation and the Colored People of Chicago.* Chicago (April, 1919), 35 pp.
A very general discussion of the housing problems of the Negroes in Chicago. Summarized in H44(a).

D22 Duncan, Hannibal G.

(a) *The Changing Race Relationship in the Border and Northern States.* Philadelphia, University of Pennsylvania Thesis (1922), 127 pp.
A broad study of economic and social discrimination against Negroes, maintaining that race prejudice increases with growth in the size of the colored group. Migration up to 1910 is discussed in Chap. i, and that since 1910 in Chap. viii. The rest of the volume deals with manifestations and increase of discrimination in the social and economic structure its casual relation with migration being implied

(b) *Race and Population Problems.* New York, Longmans, Green and Co. (1929), 424 pp.
Deals with such general problems as the rise and spread of human groups and races biology of race problems inferiority, etc.), movements of population, diffusion of culture leading theories of population, methods of control of growth of population, etc

D23 Dunn, Robert W.

(a) *Labor and Automobiles.* New York International Publishers (1929), 224 pp.
Material on the Negro largely a summary of the economic aspects of D8(a), but containing some new material.

D24 Dunne, William F.

(a) "Negroes in American Industries," *Workers Monthly*, IV, 206-8, 257-60 (March and April, 1925).
An interesting treatise by a Communist describing the fact of migration to the North and its effect on occupations and organized labor. Shows the failure of American organized labor to face the problem of the Negro in industry, and urges their organization within the Communist party and its labor groups.

D25 Dunning, William A.

(a) *Reconstruction: Political and Economic, 1865-1877.* New York, Harper and Bros. (1907), 378 pp.

The most authoritative account of the political troubles of the years following the close of the Civil War up to the withdrawal of the troops. Contains an account of mob violence by the Ku Klux Klan but ends before the dis franchisement of Negroes

D26 Durham John Stephens

(a) "The Labor Unions and the Negro," *Atlantic Monthly*, LXXXI 222-31 (February, 1898).

A general presentation of relations then existing between organized labor and the Negroes, tracing the history of this relationship and its development into a policy of discrimination against colored workers

D27 Dutcher, Dean

(a) *The Negro in Modern Industrial Society.* Lancaster, Pennsylvania, The Science Press (1930), 137 pp.

Presents an exhaustive analysis of 1910 and 1920 census figures on occupations of Negroes in the United States Is particularly valuable for its classification of these occupations (1) into those in which the number of Negroes was decreasing, moderately increasing, and strikingly increasing; and (2) into various social-economic groupings. The entire volume shows the effects of migration upon the nature of the occupations of colored people Incidentally discusses extent and causes

Eaton, Isabel, *see* D18(i).

E1 Eckenrode, Hamilton J.

(a) *Political History of Virginia during the Reconstruction.* Baltimore, Johns Hopkins Press (1904), 127 pp. Johns Hopkins University Studies in Historical and Political Science, Vol. XXII

A monograph on the political phases of Reconstruction days in Virginia. Mentions vagrancy and shows the effects of this roaming on agricultural conditions.

E2(a) "Economic Causes of the Negro Exodus," *Literary Digest*, LXXVIII, 14-15 (August 18, 1923).

A summary of editorial comment concerning the economic reasons for the migration.

E3(a) "Economic Condition of the Negro in West V rginia," *Monthly Labor Review*, XVI, 713-15 (April, 1923).

A brief discussion of the increase in Negro population due to migration, and of the condition of the newcomers in industry, particularly mining. Covers the same material as W14(a).

E4(a) "Economic Position of the Negro in West Virginia," *Monthly Labor Review*, XXV, 251-53 (August, 1927).

A summary of the report of the West Virginia Bureau of Negro Welfare and Statistics for 1925-26. For full report, see W14(c).

E5(a) "Economic Status of the Negro," *Monthly Labor Review*, XXXII, 847-51 (April, 1931).

A summary of W41(k), which is not readily available

E6(a) "Editorial," *Survey*, LIII, 698-99 (March, 1925).

A lengthy editorial on the nature of welfare agencies which are working for the improvement of conditions in Harlem.

E7 Edmonds, R. W.

(a) "The Negro Exodus: Will It Be Permanent?" *Manufacturers Record*, LXXXV, 77-78 (April 17, 1924).

An intelligent discussion of the extent of migration, of the reports that Negroes are returning South, and of the results of the movement. *See also* N52(a).

E8(a) "Education and Crime among Negroes," *Review of Reviews*, LV, 318-20 (March, 1917).

A summary of S54(a).

E9 Edwards, Thomas J.

(a) "The Tenant System and Some Changes since Emancipation," *Annals*, XLIX, 38-46 (September, 1913).

Description of the tenancy system.

E10 Edwards, William J.

(a) *Twenty-Five Years in the Black Belt.* Boston, Cornhill Co. (1918), 143 pp.

A personal narrative of the author's life, and a general, emotional and rather religious presentation of his views on various phases of the Negro's situation in the United States One short chapter (pp. 94-99) gives an account of the movement north and of its social and economic causes

E11 Eleazer, Robert B.

(a) *An Adventure in Good Will.* Atlanta, Commission on Interracial Coöperation, 3 pp. (no date.)

A history of the origin and work of the Commission on Interracial Cooperation.

(b) "Trends in Race Relations in 1926," *Opportunity*, V 16-17 (January, 1927).

A discussion of what various agencies in the South are doing to improve race relations, and a summary of some of the race troubles in the North due to migration

E12 Ellis, George W.

(a) "The Negro in the Chicago Primary," *Independent*, LXXII 890-91 (April 25, 1912).

An account of the Negro's political weight in Chicago.

E13 Ellison, J. Malcus

(a) "The Negro Church in Rural Virginia," *Southern Workman*, LX, 67-73, 176-79, 201-10, 307-14 (February, April, May, and July, 1931).

Survey of the status of the Negro church in rural Virginia, showing number of churches financial obligations, activities and the place of the church in the life of the people.

E14 Elwang, William W.

(a) *The Negroes of Columbia, Missouri*. Columbia, University of Missouri (1904), 69 pp.

An original investigation in Columbia, valuable but with an interpretation not always objec ive and unbiased Uses United States census figures for increase of Negro population and presents local findings regarding occupations, wages, churches, societies schools health and vital statistics, housing and rents crime and political activities

E15 Elzy, Robert L.

(a) "Adjusting the Colored Migrant from the South to Life in a Northern City," *Opportunity*, V, 175-76 (June, 1927).

An abstract of a paper read at the 1927 Conference of the National Urban League Summarizes, particularly for New York City the causes of migration and some of the resulting problems. The original paper is usually not available in libraries

(b) "Social Work in Brooklyn," *Opportunity*, V 238-39 (August, 1927).

An account of the work carried on by the National Urban League in Brooklyn

E16 Embree, Edwin R.

(a) "Negro Illness and Its Effect upon the Nation's Health," *Modern Hospital*, XXX, 49-54 (April, 1928).

A description of the inadequate hospital facilities for Negroes in the whole country Deals with the health and vital statistics of Negroes and the effect of migration on the problem.

E17 Emlen, John T

(a) "Movement for the Betterment of the Negro in Philadelphia," *Annals*, XLIX, 81-92 (September, 1913).

A discussion of the social and economic problems in Philadelphia resulting from migration

(b) "Negro Immgration in Philadelphia," *Southern Workman*, XLVI, 555-57 (October, 1917).

Discusses the influx of Negroes, some of the problems created, and the organization of a committee to handle the migrants

E18(a) "Employment of Negroes in Pennsylvania Industries," *Monthly Labor Review*, XII, 206 (January, 1921).

A table giving statistics for eleven counties in Pennsylvania to show the decrease in the number of foreigners and the increase in the number of Negroes employed in the state during 1919 as compared with

E19 Epstein, Abraham

(a) *The Negro Migrant in Pittsburgh*, Pittsburgh, University of Pittsburgh (1918), 74 pp.

An original investigation of the conditions among Negro migrants in Pittsburgh based on a schedule study of 500 Negro migrants Discusses living conditions, labor, delinquency and health problems of the Negro migrants in Pittsburgh, and gives some constructive suggestions toward the soluti n of the problem of race coöperation. Not an intensive survey but suggestive and valuable. *See also* N40(a).

Erickson, Ethel, *see* U3(2a).

E20(a) "Escaping Slaves," *Crisis*, XIII, 22-24 (November, 1916).

Quotations from newspapers showing the attitude of the South and of the North toward the economic problems created by migration.

E21 Ethridge, Willie S

(a) "Salesmen of Violence," *Outlook*, CLVI, 457-59 (November 19, 1930).

An account of race antagonism in the South with instances of lynching and riots; ascribes the increasing tension to economic competition.

(b) "Southern Women Attack Lynching," *Nation*, CXXXI, 647 (December 10, 1930).

A brief article on the organization of southern white women to combat lynching.

E22 Eutsler, Roland B.

(a) "Agricultural Credit and the Negro Farmer," *Social Forces*, VIII, 416-25, 565-73 (March and June, 1930).
An intensive analysis of the present working of the credit system in the South and ways in which it affects the Negro's economic situation.

E23 Evans, Leona M.

(a) "In the Promised Land," *Opportunity*, V, 114-15 (April, 1927).
A report of the social service work being done among Negroes in St. Louis showing that most of the dependent families were migrants, and revealing some of the problems of adjustment to city life

E24 Evans, Maurice Smethurst

(a) *Black and White in the Southern States*; A Study of the Race Problem in the United States from a South African Point of View. New York, Longmans, Green and Co. (1915), 299 pp.
An outsider s view of the Negro problem. Discusses social, political, economic and educational conditions in the South

E25 Evans, William L.

(a) "The Negro in Chicago Industries," *Opportunity*, I, 15-16 (February, 1923).
The Secretary of the Chicago Urban League discusses the nature of occupations of Negro men and women in Chicago and shows their retention as employees in times of depression

E26(a) "Exodus," *Crisis*, XIII, 290-91 (April, 1917).
Extracts from three periodicals showing public opinion on the economic condition of the South

E27(a) "Exodus," *Crisis*, XXVI, 202 (September, 1923).
A satirical summary of the South s opinion of the migration. Quoted in C34(a).

E28(a) "Exodus," *Opportunity*, II 27-28 January, 1924).
A quotation from a St. Louis editorial on the effect of migration on southern labor.

E29(a) "Exodus Costing State $27,000,000. That Is the Estimated Loss of Wealth from the Farms of Georgia This Year Due to the Departure of 77,500 Negroes," *American Bankers Association Journal*, XVI, 51-52 (July, 1923).
A summary of the report of the Georgia Bankers Association stating the extent of migration in 1923, the causes and the measures necessary to stop the movement Original report not available in most libraries

E30(a) "Exodus in America," *Living Age*, CCXCV, 57-60 (October 6, 1917).

Later printing of E31(a).

E31(a) "Exodus in America," *New Statesman*, IX, 393-95 (July 28, 1917).

A British summary of the causes and problems of the war-time migration of Negroes. For same article see also E30(a).

E32(a) "Exodus of Negroes," *Opportunity*, IV, 399 (December, 1926).

Brief quotation from Bulletin 7 of the Industrial Relations Department of the National Urban League on the recent migration and its effect on labor in the South Original report not easily available

E33(a) "Exodus Without Its Canaan — But Not Without Its Lessons," *Coal Age*, XI, 258 (February 10, 1917).

A let er by a Southerner commenting on the exodus of Negroes from the coal fields of Birmingham and pointing out the lessons southern mine managers, northern mine managers and Negroes may learn. The basic idea is that the Negro's place is in the South Mentions the necessity of finding out the causes of the exodus. *See also* N59(a).

E34(a) "Exploitation That Is Getting Dangerous," *World Outlook*, V, 14 (October, 1919).

A discussion of housing problems that resulted in n rthern cities after the migration of Negroes from the South

E35(a) "Extensive Migration of Negro Labor from the Southern States," *Economic World*, XCVIII, 549-50 (October 28, 1916).

An editorial giving a summary of the causes and general character of the early war-time migration.

F1 Fanning, John W.

(a) *Negro Migration*. Bulletin of the University of Georgia, Vol. XXX, No. 8B (June, 1930), 39 pp. Phelps-Stokes Fellowship Studies, No. 9.

An excellent and exhaustive study of the migration of Negroes between 1920 and 1925 from middle Georgia counties as influenced or determined by existing economic conditions. Uses census figures interviews and investigations.

F2 Farnham, Dwight T

(a) "Negroes, a Source of Industrial Labor," *Industrial Management*, LVI, 123-29 (August, 1918).

A discussion of some of the outstanding traits of the Negro's personality which must be taken into account when colored labor is employed

F3 Favrot, Leo M.

(a) "Constructive School Work for the Colored Schools of Louisiana," *Southern Workman*, XLVIII, 386-88 (August, 1919).
A brief review of the new school building projects for colored children in Louisiana, and the coöperation of colored people in improving the situation

(b) "Negro Education in Coahoma County," *Southern Workman*, LIV, 489-96 (November, 1925).
A detailed description of the condition of colored schools in Coahoma County Mississippi, with an account of improvements which have been made in recent years and plans for the future Mentions migration as causing more interest in the educational facilities available for Negroes.

(c) "Some Facts about Negro Schools and Their Distribution and Development in 14 Southern States," *High School Quarterly*, XVII, 139-54 (April, 1929).
A statistical analysis of the conditions of Negro high schools in 14 southern states. *See also* T7(a).

(d) *A Study of County Training Schools for Negroes in the South.* Charlottesville, Va. (1923), 85 pp. John F. Slater Fund Occasional Papers No. 23.
A careful statistical study of the training schools for Negroes—their organization, administration and support financial statistics, attendance etc and a discussion of the problems faced by these schools Contains recommendations for their improvement

F4 Federal Council of the Churches of Christ in America: Commission on the Churches and Race Relations.

(a) *Better Houses for Negro Homes.* New York, Federal Council of Churches (September, 1925), 24 pp.
A presentation of the housing problems which confront Negroes and an account of how certain towns and industrial concerns are trying to meet the situation.

(b) *Toward Interracial Coöperation.* New York, The Council (1926), 192 pp.
A report of the National Interracial Conference held by the Commission on the Church and Race Relations, and the Commission on Interracial Coöperation, at Cincinnati, Ohio, March, 1925. Reports discussions of publicity and race relations health, housing, interracial coöperation, social agencies church industry courts and schools, as each is affected by and affects race relations

F5 Federal Reserve Bank of Richmond

(a) *Monthly Review: General Business and Agricultural Conditions* (1918-24). Richmond, Federal Reserve Bank.

Each monthly review summarizes general conditions of crops, banks, labor, industries, cotton, coal, textiles etc Occasional reference to migration of Negroes to the North in discussions of labor conditions and labor shortage or general supply. Valuable for first-hand information of the labor situation and inferences of migration. The December 30, 1922, issue contains a brief statement of the agricultural depression due to the boll weevil and the consequent migration of Negroes to northern cities Similar monthly reports published by the Federal Reserve Banks of Atlanta, Dallas and St Louis. *See also* M31(a).

F6 Feldman, Herman

(a) *Racial Factors in American Industry.* New York, Harper and Bros. (1931), 318 pp.

An analysis of the economic status and handicaps of various racial elements such as Negroes, Orientals, Mexicans and immigrants, with a proposal of social and industrial remedies The section on the Negro, pp. 11-77, deals with the nature of occupations, relations to unions, relations with white workers, wages and success

F7 Ferguson, George Oscar

(a) *The Psychology of the Negro*: An Experimental Study. New York, Science Press (1916), 138 pp. Columbia University Contributions to Philosophy and Psychology, Vol. XXV, No. 1, Archives of Psychology No. 36 (April, 1916).

Reviews the work previously done in the field, gives the tests used in this study and the results of this survey of children in Richmond, Fredericksburg and Newport News Virginia.

F8 Fertig, James W.

(a) *The Secession and Reconstruction of Tennessee.* University of Chicago Press (1898), 108 pp.

A history of Reconstruction Days in Tennessee

F9 Ficklen, John R.

(a) *History of Reconstruction in Louisiana.* Baltimore, Johns Hopkins Press (1910), 234 pp. Johns Hopkins University Studies in Historical and Political Science, Series 28, No. 1.

Gives a picture of the political struggles of Reconstruction Days through 1868. Describes the departure of Negroes from plantations during the Civil War (pp. 118-20, 125-27).

F10 Fisher, Isaac

(a) "Negro Migration, an Opportunity for Biracial Statesmanship in the South," *National Conference of Social Work Proceedings* (1924), 75-82.

A brief paper on recent migrations, presenting some of their causes and effects, and emphasizing the increased necessity for interracial coöperation because of these movements

For other works by this author, *see* W42(a).

F11 Fisher, Rudolph

(a) "The South Lingers On," *Survey*, LIII, 644-47 (March, 1925).

A collection of brief sketches of five individuals showing the problems of adjustment faced by migrants from the South who come to Harlem.

F12 Fleming, Walter L.

(a) *The Civil War and Reconstruction in Alabama*. Cleveland, Arthur H. Clark Co. (1911), 815 pp. (First ed. 1905, Columbia University Press.)

An analysis of conditions in Alabama before, during and just after the Civil War, including a description of the Union League and Negro political participation, and the problems of reconstruction in education, the church agriculture etc

(b) *Documentary History of Reconstruction*. Cleveland, Arthur H. Clark Co. (1907), 2 vols.

A collection of contemporary documents showing the problems of Reconstruction Days in the South and attempts and proposals as to how to solve them. Gives contemporary impressions and accounts of Negro suffrage, position of Negroes before the courts, mob violence, Jim Crow segregation, Negro and Republican control, etc

(c) "'Pap' Singleton, The Moses of the Colored Exodus," *American Journal of Sociology*, XV, 61-82 (July, 1909).

A very good account of the exodus of 1879— its causes and general results with emphasis on the influence of leadership.

F13 Fletcher, Frank H.

(a) *Negro Exodus*. Report of agent appointed for the purpose of obtaining information in regard to colored emigration (undated), 24 pp.

A report of an investigation of the condition of the Negroes in Kansas shortly after the 1879 movement, consisting chiefly of statements by the Negroes giving their reasons for leaving the South and describing their condition in Kansas. Interesting contemporary material.

F14(a) "Flight into Egypt," *Crisis*, XIV, 136 July, 1917).

Extracts from southern newspapers discussing the causes of migration.

F15(a) "Flight of Negroes," *Nation*, XXVIII, 242 (April 10, 1879).
An editorial on the 1879 exodus stating the economic and political conditions which brought about the movement

F16(a) "For the Negroes of Pittsburgh," *Survey*, XLIII, 416-17 (January 17, 1920).
An editorial on phases of settlement work among the Negroes of Pittsburgh in a rapidly growing Negro section.

F17 Fortson, Blanton, and William Pickens

(a) "Negro Migrations: A Debate," *Forum*, LXXII, 593-607 (November, 1924).
Popularly written papers debating the wisdom of migration, mentioning causes of the movement

F18 Foster, A. L.

(a) "A Coöperative Adventure in the Field of Race Relations," *Opportunity*, VII, 98-99 (March, 1929).
A description of the work of the Chicago Urban League, especially of its efforts to improve race relations

Foster, Austin P., *see* M52(a).

F19 Foster, H. M.

(a) "Negro Chain Stores," *Nation*, CXXXII, 271-72 (March 11, 1931).
A description of recent movements in Negro business in the attempt to train Negroes to conduct stores etc Gives a history of the Colored Merchants Association and shows conditions of business, particularly in Harlem.

F20 Frankel, Emil

(a) "Social Work among Negroes in New Jersey," *Hospital Social Service*, XXI, 339-46 (1930).
Brief report of a general survey of conditions among Negroes in New Jersey made by questionnaires sent to leading white and colored citizens Emphasis is on social and health activities among Negroes Discusses the work of social agencies, housing, occupations, crime, dependency and health

(b) "Social Work among Negroes in New Jersey," *New Jersey Conference of Social Work Bulletin*, I: 1-7 (May 30, 1930).
Another printing of F20(a).

F21 Frazier, E. Franklin

(a) "The Changing Status of the Negro Family," *Social Forces*, IX 386-93 (March, 1931).

A comparison of the status of the Negro family in the days of slavery and at the present time, emphasizing the effects of migration upon family life Also mentions the effect of migration on the attitude of northern Negroes and on living conditions

(b) "Chicago: A Cross Section of Negro Life," *Opportunity*, VII, 70-73 (March, 1929).

A general picture of the economic and social life of Negroes in Chicago, dealing briefly with the increase in population and the effect of migration on business, on occupations on the attitude of northern Negroes, and on churches

(c) "Family Disorganization among Negroes," *Opportunity*, IX 7 (July, 1931).

A sane analysis of the effect of migration upon family disorganization, delinquency and dependency among Negroes, with particular reference to conditions in Chicago.

(d) "Family Life of the Negro in the Small Town," *Hospital Social Service*, XIV, 468-73 (December, 1926).

A discussion of the status of the Negro family in the small towns of the South, mentioning the effect of migration to towns and of occupations and housing upon family life

(e) "Family Life of the Negro in the Small Town," *National Conference of Social Work Proceedings* (1926), 384-88.

Deals with migration to towns it affects family life

(f) "How Present Day Problems of Social Life Affect the Negro," *Hospital Social Service*, XIII, 384-93 (April, 1926).

A discussion of the effect on the Negro of the present disorganization of the family, poverty and problems of health Mentions the effect of migration upon family life, and upon the control of the church over its members

(g) "The Negro Community: A Cultural Phenomenon," *Social Forces*, VII, 415-20 (March, 1929).

A brief picture of the Negro community in Chicago as a cultural phenomenon, describing its spacial distribution, the nature of its economic, social, religious and political organization, and the status of the Negro family.

(h) "The Negro Family," *Annals*, CXL, 44-51 (November, 1928).

A brief presentation of various statistical aspects of the Negro family and the development of family life among them. Mentions the need for studying the effect of migration on the family.

(i) "A Negro Industrial Group," *Howard Review*, I, 126-211 (June, 1924).

A careful, first-hand study of economic, social and living conditions of the Negro longshoremen in New York City. *See also* Z16(a).

(j) "Occupational Classes among Negroes in Cities," *American Journal of Sociology*, XXXV, 718-38 (March, 1930).

A careful analysis of occupational classifications among Negroes in selected cities North and South Contends stratification is due largely to migration to cities

(k) "The Occupational Differentiation of the Negro in Cities," *Southern Workman*, LIX, 195a-200a (May, 1930).

A discussion of class distinctions among Negroes and the effect of migration upon this economic and social differentiation.

(l) "Three Scourges of the Negro Family," *Opportunity*, IV, 210-13 (July, 1926).

Sensible discussion of the present status of the Negro family

F22 Frey, John P.

(a) "Attempts to Organize Negro Workers," *American Federationist*, XXXVI, 296-305 (March, 1929).

Presents the viewpoint of the A F. of L concerning the problems involved in trying to include Negroes

F23(a) "From a Report on Negro Labor: Based on a Questionnaire of the Pennsylvania Bureau of Employment," *Bloomfield's Labor Digest*, XX, 3419-21 (March 20, 1926).

A report of results secured from a questionnaire concerning the nature of occupations of Negroes in industry in Pennsylvania and their success in adapting themselves to industrial conditions.

F24(a) "From Kitchen to Factory," *World Outlook* V, 29 (October, 1919).

A brief account of the entrance of colored women into industries

F25 Fry, C. Luther

(a) "The Negro in the United States—A Statistical Statement," *Annals*, CXL, 26-35 (November, 1928).

A statistical survey of the Negro population, its rate of growth, age and sex composition, and distribution. Emphasizes the urban movement

G1 Gannett, Henry

(a) *Occupations of the Negroes.* Baltimore, Maryland (1895), 16 pp. John F. Slater Fund Occasional Papers No. 6.

A statistical analysis and graphic presentation of the occupations of Negroes in the United States as a whole and in specific states in 1890.

Also in United States Bureau of Education, *Report, 1894-95*, Vol. II, pp. 1384-96.

(b) *Statistics of the Negroes in the United States.* Baltimore, The Trustees (1894), 28 pp. John F. Slater Fund Occasional Papers No. 4.

A general discussion of the census figures on the growth and distribution of Negroes in the United States up to 1890, giving the history of the Negro in each slave state, and showing the per cent of Negroes in the total population of each at various decades Discusses migrations of Negroes from 1880-90 and the direction and extent Has many charts

Also in United States Bureau of Education, *Report, 1894-95*, Vol II, pp. 1396-1415.

G2 Garner, George

(a) "The Negro Question as It Relates to Negroes in the North and in the South," *Manufacturers Record* XCII, 63-64 (December 1, 1927).

A contention by a Northerner that race dificulties in the North and the dangers of migration are due to the fact that Northerners are ignorant of the Negro's racial characteristics and hence tend to treat him as a social and political equal.

G3 Garner, James W.

(a) *Reconstruction in Mississippi.* New York, Macmillan Co. (1901), 422 pp.

A history of political troubles and the economic and social problems of Reconstruction.

G4 Gee, Wilson, and John J. Corson

(a) *Rural Depopulation in Certain Tidewater and Piedmont Areas of Virginia.* Charlottesville (1929), 104 pp. University of Virginia Institute for Research in Social Sciences No. 3.

A valuable detailed study of the problem of migration from rural counties of Virginia. Deals with population trends by counties, 1790-1920, some causative factors, conditions among the migrants such as their social origins, education, occupation, age, size of farm, etc., present residence and occupation the composition of the non-migrants and their education, occupation, etc Gives total number of Negroes in occupations entered after migration — no geographical distinction, but minute classification of jobs In every

discussion compares the status of whites and Negroes who have migrated or are among the non-migrants

G5 Gehlke, Charles E.

(a) "Negro in Detroit," *National Municipal Review*, XVI, 748-51 (December, 1927).
A review of D8(a), which is not readily available

G6(a) "Georgia Plantation," *Scribners*, XXI, 830-36 (April, 1881).
A description of life on the plantation owned by Mr Barrow of Oglethorpe, Georgia, and the changes that had occurred between the Civil War and 1880. A good description of the early tenancy system of farming.

G7 Georgia State Department of Commerce and Labor

(a) *Fifth Annual Report of the Commissioner of Commerce and Labor* (for the year ending December 31, 1916).
On pp. 5-7 the labor situation and shortage due to the migration of Negroes is mentioned and a tax on labor agents advocated
No mention of migration in Sixth to Sixteenth Reports, 1917-28.

G8 Gilbert, John W.

(a) "City Housing of Negroes in Relation to Health," *Southern Sociological Congress: The New Chivalry* (1915), pp. 405-12.
A discussion of the effect of poor housing conditions on Negro health in cities North and South

G9 Gilliam, E. W.

(a) "Negroes in the United States," *Popular Science Monthly*, XXII 433-44 (February, 1883).
Deals with population figures for 1830 to 1880, showing increase and distribution of blacks with general conclusions on the status and future place of the Negro politically and economically

G10 Gilligan, Francis J.

(a) *The Morality of the Color Line*. Washington, D.C., Catholic University of America (1928), 222 pp.
A synthetic study discussing discrimination, particularly in trains, schools, industries housing, etc., with casual mention of the effect of migration on this problem. Attempts to prove the non-Christian nature of such discrimination

G11 Gist, F. W.

(a) "Migratory Habits of the Negro under Past and Present Condi-

tions," *Manufacturers Record*, LXXXV, 77-79 (March 13, 1924).
An excellent statistical view of the naturalness of migrations and the economic causes and results of the recent Negro movement

G12 Godkin, E. L.

(a) "The Flight of the Negroes," *Nation*, XXVIII, 242 (April 10, 1879).
A brief discussion of some of the causes of the 1879 migration from a somewhat biased viewpoint

G13 Gold, H. R., and B. K. Armstrong

(a) *A Preliminary Study of Interracial Conditions in Chicago*. New York, Home Missions Council (1920), 15 pp. (unnumbered)
A superficial treatment of some of the housing, social and industrial problems in Chicago resulting from migration, with suggestions as to ways in which the churches may aid in clarifying the racial situation

Goldenweiser, E. A., *see* U3(5a), U3(15a).

Gover, Mary, *see* U3(16a).

G14(a) *Governor Dorsey's Statement as to the Negro in Georgia* (April 22, 1921), 24 pp. (unnumbered
An official document instancing cases of mistreatment of Negroes in Georgia.

G15 Graham, Irene J

(a) "Family Support and Dependency among Chicago Negroes: A Study of Unpublished Census Data," *Social Service Review*, III, 541-62 (December, 1929).
An exhaustive analysis of unpublished census data on Chicago Negroes, dealing with the problem of family support and dependency Includes tables of occupations, and information on sources of income and the e fect of economic conditions on family life

(b) "The Negro Family in a Northern City," *Opportunity*, VIII 48-51 (February, 1930).
An analysis of the make-up of families in Chicago on the basis of Census Bureau data, showing the number of children per family broken families sources of income, and effect on family life of the occupational status of the breadwinner together with comparison with a white group.

G16 Granger, Lester B.

(a) "Race Relations and the School System," *Opportunity*, III, 327-29 (November, 1925).
Presents the results of a study of Negroes in the high schools of New Jersey, comparing rates of attendance and of graduation for whites and

Negroes, and debating whether separate or mixed schools have higher rates of attendance for colored children. Incidentally discusses the separation of races

G17(a) "Great Migration," *Crisis*, XXVII, 77-78 (December, 1923).

A summary of comments in periodicals on the causes of migration and on Georgia's financial loss as a result of the movement

G18 Greater New York Federation of Churches

(a) *The Negro Churches of Manhattan:* A Study Made in 1930. New York, The Federation, 36 pp.

A first-hand survey of churches in Harlem—their number, membership, activities, and place in the life of the community. Shows trends of population in Harlem.

G19 Green, Howard Whipple

(a) "A Comparison of the Death Rates from Tuberculosis in 23 Large Cities of the United States," *American Review of Tuberculosis*, XIII, 94-96 (January, 1926).

A brief article giving death rates for southern and northern cities for colored and white

For other works by this author, *see* C21(a).

G20 Greene, Lorenzo, and Carter G. Woodson

(a) *The Negro Wage Earner.* Washington, The Association for the Study of Negro Life and History (1930), 388 pp.

Provides a detailed analysis of the occupational distribution and labor characteristics of Negroes on the basis of the census division of occupations The status of the Negro in each occupational division is discussed for the two periods 1890 to 1917, and since 1917. Each of the occupational divisions for each period, deals with number and per cent of Negroes employed rate of increase or decrease, wages, economic opportunities success relation to unions, etc The economic causes and effects of migration are discussed throughout the book in scattered references in so far as conditions in each occupation have affected or been affected by migration.

G21 Greener, R. T

(a) "Emigration of Colored Citizens from the Southern States," *American Journal of Social Science*, XI, 22-36 (May, 1880).

A contemporary discussion of the c uses and advantages of migration as an answer to the arguments against the movement by F Douglass in an article in the same issue, for which see D14(a).

G22 Guernsey, F. R.

(a) "Negro Exodus," *International Review*, VII, 373-90 October, 1879).

A detailed and impartial discussion of the causes of the exodus of 1879 and the status of the migrants in Kansas, together with suggestions for the improvement of conditions in the South

G23 Guild, June P.

(a) "The Negro in Richmond V rginia," *Southern Workman*, LIX, 51-54 (February, 1930).

Summary of R18(a).

G24 Guthrie, W. A.

(a) "Statutory Prohibition of the Emigration of Colored Laborers from North Carolina," *American Law Review*, XXXVIII, 144-45 (January and February, 1904).

A brief letter to the *Law Review* summarizing the legislation of North Carolina concerning Negro emigration and the tax on labor agents

G25 Gwinnell, William B.

(a) "Shifting Populations in Great Northern Cities," *Opportunity*, VI, 279 September, 1928).

A brief survey of the changing proportions that Negroes and the newer immigrant stocks form in the populations of large northern cities, emphasizing the important bearing of this shift on public opinion.

Hager, John M., *see* U3(17a).

H1 Hain, A. J

(a) "Our Immgrant, The Negro" *Iron Trade Review*, LXXIII 730-36 (September 13, 1923).

A sane unprejudiced discussion of recent movements their extent causes and economic results the place of the Negro in Northern industries and the attitude of employers toward him.

H2 Hall, Charles E.

(a) "The Negro Is Coming to Town," *North American Review*, CCXXIX (January, 1930).

Deals with the extent of migration from 1920 to 1925 and some of the results in northern cities

H3 Hammond, L. H.

(a) "Ignorance and the Eleven Million," *Nations Business*, VIII 38-40 (December, 1920).

An article on the necessity of educating and assisting Negroes to better their living conditions as a means of improving the labor supply. Deals largely with measures the southern states are taking to remedy conditions among Negroes in regard to health, education and race relations

H4 Hammond, Matthew B.

(a) *The Cotton Industry*. New York (December, 1897), 382 pp. American Economic Association Publications, n.s. 1.

Chaps. iv-vi give a description of the share system, tenancy credit system and the effect of these tendencies on southern agriculture and the Negro's place in that field

H5(a) "Hampton and Negro Migration," *Southern Workman*, XLVI, 330-31 (June, 1917).

An editorial explaining Hampton's attitude in sending Negro girls North for domestic service.

H6 *Hampton Negro Conference Annual Reports* (1897-1912), Nos. 1-16. Hampton, Virginia, Hampton Institute Press.

Contain records of the Annual Conferences including digests of papers on various phases of the Negro problem. Only occasional references to migration, which are listed below.

(a) *1898*: States that Negroes are flocking to cities, (p. 10); dis-discusses dangers confronting Negro girls in the North (pp. 62-69). *See also* M20(a).

(b) *1900*: Discusses conditions among Negroes in the North and mentions their coming from the South (pp. 39-41.)

(c) *1904*: States causes of migration to Chicago (p. 127); and discusses briefly m gration of Negro girls to the North (pp. 39-51).

(d) *1905*: Mentions the evil conditions attending the migration of Negro girls from V rginia (pp. 75-79).

(e) *1906*: Deals with housing in the North (pp. 52-67). *See also* W49(b).

(f) *1907*: Merely states that Negroes migrate to cities in the North (p. 97).

(g) *1911*: Mentions some of the reasons why the Negroes leave the rural districts (pp. 10, 25, 26).

(h) *1912*: States reasons for the movement to cities (pp. 10, 11, 18 ff.). *See also* H19(f), H19(h), J18(b), P25(a).

H7 Hancock, Gordon B.

(a) "Changing Status of Negro Labor" *Southern Workman*, LX, 351-60 (August, 1931).

A good general survey of the changes that are taking place in the status of Negro labor.

(b) "Our Coming Captivity," *Southern Workman*, LIX, 153-60 (April, 1930).

An article describing the increasing loss of economic opportunities for Negroes due to displacement by whites and the reasons for the growing seriousness of the Negro's economic situation.

H8(a) "Harlem" *Survey*, LIII, 629-30 (March, 1925).

An unsigned article on the significance of Harlem as the center of the modern Negro's hopes for improvement and racial uplift

Harmon, G. E., *see* U3(18a).

H9 Harmon, J. H.

(a) "The Negro as a Local Business Man," *Journal of Negro History*, XIV, 116-55 (April, 1929).

A general historical account of the status of Negro business concerns before and after 1865, and at the present time, and of factors preventing the rapid development of these concerns

H10 Harris, Abram L.

(a) "Negro and Economic Radicalism," *Modern Quarterly*, II, 198-208 (February, 1925).

A study of the Negro's attitude toward trade unions and business organization.

(b) "The Negro in the Coal Mining Industry," *Opportunity*, IV, 45-48 (February, 1926).

Discusses in detail the numerical strength of Negroes in the coal mines particularly in West Virginia, and their relation to the unions

(c) "Negro Labor's Quarrel with White Workingmen," *Current History*, XXIV, 903-8 (September, 1926).

Deals with the present relations of Negroes to the unions, showing the attitude of the A F. of L. and the locals toward Negroes, and the disadvantages su fered by colored industrial workers As a result of the unions' discrimination against Negroes they are inclined to listen to Communist c programs.

(d) "Negro Migration to the North," *Current History*, XX, 921-25 (September, 1924).

A sensible account of the economic conditions leading to migration, and of the northern migration as a part of the urban movement

(e) *The Negro Population in Minneapolis*: A Study of Race Relations. Minneapolis, Minneapolis Urban League and Phyllis Wheatly Settlement (1926), 77 pp.

A careful statistical study of Negro migration to Minneapolis up to 1925, and of race relations and the social and economic conditions of Negroes resulting therefrom.

(f) *The Negro Worker*. Progressive Labor Library Pamphlet No. 3, New York. Published by the National Executive Committee of the Conference for Progressive Labor Activities (1930), 17 pp.

A discussion of the necessity of including Negro workers in organized labor.

(g) "The Negro Worker: A Problem of Vital Concern to the Entire Labor Movement," *Labor Age*, XIX, 5-8 (February, 1930).

A discussion of the attitude of organized labor toward Negroes and of the place of Negroes in industry and the unions.

——— For other works by this author, *see* S51(a).

H11 Harris, H. L., Jr.

(a) "Health of the Negro Family in Chicago, Illinois," *Opportunity*, V, 258-60 (September, 1927).

A general account of the factors required to improve health conditions among Negroes, containing interesting charts of Negro and white death rates in Chicago for 1925.

(b) "Negro Mortality Rates in Chicago," *Social Service Review*, I 58-77 (March, 1927).

A discussion of mortality rates in Chicago based on first-hand investigations of the Health Commission. *See also* B57(a).

H12 Harrison, Shelby, and Others

(a) *The Public Employment Office*. New York, Russell Sage Foundation (1924), 685 pp.

Chap. xxxiv (pp. 605-10, "Negro Workers by F. A. King) contains a dis cussion of the relation of Negro workers to public employment offices

H13 Hart, Albert Bushnell

(a) "The Realities of Negro Suffrage," *American Political Science Association Proceedings* (1905), Vol. II, 149-65.

Describes the history of Negro suffrage before the Civil War and since, and the means by which colored voters have been deprived of the vote since Reconstruction.

H14 Hart, Hastings H.

(a) "Peonage and the Public," *Survey*, XLVI, 43-44 (April 9, 1921).
A general description of what is meant by peonage and of the necessity for investigating the conditions revealed in Georgia by the murder of Negroes in Jasper County

H15 Hartt, Rollin L.

(a) "New Negro," *Independent*, CV, 59-60 (January 15, 1921).
A very general account of the effect of war and migration on the Negro's psychology and race consciousiness.

(b) "When the Negro Comes North," *World's Work*, XLVIII, 83-89, 184-92, 318-23 (May, June and July, 1924).
A popularly written group of articles on the extent, causes and effects of recent migration.

H16 Hartzell, J. C.

(a) "Negro Exodus, 1879," *Methodist Quarterly Review*, XXXIX 722-47 (October, 1879).
An interesting contemporary account of the 1879 exodus showing in great detail the conditions which caused the migration. Written from the religious point of view

H17 Haygood, Atticus

(a) *Our Brothers in Black* New York, Phillips and Hunt (1881), 252 pp.
A southern man's personal opinions on the Negro problem and the necessity for the education of the blacks. Chap. iii denounces the idea of colonization.

H18 Haynes, Elizabeth R.

(a) "Negroes in Domestic Service in the United States," *Journal of Negro History*, VIII, 384-442 (October, 1923).
An exhaustive analysis of the status of colored women workers in th s field

(b) "Two Million Negro Women at Work," *Southern Workman*, LI, 64-72 (February, 1922).
A general presentation of the nature of occupations in which Negro women are found in the country as a whole describing the conditions of labor and wages in each of the main fields

H19 Haynes, George E.

(a) "Church and Negro Progress," *Annals*, CXL, 264-71 (November, 1928).
A discussion of the membership and activities of the Negro church and its influence upon Negro life

(b) "The Church and the Negro Spirit," *Survey*, LIII, 695-97 (March, 1925).

An article on the place of the church in the life of the Negroes of New York

(c) "Conditions among Negroes in the Cities," *Annals*, XLIX, 105-19 (September, 1913).

Sympathetic sensible discussion of the causes of, and problems aroused by the urban movement of Negroes, such as segregation, housing conditions, economic opportunities health and education.

(d) "Effect of War Conditions on Negro Labor," *Academy of Political Science Proceedings*, VIII, 299-312 (February, 1919).

A thoughtful unbiased consideration of the effect of the War on relations between Negroes and whites Includes a survey of causes and results of migration under (1) the change in the relation of the Negro wage earners to white employers North and South (2) the change in the relation of Negro wage earners to white wage earners and (3) the change in the Negro himself

(e) "Migration of Negroes into Northern Cities," *National Conference of Social Work Proceedings* (1917), 494-97.

Brief discussion of the general character and causes of migration.

(f) "Movement of Negroes from the Country to the City," *Southern Workman*, XLII, 230-36 (April, 1913).

An excellent discussion of census figures showing movements of wh tes and Negroes, and causes and remedies of such movements. Same material contained in H19(h), and much the same in H6(h).

(g) "The Negro at Work," *American Review of Reviews*, LIX, 389-93 (April, 1919).

A general treatment of the work Negroes did during the War, the effect of war conditions on them, and activities of the Division of Negro Economics.

(h) *The Negro at Work in New York City*. New York, Columbia University Press (1912), 159 pp. Columbia University Studies in History, Economics and Public Law No. 124.

An unbiased statistical study and original investigation of the Negro as a wage earner in New York City. The first chapter gives a good discussion of the causes of migration to cities and the rate of increase of urban colored population, which is similar to H6(h) and H19(f).

(i) "Negro Laborer and the Immigrant," *Survey*, XLVI, 209-10 (May 14, 1921).

Discusses the possible future supply of immigrant labor, its effect on the Negro's place in industry, and the Negro's success in northern industry

(j) *Negro Migration and Its Implications North and South.* An address before the Seventy-seventh Annual Meeting of the American Missionary Association, Springfield Massachusetts (October 23, 1923), 15 pp.

An account of the extent direction, causes and results of the migration, dealing with conditions in the North and in the South. *See also* H19(k).

(k) "Negro Migration and Its Implications North and South," *77th Annual Report of the American Missionary Society* (1923), 14-17.

A comprehensive extract of an address discussing the nature of the movement, some of its results, and the Negro's place in industry

Summarizes H19(j), which is not always available in libraries

(l) "Negro Migration—Its Effect on Family and Community Life in the North," *National Conference of Social Work Proceedings* (1924), 62-75.

A discussion of the character of the recent migration and its place in the whole problem of internal migration, including material on types of migrants and of localities from which they came, as well as on housing, health and similar problems in the North

Also reprinted in pamphlet form.

(m) "Negro Migration: Its Effect on Family and Community Life in the North," *Opportunity*, II, 271-74, 303-6 (September and October, 1924).

Practically the same article as H19(l).

(n) *Negro Newcomers in Detroit.* New York, Home Missions Council (1918), 42 pp.

An excellent preliminary survey of the condition of the Negro in Detroit with a brief summary of causes of migration Includes a program of action for the churches in aiding the migrants

(o) "Negroes Move North," *Survey*, XL, 115-22 (May 4, 1918); XLI, 455-61 (January 4, 1919).

The first section gives an account of the causes and characteristics of migration and of results in the South while the second discusses conditions of Negro labor in the North

(p) "Race Riots in Relation to Democracy," *Survey*, XLII, 697-99. (August 9, 1919).

A thoughtful discussion of the relation between race conflicts and the lack of right contacts between the races

(q) *The Trend of the Races.* New York, Council of Women for Home Missions and Missionary Education Movement of the United States and Canada (1922), 205 pp.

Chiefly a discussion of the progress the Negroes have made since the Civil

War. Chap. ii gives a concise, impartial summary of the causes and effects of migration during later years, and the types of migrants

(r) "What Negroes Think of the Race Riots," *Public*, XXII, 848-49 (August 9, 1919).
A picture of the reaction of Negroes toward the Washington and Chicago riots, showing their increasing feeling of the necessity for militancy in protecting themselves, and discussing in general the problem of race relations

——— For other works by this author, *see* U3(19a).

H20(a) "Health Campaign among Negroes," *New York City Department of Health Weekly Bulletin*, VI, 105 (April 7, 1917).
A brief article on death rates in New York City among Negroes and whites and plans for an educational campaign among Negroes.

H21(a) "Health of Negroes in New York City," *New York City Department of Health Weekly Bulletin*, XV, 89-91 (June 5, 1926).
A discussion of deaths of Negroes compared to those of whites in New York City in 1925, by certain causes with reasons why their mortality is higher in specific diseases

H22(a) "Hegira (or The Exodus)," *Crisis*, XIII, 134-35, 179-82, 233-34 (January and March, 1917); XIV, 23-25 (May, 1917).
Quotations from northern and southern newspapers on the causes of migration, showing the attitude of the North, the South and the Negro.

H23(a) "Helping Negro Workers to Purchase Homes," *Opportunity*, II, 23-24 (January, 1924).
An account of a corporation established in Baltimore to help Negroes buy homes.

H24(a) "Helping the Negro Migrant," *Southern Workman*, XLVI, 527 (October, 1917).
An editorial summarization of W9(e). *See also* L15(a).

H25 Henry, Alice

(a) *Women and the Labor Movement*. New York, George H. Doran Co. (1926), 241 pp.
Chap. xi (pp. 202-11, The Negro Woman) discusses the effect of the War and migration upon women as industrial workers in various industries. Material is taken largely from U3(32a).

H26 Henry, Waights G.

(a) *The Negro as an Economic Factor in Alabama*. Nashville, Tennessee, Printed for the author, Publishing House of the Methodist Episcopal Church, South (1919), 111 pp.
A general discussion of the social and economic condition of the Negro in

Alabama, together with a statistical survey of the Negro's place in Alabama industries

H27 Herskovits, Melville J.

(a) *The American Negro*: A Study in Race Crossing New York Alfred A. Knopf (1928), 92 pp.

A study of race traits and race amalgamation, and of the physical type Negroes are developing as a result of such mingling.

H28 Hill, Joseph A.

(a) "Effects of the Northward Migration of the Negro," *American Sociological Society Proceedings*, XVIII, 34-46 (1923).

A preliminary and briefer treatment of material in H28(b).

(b) "Recent Northward Migration of the Negro," *Monthly Labor Review*, XVIII, 415-88 (March, 1924).

Discusses the volume and characteristics of the movement of Negroes to the North during the World War with a brief history of earlier movements to the Southwest and to the North showing the unprecedented volume of recent migration to the larger northern cities and from the far South Gives tersely the effect on the nature of occupations, and on birth and death rates. *See also* H28(a), H28(c), U3(29a).

(c) "Recent Northward Migration of the Negro," *Opportunity*, II 100-5 (April, 1924).

Another printing of H28(b) with several numerical differences and text changes

——— For other works by this author, *see* U3(20a), U3(44a).

H29 Hill, T. Arnold

(a) "Labor," *Opportunity*, VII, 23 (January, 1929).

A report of the Secretary of the Industrial Relations Department of the National Urban League on the current outstanding features of labor conditions among Negroes This article discusses the employment situation and economic opportunities in Pittsburgh, with slight references to conditions in Detroit.

(b) "Labor," *Opportunity*, IX October, 1931).

Summary of the unemployment situation among Negroes and résumé of the increase of Negro population in northern cities 1920-30.

(c) "Labor: Dayton, Ohio," *Opportunity*, VI, 343 (November, 1928).

A short article giving instances of discrimination against Negroes in schools, theaters, occupations, etc., in Dayton, Ohio.

(d) "Negro in Industry," *American Federationist*, XXXII, 915-20 (October, 1925).

A good summary of the movement to northern cities its relation to the entrance of Negroes into industry, and to the problems of organized labor.

(e) "The Negro in Industry, 1926," *Opportunity*, V, 51-52 (February, 1927).

A report of the Negro's gains and losses in industry and of his relation to the unions during 1926 as these conditions were found by various branches of the Urban League. Discusses briefly the localities affected by migration during the year.

(f) "Negro Labor," *American Federationist*, XXXV, 1452-56 (December, 1928).

Discusses the nature of the occupations of Negroes in various states North and South the gains in industrial pursuits wages, and relation to unions

(g) "Negroes in Southern Industry," *Annals*, CLIII, 170-81 (January, 1931).

A discussion of the Negro's present place in the industrial life of the South dealing with the nature of his occupations, his relation to the unions his economic opportunities etc Treats of the urban trend both before and since 1920, showing its e fect on unemployment and occupation

(h) *Occupations for Negroes.* New York, National Urban League (1928), 8 pp.

A pamphlet describing the work and program of the Industri l Relations Department of the Urban League

(i) "Present Status of Negro Labor," *Opportunity*, VII, 143-45 (May, 1929).

A fair-minded discussion of unemployment arnong Negroes, showing its relation to the general industrial situation and factors producing the present conditions. Discusses occupations in which Negroes are found in various cities with casual mention of migration

(j) "Present Status of the Negro in Industry," *United States Department of Labor Bulletin 501*, pp. 94-105 (1929).

Proceedings of the Sixteenth Annual Meeting of the International Association of Public Service Employment Agencies held in Cleveland, September 1928. An address presenting the nature of occupations of the Negro, his entrance into industry economic dead lines in occupations and in labor unions, and the need for vocational training.

(k) "Recent Developments in the Problem of Negro Labor," *National Conference of Social Work Proceedings* (1921), 321-25.

A discussion of the effect of recent migrations on the relation of Negroes to industry, to unions, and to communities in the North

(l) "Richmond — Louisville — Cincinnati," *Opportunity*, IX 218 (July, 1931).

A brief discussion of the status of Negroes in Richmond, Louisville and Cin cinnati, maintaining that Richmond is losing its Negro population because of the attitude of whites. For an answer see S23(a).

(m) "Why Southern Negroes Don't Go South," *Survey*, XLIII, 183-85 (November 29, 1919).

An article provoked by rumors that Negro migrants were returning South Shows efforts to induce migrants to return and reasons why Negroes stayed in the North

Hill, T. Edward, *see* W14(a-c).

H30 Hill, W. B.

(a) *Rural Survey of Clarke County, Georgia, with Special Reference to the Negroes*, (March, 1915), Bulletin of the University of Georgia, Vol. XV, No. 3, 63 pp. Phelps-Stokes Fellowship Studies No. 2.

Discusses the location, topography and early history of Clarke County economic conditions such as tenancy farm ownership, value of farms, etc educational, religious and social conditions.

H31 Hobbs, Samuel H., Jr

(a) *North Carolina, Economic and Social*. Chapel Hill, University of North Carolina Press (1930), 403 pp.

An exhaustive description of North Carolina — its physical resources, population composition, physical and social-economic areas industrial, agricultural, and financial institutions wealth, literacy, government etc Discusses urban trend for the total population, mentioning movement to the state, 1910-25. Contains a good discussion of the tenancy system.

H32 Hoffman, Frederick L.

(a) "The Negro Health Problem" *Opportunity*, IV, 119-21 (April, 1926).

A discussion of the Negro's progress in health, pointing out factors tending to improve it

(b) *Race Traits and Tendencies of the American Negro*. New York Macmillan Co. (1896), 329 pp. Also published in American Economic Association Publications Vol. XI, Nos. 1-3.

A careful analysis of population and vital statistics economic and social c nditions and problems of race amalgamation, particularly as shown in the Census One of the best of the early scientific studies but somewhat marred by dogmatic treatment of questions now recognized as moot. *See also* M39(p).

(c) "Vital Statistics of the Negro," *Arena*, V, 529-42 (April, 1892).

A statistical account of vital statistics of the colored population through the Census of 1890, emphasizing the drift to cities of the South as a cause of high mortality. Chiefly a discussion of mortality rates

H33 Hollis, John P.

(a) *The Early Period of Reconstruction in South Carolina.* Baltimore, Johns Hopkins Press (1905), 129 pp. Johns Hopkins University Studies in Historical and Political Science, Series 23.

Deals with the effect of the Civil War upon the economic and political life of South Carolina, its chief features of political life, 1865-68, and activities of the Freedmen's Bureau.

H34 Holmes, George K.

(a) "The Supply of Farm Labor," *Annals*, XXXIII, 362-72 (March, 1909).

Describes the nature of farm labor and migration to cities; mentions the Negro's migratory tendency

H35 Holmes, Samuel J.

(a) "The Biological Trend of the Negro," *University of California Chronicle*, XXXII, 38-70 (January, 1930).

Discusses the trend of Negroes health, and of their birth and death rates, and their tendenc es to specific diseases, particularly as these have been affected by migration

(b) "Will the Negro Survive in the North?" *Scientific Monthly*, XXVII, 557-61 (December, 1928).

A discussion of vital statistics of Negroes living in the North, showing that Negro mortality is decreasing in northern cities and that in 1924-25 many northern states showed an increase of births over deaths

H36 ——— and S. L. Parker

(a) "Stabilized Natural Increase of the Negro," *Journal of the American Statistical Association*, XXVI, 159-71 (June, 1931).

A statistical treatment of the rates of increase among Negroes both North and South with some consideration of the influence of migration on these rates.

H37 Holsey, Albon L.

(a) "The C. M. A. S ores Face the Chains," *Opportunity*, VII, 210-13 (July, 1929).

An account of the organization of the Colored Merchants Association and what it has done for Negro business in Montgomery Alabama, and Winston-Salem, North Carolina.

(b) "Negro in Business Aided by Racial Appeal," *Forbes*, XXI, 42-48 (January 15, 1928).

An account of the work of the National Negro Business League and of the nature and progress of Negro business concerns showing efforts to stimulate Negroes to support the enterprises of their own race

(c) "What the Negro Is Doing in Business," *Forbes*, XXIII (May 1, 1929).

Report of a survey made by the National Negro Business League, revealing the condition of Negro business enterprises in the North and South

H38 Holtzclaw, William W.

(a) "Present Status of the Negro Farmer in Mississippi," *Southern Workman*, LIX, 339-44 (August, 1930).

A picture of present conditions among Negroes in the cotton districts of Mississippi, showing the effect of migration upon the attitude of the South toward the Negro.

H39 Home Missions Council

(a) *Annual Report, 1918.* New York, Home Missions Council (1918), 21-32.

Three addresses on "Negro Migration to the Industrial Centers of North and East," giving the causes of and presenting the viewpoint of the South by John M Moore), of the Negro (by John Hope) and of the North by Willard Beahan).

(b) *The Negro Migration.* Repor of Committee on Negro Work New York, Home Missions Council (January, 1919), 9 pp. (unnumbered.)

A report of the religious needs of migrants

H40 Hope, John, and T. J. Woofter, Jr

(a) *Relations between the Black and White Races in America.* Preliminary draft for the Jerusalem Meeting of the International Missionary Council (March 24-April 8, 1928), 63 pp.

The paper by Woofter on "Agencies for Interracial Coöperation in the United States," discusses some of the problems arising from race prejudice and describes the development of forces and agencies which operate to increase understanding and friendship between the races, particularly the work of the Phelps-Stokes Fund extension agencies in agriculture the National Urban League and the Interracial Commission.

——— For other works by John Hope, *see* H39(a).

H41 Horwill, H. W.

(a) "Negro Exodus," *Contemporary Review*, CXIV 299-305 (September, 1918).

A fair and sympathetic treatment of the causes and results of migration, emphasizing increased prejudice and race riots.

H42 Houghteling, Leila

(a) *The Income and Standard of Living of Unskilled Laborers in Chicago*. Chicago, University of Chicago Press (1927), 224 pp.
A careful investigation of the subject including a study of the chief wage earners of the families, family composition, income and standards of living. See index for information relating to Negroes

H43(a) "Housmg and the Cincinnati Experiment," *Buffalo Foundation Forum*, I, 4-5 (February, 1921).
A statement of the undesirable housing conditions among Negroes in Buffalo and quotation from the Annual Report for June, 1926, of the Cincinnati Model Homes Company) a description of what has been done in Cincinnati to better such conditions among the colored population.

H44(a) "Housing of Colored People," *Chicago City Club Bulletin*, XII, 169-70 (August 18, 1919).
Summary of D21(a).

H45(a) "Housing Problem and the Negro," *Charities*, XV (October 7, 1905).
An editorial on the housing troubles of Negro migrants to northern cities

H46(a) "Housing the Migrants," *Opportunity*, I, 290 (October, 1923).
An editorial on the serious housing shortage due to northern migration.

H47(a) "Housing War," *Opportunity*, III 323-24 (November, 1925).
An editorial commenting on the race friction which has developed over the housing situation in various northern cities since the influx of Negroes

H48 Houze, J. O

(a) "Negro Labor and the Industries," *Opportunity*, I, 20-22 (January, 1923).
The personnel manager of the National Malleable Castings Company re ports on his experience with Negro labor.

H49 Hovey, George R.

(a) "Negro Americans," *Missionary Review*, XLV, 824 (October, 1922).
A discussion of the extent of migrations, 1910-20, to northern and southern cities, and the work of the National Urb n League

H50(a) "How Can the South Meet the Negro Migration Movement?" *Manufacturers Record*, LXXXIII, 88-90 (May 3, 1923).
An intelligent discussion of social and economic conditions in the South emphasizing the steps the South must take to retain its Negroes. *See also* P34(a).

H51(a) "How the Negroes Were Duped," *Journal of Negro History*, IV, 55 (January, 1919).

A letter dated 1879 showing how the Negroes were led to migrate by false pictures of the ideal conditions in Kansas.

H52(a) "How the War Brings Unprophesied Opportunities to the Negro Race," *Current Opinion*, LXI, 404-5 (December, 1916).

Extracts from various newspaper articles North and South discussing some of the probable effects of migration.

H53 Hoyer, H. A.

(a) "Migration of Colored Workers," *Survey*, XLIV, 930 (March 26, 1921).

A description of how Louisville Kentucky, took care of impecunious Negroes trying to return South

H54 Hubert, James H.

(a) "Harlem Faces Unemployment," *Opportunity*, IX, 42-45 (February, 1931).

A description of the unemployment situation in Harlem.

(b) "The Urban League Movement," *Southern Workman*, LV, 24-31 (January, 1926).

A history of the National Urban League and its activities

H55 Hughes, Elizabeth

(a) *Living Conditions of Small Wage Earners in Chicago.* Chicago Department of Public Welfare (1925), 62 pp.

A study of living conditions of Negroes and Mexicans. Mentions migration of Negroes to fill the labor gap during the World War and the effect of this movement on housing conditions. Deals with the length of residence of Negroes in Chicago, composition of the Negro group, lodgers, congestion, housing conditions, rents, and a little information on occupations and wages. Summarized in U3(25a).

H56 Huiswoud, Otto

(a) "The Negro and the Trade Unions," *Communist*, VII, 770-75 (December, 1928).

A summary and brief discussion of migration to the North, 1865-1910, and since 1910, and its effect upon the relations between Negroes and organized labor, with emphasis upon the necessity of including Negroes in organizations of Communists

Hunter, W. D., *see* U3(21a).

H57 Hussey, L. M.

(a) "Aframerican, North and South," *American Mercury*, VII, 196-200 (February, 1926).

A discussion of the status of the intelligent, educated colored man in the North and South showing the dangers of his unprotested migration from the South in leaving the masses of Negroes without intelligent leaders

Husted, Harold, *see* B53(a).

I1(a) "In the South," *Opportunity*, II 126-27, 190-91 (April and June, 1924).

Quotations from newspapers showing some of the results of the migration.

I2(a) "Increase of Negro Prisoners in Cleveland," *Survey*, XXXVIII 511-12 (September 8, 1917).

A very brief statement of the increase of Negro crime as a result of migration.

I3(a) "Industrial Employment of the Negro in Pennsylvania," *Monthly Labor Review*, XXII, 1224-27 June, 1926).

A short discussion of the status of the Negro in the steel industry

I4(a) "Industrial Problems in Cities," *Opportunity*, IV, 68-72, 93-94 (February and March, 1926).

A collection of reports from secretaries of Urban League Branches in various northern cities concerning the industrial status of the Negroes in those industrial centers

I5 Ingle, E.

(a) *The Negro in the District of Columbia.* Baltimore, Johns Hopkins Press (1893), 110 pp.

A general discussion of the situation of the Negro in the District of Columbia in 1893, particularly of his political status Gives a general estimate of the extent of the migration of Negroes to the District of Columbia (pp. 19-22).

I6 Irwin, Marjorie F.

(a) *The Negro in Charlottesville and Albermarle County.* University of Virginia (1929), 94 pp. Phelps-Stokes Fellowship Papers No. 9.

An investigation of Negro life in this section including material on the physical setting, history of the Negro in this county the social organization, churches schools, etc Chap. iv discusses migration from the county in 1870-80, 1888-89, 1916-17; and deals with the fact of migration and the economic, social and socio-psychological causes

I7(a) "Is the Negro Moving North?" *World's Work*, III, 1815 (March, 1902).

An editorial comment on census figures showing the increase of Negro population in various cities

J1 Jacobs, Thornwell

(a) "South Benefits from Migration," *American Bankers Association Journal*, XVI, 181-84 September, 1923).

Broad generalizations picturing the migration as beneficial from every view point

J2(a) "Jim Crow Cars," *Crisis*, XXXIII, 159 (January, 1927).

An extract from an editorial in a Negro Texas paper describing conditions in the Jim Crow cars and giving discrimination as one reason for migration

John F. Slater Fund, *see* F3(d), G1(a), G1(b).

J3 Johnsen, Julia E.

(a) *Selected Articles on the Negro Problem*. New York, H. W. Wilson Co. (1921), 370 pp.

A compilation of articles on various phases of the Negro problem; those on migration are quoted largely from S11(c).

J4 Johnson, Charles S.

(a) "The American Migrant: The Negro," *National Conference of Social Work Proceedings* (1927), 554-58.

Emphasizes the economic nature of Negro migration and connects it with the general trend of foreign and Mexican labor movements

(b) "The Balance Sheet," *World Tomorrow*, XI, 13-16 (January, 1928).

In a general discussion of present race relations the results of migration are shown in increased antagonism in the North and in the work of the Interracial Committees in the South

(c) "Black Workers and the City," *Survey*, LIII, 641-43 (March, 1925).

A popularly written, sane discussion of the problems involved in the adjust ment of Negro migrants to city life, particularly in New York Deals with the nature of occupations, new industrial openings, limitation of occupations and the attitude of unions toward colored workers

(d) "Changing Economic Status of the Negro," *Annals*, CXL, 128-37 (November, 1928).

A general survey of the Negro's entrance into industrial pursuits with occupational statistics Discusses the economic effects of the migration and the relation of Negro labor to foreign immigrant labor. Much of the material in this article is also to be found in the first few chapters of J4(h).

(e) "How Much Is the Migration a Flight from Persecution?" *Opportunity*, I, 272-74 (September, 1923).

A worth while unbiased discussion of migration and its causes usin census figures

(f) "How the Negro Fits in Northern Industries," *Industrial Psychology*, I, 399-412 (June, 1926).

A very good account of the migration and its causes, problems in northern industry, and results on health, housing and race relations. For summary, see A3(a).

(g) "Negro Health in the Light of Vital Statistics," *National Conference of Social Work Proceedings* (1928), 173-75.

A concise statement of mortality rates for Negroes at various periods in the United States as a whole and in different sections, with figures for deaths from chief causes

(h) *The Negro in American Civilization*: A Study of Negro Life and Race Relations in the Light of Social Research. New York, Henry Holt and Co. (1930), 538 pp. and b bliography.

This book is an attempt "to construct a reasonably faithful contemporary picture of Negro life and relationships with the white race in the United States," and is the result of material gathered under the auspices of the Social Science Research Council and the Russell Sage Foundation, and presented before the National Interracial Conference Washington D C., December, 1928. In the first part of the volume the author, as research secretary for the Conference, has compiled a vast amount of material from many sources dealing with various problems and phases of Negro life while the second part of the book contains an account of the leading addresses given at the Conference together with a summary of discussions and ques tions raised The compendium is a valuable source of material, throwing light on movements of the colored population, the Negro's economic status, health, housing, education, recreation, law observance citizenship rights, and race relations It affords an excellent picture of Negro life to any one interested in the study of the causes results and conditions surrounding the movements of Negroes. *See also* C3(c), N25(a).

(i) "The Negro Migration," *Buffalo Foundation Forum*, XXVIII 10-12 (November, 1923).

Extracts from an address given bef re the Buffalo Council of Social Agencies discussing the causes of the migration

(j) "The Negro Migration: An Economic Interpretation," *Modern Quarterly*, II, 314-26 (July, 1925).

A thoughtful consideration of the causes of migration with emphasis on the economic phases, and on congestion of population in the South

(k) "The Negro Population of Waterbury, Connecticut," *Opportunity*, I, 298-302; 338-42 (October and November, 1923).

The report of a survey made by the National Urban League on the condition of Negroes in Waterbury. *See also* Z35(m).

(l) "Negro Workers and the Unions," *Survey*, LX, 113-15 (April 15, 1928).

Deals with the relation of Negroes to organized labor.

(m) "Negro Workers in Los Angeles Industries," *Opportunity*, VI 234-40 (August, 1928).

A first-hand study of the status of Negroes in Los Angeles industries their occupations, wages, relation to unions success race relations in industry etc *See also* Z35(d).

(n) "Negroes at Work in Baltimore, Maryland," *Opportunity*, I, 12-19 (June, 1923).

A study of the industrial situation, giving statistics on occupations, type of industries employing Negroes, reasons Negroes are not employed in some concerns, and the relation of Negroes to the unions

(o) "Present Trends in the Employment of Negro Labor," *Opportunity*, VII 146-48 (May, 1929).

A general discussion of trends in industry in so far as they affect Negroes, showing the lines in which Negroes are failing to hold their own and the sort of positions they are occupying, with illustrations from Nashville Tennessee

(p) "Public Opinion and the Negro," *National Conference of Social Work Proceedings* (1923), 497-502; and also in *Opportunity*, I, 201-6 (July, 1923).

Considers and refutes some of the most generally held beliefs about the Negro.

(q) "Some Economic Aspects of Negro Migrations," *Opportunity*, V 297-99 (October, 1927).

Emphasizes the economic character of Negro migrations and shows the similarity and relation of Negro movements to European and Mexican immigration.

(r) "Substitution of Negro Labor for European Immigrant Labor," *National Conference of Social Work Proceedings* (1926), 317-27.

An excellent discussion of the transition from immigrant to Negro labor and the place of Negro labor in northern industry Much the same material as Chaps. ii and iii of J4(h).

(s) "When the Negro Migrates North,"' *World Tomorrow*, VI, 139-41 (May, 1923).

A thoughtful account of the economic condition of Negroes in the North giving some of the results of migration.

J5 Johnson, E. Polk

(a) *A History of Kentucky and Kentuckians*. Chicago and New York, Lewis Publishing Co. (1912), 3 vols.

A detailed account of the history of Kentucky. Vols. II and III give biographical accounts of prominent Kentuckians Gives a description of the political troubles of Reconstruction.

J6 Johnson, Everett

(a) "A Study of the Negro Families in the Pinewood Avenue District of Toledo, Ohio," *Opportunity*, VII, 243-45 (August, 1929).
A small scale original investigation showing the migratory nature of the colored population, sources of migration, housing conditions, marital composition, churches recreational and industrial status. *See also* Z35(p).

J7 Johnson, Franklin

(a) *Development of State Legislation Concerning the Free Negro.* New York, Arbor Press (1918), 207 pp.
A collection and digest of laws by states relating to the restrictive and protective legislation concerning the Negro in regard to civil rights, education, transportation, etc Contains an historical account of the development of both protective and restrictive legislation.

J8 Johnson, Guy B.

(a) "Negro Migration and Its Consequences," *Social Forces*, II, 404-8 (March, 1924).
Discusses the causes and consequences both immediate and eventual, of migration.

J9 Johnson, James Weldon

(a) *Black Manhattan.* New York, Alfred A. Knopf (1930), 284 pp.
A delightful story of Negro life in New York City and the historical background of Negro sections with many anecdotes of Negroes who have become famous in literary, artistic and dramatic life, and in similar fields Chap. xiii deals particularly with the growth of Harlem during and since the World War because of migration from the South showing the effects on housing, employment etc

(b) "Changing Status of Negro Labor," *National Conference of Social Work Proceedings* (1918), 383-88.
A brief discussion of the Negro's introduction into modern industry and his relation to the unions

(c) "The Gentleman's Agreement and the Negro Vote," *Crisis*, XXVIII, 260-64 October, 1924).
Shows how Negroes are disfranchised in the South by registration and poll tax requirements etc., and in some localities in the North by the Gentleman s Agreement Demands that Negroes become independent of parties and thus increase their political power

(d) "The Making of Harlem," *Survey*, LIII, 635-39 (March, 1925).
A popular description of the growth and present condition of Harlem.

(e) "The Negro Looks at Politics," *American Mercury*, XVIII, 88-94 (September, 1929).

A general picture of the Negro's political status

J10 ——— and Herbert J. Seligmann

(a) "Legal Aspects of the Negro Problem," *Annals*, CXL, 90-97 (November, 1928).

A discussion of court decisions in regard to questions involved in the relationships of whites and blacks

J11 Johnson, M. K.

(a) *School Conditions in Clarke County, Georgia, with Special Reference to Negroes*. Bulletin of the University of Georgia, Vol. XVI No. 11A (August, 1916), 49 pp. Phelps-Stokes Fellowship Studies No. 3.

A survey of general social and economic conditions in the county discussing school conditions school work and progress and the results of general intelligence tests

J12 Johnston, V D.

(a) "The Migration and the Census of 1920," *Opportunity*, I, 235-38 (August, 1923).

A statistical analysis of the census figures on population, and of the ef ect of migration on wages in the South

J13(a) "Johnstown's Flood of Negro Labor," *Literary Digest*, LXXIX, 18 (October 6, 1923).

Editorial comment on a Johnstown Mayor's edict that all Negroes should leave

J14 Joiner, W. A.

(a) *A Half Century of Freedom of the Negro in Ohio*. Xenia, Ohio, Smith Publishing Co. (1915), 134pp.

A publication of Wilberforce University, giving a statistical report of sex age, industries etc., of the Negroes in Ohio.

J15 Joint Committee on Negro Child Study in New York City

(a) *Study of Delinquent and Neglected Negro Children Before the New York City Children's Court in 1925*. New York, The Committee (1927), 48 pp.

An important monograph which studies the Negro children brought before the court during 1925. Deals with age, sex charges against the delinquents and causes of delinquency. *See also* P28(a).

J16 Jones, Eugene Kinckle

(a) "Housing and Race Friction," *American Architect*, CXVI, 445-46 October 1, 1919).

A discussion of the housing problems created by the migration of Negroes to the North and the resulting increase of race friction

(b) "National Urban League," *Opportunity*, III, 12-15 January, 1925).

An account of the origin and development of the National Urban League, showing how its activities have been influenced by migration

(c) "Negro in Community Life," *National Conference of Social Work Proceedings* (1929), 388-98.

A summary of National Urban League surveys of social conditions among Negroes in the five cities of Gr nd Rapids Albany Tulsa, Worcester, and Denver Pictures the nature of occupations, conditions of housing, health crime, recreation, race relations, the number of Negroes in the schools, mortality rates, and the attitude of welfare agencies toward Negroes. *See also* A4(a), M55(a), R12(a), R12(e), R12(f), T10(a), Z35(a), Z35(b), Z35(g), Z35(t), Z35(z).

(d) "Negro in Industry," *National Conference of Social Work Proceedings* (1919), 438-41.

An address presenting the economic status of the Negro, the nature of his occupations and limitation of opportunity success where given a chance to enter industry attitude of unions toward colored workers, and suggested remedies for present handicaps of Negroes

(e) "Negro in the North," *Current History*, XV 969-74 (March, 1922).

A discussion of the results of the northward movement as seen after a period of industrial depression; an optimistic account showing what the Negroes have accomplished

(f) "Negro Migration in New York State," *Opportunity*, IV, 7-11 (January, 1926).

An excellent discussion of the causes of migration, the extent of the movement to New York, the condition of the migrants, and the general attitude of New York to the movement

Also in *New York Conference of Charities and Correction Proceedings* (1925), 29-39.

(g) "Negroes, North and South: A Contrast," *Missionary Review*, XLV, 479-82 (June, 1922).

A general comparison of the social, economic and politic l conditions of Negroes, North and South; mentions the effect of migration upon the attitude of the Negroes aod whites toward each other

(h) "Negro's Opportunity Today," *Opportunity*, VI, 10-12 January, 1928).

A general review of the advances made by Negroes in art, health home ownership, occupations, literature, music etc One paragraph mentions migration and its effect on occupations, particularly in New York City

(i) "Problems of the Colored Child," *Annals*, XCVIII, 142-47 November, 1921).

A brief account of some of the chief problems relating to Negro children illiteracy educational problems in the North infant mortality juvenile delinquency etc Mentions recent migrations in showing the effect of such movements upon educational problems in the North

(j) "Social Work among Negroes," *Annals*, CXL, 287-93 (November, 1928).

A history of the development and activities of various social agencies and organizations working among Negroes

(k) "Twenty Years After: A Record of Accomplishments of the National Urban League During 1929," *Opportunity*, VIII, 77-85, 112-14 (March and April, 1930).

A detailed account of what the Urban League sponsored and accomplished in various localities during the year 1929. A similar but smaller annual report of the activities of the Urban League is to be found in the March or April issue of *Opportunity* of each year.

J17 Jones, Lance G. E.

(a) *Negro Schools in the Southern States.* Oxford, Clarendon Press (1928), 160 pp.

A report of a careful survey, made by an Englishman, of Negro education in the southern states Considers the status of public school education for Negroes, the industrial schools and the leading institutions.

J18 Jones, Thomas Jesse

(a) "Negro Population in the United States," *Annals*, XLIX, 1-9 September, 1913).

A statistical discussion on the basis of the 1910 Census of the increase of Negro population and its distribution. Discusses comparative movements of Negroes to the North during 1900-10 and before 1900, the gains and losses in specific states, and the urban movements of Negroes

(b) "Negroes and the Census of 1910," *Southern Workman*, XLI, 459-72 (August, 1912).

An analysis of the 1910 census statistics with reference to Negro population figures Contains brief mention of the movement of Negroes

Also in Hampton Bulletin 1912: 18-34. *See also* H6(h).

(c) "Negroes in the Country at Large," *Charities*, XV, 88-96 (Octoher 7, 1905).
Mainly a summary of U3(34a).

For other works by this author, *see* U3(23a), U3(23b).

J19 Jones, William H.

(a) *Housing of Negroes in Washington, D. C.* Washington, Howard University Press (1929), 191 pp.
A careful original investigation of housing conditions made under the auspices of the Interracial Committee of the Washington Federation of Churches

(b) *Recreation and Amusement among Negroes in Washington, D. C.* Washington, Howard University Press (1927), 216 pp.
Presents the conclusions derived from a study of the leisure time activities of Negroes in Washington The chief sections of the volume deal with (1) non-commercialized recreation and amusement, (2) commercialized amusements, and some behavior consequences of inadequate recreational and amusement facilities

K1 Kellor, Frances A.

(a) "Assisted Emigration from the South: The Women," *Charities*, XV, 11-14 (October 7, 1905).
A discussion of efforts to protect Negro women migrants and assist them in adjusting to northern conditions.

(b) "The Criminal Negro," *Arena*, XXV, 59-68, 190-97, 308-16, 419-28, 510-20 (January-May, 1901); XXVI, 56-66, 304-10, 521-27 (July, September and November, 1901).
An original study of criminality among Negroes, including a comparison of conditions in the South with those in the North, and a description of conditions in the South that influence high rates of crime among Negroes

K2 Kelsey, Carl

(a) "Evolution of Negro Labor," *Annals*, XXI, 55-76 (January, 1903).
Discusses the effect of slavery upon the type of occupations in which Negroes are now found and on their work habits, and the effect of their geographical segregation upon their economic development

(b) *The Negro Farmer*. Chicago, Jennip and Pye (1903), 103 pp.
An intelligent description of the social and economic conditions among the Negro farmers of the South

(c) "Some Causes of Negro Em gration," *Charities*, XV, 15-17. (October 7, 1905).

A brief early treatment of the extent and causes of migration, particularly from Virginia. *See also* N73(a).

K3 Kennedy, Louise V

(a) *The Negro Peasant Turns Cityward*. New York, Columbia University Press (1930), 270 pp. Columbia University Studies in History, Economics and Public Law No. 329.

A study of the effects of recent Negro migration to northern cities Deals with the problems raised by such movements in the fields of industrial employment relation of Negroes to unions, housing, health education, etc Synthesizes surveys of specific cities and available material on the subject

K4 Kent, Frank R.

(a) *The Democratic Party*: A History. New York, Century Co. (1928), 568 pp.

A journalistically written history of the Democratic party

K5 Kent, J. F.

(a) "Labor Appreciates the Human Element," *Iron Trade Review*, LXI, 774-75 (October 11, 1917).

A description of the welfare work done by the American Cast Iron Pipe Company in Brimingham, Alabama, for their colored employees Maintains that as a result the Negro laborers are dependable and satisfactory.

K6 Kerlin, Robert T

(a) "America's Race Problem" *Southern Workman*, LVIII, 489-92 (November, 1929).

A general review of results of migration both in the South and in the North showing in particular the increase of race friction in the North and the increased effort toward racial adjustment in the South

(b) *The Voice of the Negro, 1919*. New York, E. P. Dutton and Co. (1920), 188 pp.

A valuable compilation of extracts from Negro newspapers on various subjects, including reactions of the Negro press on such aspects of migration as the northern urban movement the Chicago riot, lynchings, peonage, labor agents, etc. Contains a statement of the causes of migration as presented by the Negro newspapers (pp. 137-45).

Kerns, J. Harvey, *see* S60(a).

King, F. A., *see* H12(a).

K7 King, Willis J.

(a) *The Negro in American Life.* New York, Methodist Book Concern (1926), 154 pp.

A general discussion of the status of the Negro. Chap. ix gives an intelligent summary treatment of the history, causes and results of the migration. Chap. viii refers to the economic problems aroused by migration.

K8(a) "King Cotton, the Negro and the Nation," *Opportunity*, I, 196 (July, 1923).

An editorial on the migration and its effect on southern industry

K9 Kingsley, Harold M.

(a) "The Negro Goes to Church," *Opportunity*, VII, 90-91 (March, 1929).

A description of the Negro church in Chicago.

(b) *The Negro in Chicago*: A Spiritual Interpretation of an Economic Problem. Chicago Congregational Missionary and Extension Society, 16 pp. (No date.)

A discussion of Negro migration to Chicago, and the relation of the church to resulting problems. Mentions occupations particularly

K10 Kiser, Clyde Vernon

(a) *Sea Island to City.* New York, Columbia University Press (1932), 272 pp. Studies in History, Economics and Public Law No. 368.

A valuable first-hand investigation, through personal interviews with several hundred Negroes, of the causes, operation and results of Negro migration as exemplified in the movement from St. Helena Island, South Carolina, to Harlem and other urban centers Is particularly important for its presentation of the personal testimony of migrants. *See also* W41(b).

K11 Klein, Philip

(a) *The Burden of Unemployment*: A Study of Unemployment Relief Measures in 15 American Cities, 1921-1922. New York, Russell Sage Foundation (1923), 260 pp.

For references to the situation of Negroes during the crisis of 1920-22 and the work of welfare agencies see index

K12 Klineberg, Otto

(a) *An Experimental Study of Speed and Other Factors in "Racial" Differences.* Archives of Psychology, No. 93 (1928), 111 pp.

A report of intelligence and learning tests applied to Indians, Negroes and whites Emphasizes comparison of groups w thin the same race living in differing environments in order to see effect of the latter on what seem to be racial characteristics Mentions migration may draw faster Negroes

(b) "The Question of Negro Intelligence," *Opportunity*, IX 366-68 (December, 1931).

A discussion of differences in race mentality summarizing various studies that have been made and dealing with the mental status of migrants Maintains that migration is not selective whereby only the more intelligent migrate. The material is drawn largely from a study of New York Negroes

K13 Klugh, Eolyn C.

(a) "Colored Girls at Work in Boston," *Opportunity*, VI, 295-99 (October, 1928).

A small-scale original investigation of the occupations and wages in Boston of colored girls with high school or college training.

K14 Knapp, J. W.

(a) "An Experiment with Negro Labor," *Opportunity*, I, 19-20 (February, 1923).

Narrates the experiences of the personnel director of the Bethlehem Steel Corporation in handling Negro labor.

K15 Knight, Charles L.

(a) *Negro Housing in Certain Virginia Cities*. University of V rginia (1927), 158 pp. Phelps-Stokes Fellowship Papers, No. 8.

Pre ents in detail the housing and living conditions of Negroes in Richmond Lynchburg and Charlottesville, particularly the condition of houses crowd ing, lodgers, rents, and ownership. Also discusses the general characteristics of the urban trend among Negroes, incidentally showing reasons for migration.

K16 Knox, J H. M.

(a) "Morbidity and Mortality in the Negro Infant," *Archives of Pediatrics*, XLII, 242-47 (April, 1925).

Compares infant mortality rates of colored and whites, causes of Negro infant deaths, and whether high rates are due to racial inferiority

L1 (a) "Labor Aspects of the Negro Migration," *City Club Bulletin of Chicago*, X, 232-34 (October 31, 1917).

An article briefly mentioning race riots and labor problems arising from migration.

L2 Lamar, Lucius Q. C.

(a) "Speech in the Senate of the United States, June 14, 1880," *Congressional Record*, X, 4527-33 (Part 5) 46th Congress, 2nd Session. Washington, Government Printing Office (1880).

An oratorical criticism of Senator Windom's presentation of the minority report of the committee appointed to investigate the 1879 exodus. *See also* U3(38a).

L3 Landis, H. M. R.

(a) "Tuberculosis and the Negro," *Annals*, CXL, 86-89 (November, 1928).
Emphasizes the necessity of educating colored people in prevention and treatment of tuberculosis.

(b) "The Tuberculosis Problem and the Negro," *National Tuberculosis Association Transactions* (1926), 376-79.
Report of the work of Phipps Institute in dealing with the tuberculosis problem among Negroes in Philadelphia.

L4 Lane, Winthrop D.

(a) "Ambushed in the City: The Grim Side of Harlem," *Survey*, LIII, 692-94 (March, 1925).
A description of various ways in which Negroes are exploited such as in playing the numbers high rents, patent medicines fake drug stores, dishonest doctors, etc Mentions migration to the North in showing how the arrival of unsophisticated, ignorant migrants provides a fertile field for such exploitation and also increases the difficulties of adjustment which lead to sickness and high mortality rates

Lanie, Lyle H., *see* P12(a).

L5 Lansdale, Robert T

(a) "The Negro as a Social Problem in Northern Cities," *Governmental Research Association Proceedings* (1928), 41-53.
A discussion of the social problems faced by northern municipalities as a result of the migration of Negroes Deals with the composition of the population, the source of migration, race relations housing, health and vital statistics crime and the activities of social agencies

L6 Lasker, Bruno

(a) "The Negro in Detroit," *Survey*, LVIII, 72-73 (April 15, 1927).
A good summary of D8(a).

L7 Latham, Henry

(a) *Black and White*, A Journal of Three Month's Tour in the United States. London, Macmillan and Co. (1867), 304 pp.
A diary written by an Englishman during his tour of America, only in part concerned with the South. Has one chapter (pp. 263-79) on the Negro, discussing his status before and since the Civil War. Mentions seeing Negroes migrating west to Mississippi and Texas on pp. 140-41, 269.

L8 Lattimore, Florence L.

(a) "Liberty and the Pursuit of Happiness," *World Outlook*, V, 7-8 (October, 1919).

An account of the effect of migration on the problem of adequate recreation for Negroes in the North

L9(a) "Law and Order for the Negro," *Survey*, XXXVIII, 442-43 (August 18, 1917).

A news item of a Conference on Mob Violence with a brief discussion of the relation of lynching to migration

Laws, J. B., *see* U3(24a).

L10 Lea, M. S.

(a) "Across the Color Line," *American Mercury*, XVI, 282-86 (March, 1929).

Stories of light-colored Negroes who have passed over into the life of the white group.

L11 Leavell, R. H.

(a) "Boy That Quit Roamin'," *Outlook*, CXXXV, 590-92 (December 5, 1923).

A popularly written story of how one southerner kept his Negro laborers on the farm.

(b) "What Does the Negro Want," *Outlook*, CXXII, 604-6 (August 20, 1919).

A description of a colored school in Cincinnati involving problems of education resulting from the migration.

——— For other works by this author, *see* U3 (30a).

L12 Lee, Guy Carleton

(a) "Negroes under Northern Conditions," *Gunton's Magazine*, X 52-64 (January, 1896).

A survey of conditions among Negroes in Carlisle Pennsylvania, showing conditions of housing, rents standard of living, occupations, wages, crime, churches, and schools.

L13 Lee, Porter R., and Walter W. Pettit

(a) *Report of a Study of the Interrelation of the Work of National Social Agencies in 14 American Communities*. New York, National Information Bureau, 157 pp. (No date.)

A study made in 1921-22 of activities of national organizations in fourteen communities their interrelationship and local relationships. Contains surveys of four br nches of the Urban League

L14 Leigh, Frances B.

(a) *Ten Years on a Georgia Plantation since the War.* London, Richard Bentley and Son (1883), 347 pp.

A personal account of life on a Georgia plantation following the war, describing the economic and social conditions of Reconstruction Days

L15 Leonard, Oscar, and F. B. Washington

(a) "Welcoming Southern Negroes: East St. Louis and Detroit—A Contrast," *Survey*, XXXVIII, 331-35 (July 14, 1917).

I The East St Louis Pogrom: A brief discussion of the causes and events of the East St Louis riot.

II. Detroit Newcomers Greeting: A discussion of the migration to Detroit and of the Urban League's attempts to aid the migrants. *See also* H24(a), L17(a), W9(e).

L16 Lescohier, Don D.

(a) "The Race Problem in the United Statcs," *American Review*, IV 495-506 (December, 1926).

Pictures migration as part of the tendency of Negroes to become more selfconscious and more determined to better themselves, and at the same time mentions extent and direction of recent movements the general social and economic causes and some of the results

L17(a) "Lesson of Detroit," *Crisis*, XIV, 239-41 (September, 1917).

Summary of L15(a).

L18 Lett, Harold A.

(a) "Migration Difficulties in Michigan," *Southern Workman*, LVI, 231-36 (May, 1927).

Discusses the social and economic problems created by the influx of Negroes and Michigan s attempt to meet the situation through its Division of Negro Welfare and Statistics

(b) "Negro Welfare in Michigan," *Southern Workman*, LV, 206-8 (May, 1926).

A popular story of how Michigan met the problem of a large influx of Negroes

(c) "Work: Negro Unemployed in Pittsburgh," *Opportunity*, IX, 79-81 (March, 1931).

Stories of cases of the unemployed in Pittsburgh, showing the economic handicaps of the Negro.

L19(a) "Letters of Negro Migrants," *Journal of Negro History*, IV 291-340, 412-65 (July and October, 1919).

An interesting and valuable collection of letters from migrants and prospect ve migrants grouped according to general subject matter such as inquires about economic opportunities in the North, conditions in the South educational advantages, etc. *See* Z36(a).

L20 Lewis, Charles

(a) "Thirty Cent Cotton and the Negro," *Illustrated World*, XXIX 470 (May, 1918).

A brief general statement of the effect of high-priced cotton on migration.

L21 Lewis, Edward E.

(a) *The Mobility of the Negro*: A Study in the American Labor Supply. New York, Columbia University Press (1931), 144 pp. Columbia University Studies in History, Economics and Public Law No. 342.

An analysis of the economic causes of Negro migration for the period 1919-24, contrasting the relative importance of the "pull" of industrial opportunity with the "push" of agricultural disorganization to determine the future rôle of the Negro as an industrial reserve Develops a special statistical technique to measure these factors Chap. v considers the extent and direction of movements during the period studied

L22 Lilienthal, David F.

(a) "Trial of Two Races," *Outlook*, CXLI, 629-30 (December 23, 1925).

A discussion of the Sweet trial in Detroit, showing race prejudice resulting from the migration

L23 Lindsay, Arnett G.

(a) "The Negro in Banking" *Journal of Negro History*, XIV 156-201 (April, 1929).

A history of the growth of Negro banking concerns and a careful account of the present status of Negro banks

L24 Locke, Alain

(a) "Enter the New Negro," *Survey*, LIII, 631-34 (March, 1925).

Discusses the rise of and nature of the new spirit of the Negro, and his developing self respect self reliance and race consciousness.

(b) *The New Negro*: An Interpretation. New York Albert and Charles Boni (1925), 446 pp.

A collection of extracts from Negro literature and of articles dealing with various phases of the Negro's economic, social and artistic life An amplification of S63(a).

L25 Long, Francis T

(a) *The Negroes of Clarke County, Georgia, during the Great War.* Bulletin of the University of Georgia, Vol. XIX, No. 8 (1919), 56 pp. Phelps-Stokes Fellowship Studies No. 5.

A full statistical analysis of the activities of the Negroes during the War with a comparison of white and colored participation in various phases of war work Chap. v contains a discussion of the causes of migration.

L26 Lonn, Ella

(a) *Reconstruction in Louisiana after 1868.* New York, G. P. Putnam's Sons (1918), 95 pp.

An exhaustive account of the troubles chiefly political, of Reconstruction Days

L27 Louisiana. Department of Commissioner of Labor and Industrial Statistics

(a) *Biennial Reports* (1916-1930), from the Ninth through the Seventeenth, New Orleans, The Department.

Each biennial report surveys conditions of labor in Louisiana for the two years being considered dealing with such subjects as wages, strikes, legislation etc., and giving reports of specific industries Each report has a section on the shortage of common labor. The reports for 1916-18 and 1919-20 are particularly valuable

L28 Lovejoy, Owen R.

(a) "Justice to the Negro Child" *Opportunity*, VII 174-76 (June, 1929).

A picture of some of the social results of the rapid increase of Negroes in Harlem, pointing out the lack of recreational facilities high delinquency rates and poor health

(b) "The New Industrial South," *National Conference of Social Work Proceedings* (1928), 281-87.

Deals with the nature of the present industrial development in the South and the present status of agricultural and industrial conditions Mentions Negro migration to the North as a cause of the shift of interest from agriculture to industry and as affecting social and industrial problems in urban communities to which the migrants have gone.

L29 Lovestone, Jay

(a) "The Great Negro Migration," *Workers Monthly*, V, 179-84 (February, 1926).

An account of Negro migration, both 1916-18 and 1922-23, its extent, causes and results in the effort to show the necessity of organizing Negroes within the ranks of Communists as part of the class struggle against capitalist oligarchy

L30(a) "Lure of the North for the Negroes," S XXXVIII 27-28 (April 7, 1917).

A very brief comment on the immediate results of the migration of Negroes to Philadelphia.

L31 Lynch, John R.

(a) *The Facts of Reconstruction*. New York, Neal Publishing Co. (1917), 325 pp.

An account of Reconstruction Days in the South, particularly in Mississippi, by a man who was in active political life at the time.

L32(a) "Lynching Again on the Increase," *Christian Century*, XLVIII, 5 (January 7, 1931).

An editorial on the increase in lynching and its relation to migration and the economic depression.

L33(a) "Lynching Industry," *Crisis*, XIX, 183-86 (February, 1920).

Contains a list of lynchings during the year 1919; giving for each the date place, name of person lynched and the charge against him. Also gives a summary of the number of lynchings from 1885-1919.

L34 Lyons, Adelaide

(a) "Prayin' Members up North," *World Outlook*, V, 35 (October, 1919).

A story of two migrants and their cold reception in a northern Negro church showing one reason why Negroes are breaking away from the church

M1 McClelland, Ed. S.

(a) "Negro Labor in the Westinghouse Electric and Manufacturing Corporation," *Opportunity*, I, 22-23 (January, 1923).

The personnel manager tells of his experience with Negro labor.

M2 McConnell, John P.

(a) *Negroes and Their Treatment in Virginia from 1865-1867*. Pulaski, Virginia, B. D. Smith and Bros. (1910), 126 pp.

An historical account of the distribution of Negroes in Virginia, of public opinion regarding emancipation and the effect of freedom on the Negroes economically socially and legally, and of the nature of the laws passed to regulate relations between whites and Negroes Chap. i discusses migration to cities, other states and particularly to the North. There is also a discussion of migration on pp. 19-23.

M3 McConnell, W. J.

(a) "The Effect of Industrialization upon the Negro" *Southwestern*

Political and Social Science Association Proceedings (1924), 265-70.
Discusses in general the Negro's success in industry and the effect of the movement into industrial centers on birth and death rates and health.

McDougald, Gertrude, *see* N11(a), N84(a), Z30.

M4 McDowell, Arthur G.

(a) "Negro Labor and the Miners Revolt," *Opportunity*, IX, 272-75, 236-38 (August and September, 1931).
An account of the status of the Negro in the coal mines

M5 McDowell, Mary E.

(a) "Hovels or Homes?" *Opportunity*, VII, 74-77 (March, 1929).
A careful discussion of the di ficulties faced by Negroes in their attempts to secure decent homes and of the effect of migration on housing in Chicago.

M6 McGhee, Ethel

(a) "Northern Negro Family," *Opportunity*, V, 176-78 (June, 1927).
An abstract of a paper read at the 1927 Conference of the National Urban League Presents some of the di ficulties surrounding the development of normal family life among northern Negroes and the problems of adjustment faced by Negro migrants

M7 McKenzie, H. B.

(a) "South: The Cotton and the Negro: Reply to H. Snyder," *North American Review*, CCXIX, 486-95 (April, 1924).
A sensible discussion of the causes of migration and the status of the Negro, North and South. *See also* S35(a).

M8 McKinley, Carlyle E.

(a) *An Appeal to Pharaoh*: The Negro Problem, and Its Radical Solution. New York, Fords, Howard and Hulbert (1889), 205 pp.
An early presentation of the Negro problem contending that the only adequate solution is the deportation of the Negroes to Africa.

M9 MacLean, A. M.

(a) "Where Color Lines are Drawn," *Survey*, XLVIII, 453-54 (July 1, 1922).
An impressionistic narrative of personal stories of Negroes, some of them migrants, who are handicapped economically by their color in the North

M10(a) "Making a Living: What the Negro Faces," *World Tomorrow*, VI, 135-58 (May, 1923).
The entire number is devoted to the lack of economic opportunities and to the economic handicaps faced by Negroes. Articles of value for migration are

listed under authors in this Bibliography. *See also* D18(l), J4(s), M21(a), S10(a), T23(a).

M11 Manly, A. L.

(a) "Where Negroes Live in Philadelphia," *Opportunity*, I, 10-15 (May, 1923).

Shows how migration affected the housing situation in Philadelphia and how the migrants live

M12 Mark, Mary Louise

(a) *Negroes in Columbus, Ohio*. Columbus, Ohio State University Press (1928), 63 pp. Ohio State University Series, Contributions in Social Science No. 2.

A report of a survey made with the assistance of the graduate students of Ohio State University Is particularly a study of the mechanics of the migration and of the economic and social status of recent colored migrants to Columbus Considers the housing problems, occupations, educational status and health of the Negro group.

M13 Markoe, W. M.

(a) "The Great Negro Migration," *America: A Catholic Review of the Week*, XXX, 396-97 (February 9, 1924).

A brief article giving general estimates of the extent of migration, alleging mistreatment as the chief cause of the movement

M14 Marquette, Bleecker

(a) "The Health Council Idea," *National Conference of Social Work Proceedings* (1926), 244-50.

A description of the plan of organization of the Cincinnati Health Federation and its activities including a brief summary of health work among Negroes in Cincinnati

(b) "Helping the Negro Solve His Problem," *Nation's Health*, IX 19-21 (January 15, 1927).

The story of the founding of the Shoemaker Health Center in Cincinnati and of its work among Negroes.

M15 Marrs, S. M. N., G. T. Bludworth and D. B. Taylor

(a) *Negro Education in Texas*. Texas State Department of Education, Bulletin 212 (October, 1926), 28 pp.

An account of buildings, expenditures teacher training facilities, etc., for whites and Negroes.

M16 Marshall, Charles K.

(a) *The Exodus: Its Effect upon the People of the South*. Colored

Labor Not Indispensable. An address delivered before the Board of Directors of the American Colonization Society, January 21, 1880. Washington (1880), 15 pp.

An oratorical plea for the colonization of Negroes in Africa. Also mentions the exodus to Kansas and the reasons. Of value as a contemporary view of the 1879 exodus

M17 Martin, Asa Earl

(a) *Our Negro Population. A Sociological Study of the Negroes of Kansas City, Missouri.* Kansas City, Franklin Hudson Publishing Co. (1913), 189 pp. (M.A. Thesis, Wm. Jewell College, Liberty, Missouri.)

One of the better early original investigations A study of the social and economic conditions among Negroes, in Kansas City, January to April, 1912, including a personal canvass of 500 representative Negro families and giving general statements with some statistical evidence concerning the occupations, business activities, wages, expenditures, housing conditions health and morals crime, organizations religion, and education of the colored population.

M18 Maryland Interracial Commission

(a) *Report with Recommendations to the Governor and General Assembly* (1927), 23 pp.

The report of the Commission on social and economic conditions among the Negroes in Maryland with recommendations as to what should be done to improve race relations

M19 Massachusetts Bureau of Statistics and Labor

(a) *The Social and Industrial Condition of the Negro in Massachusetts. Thirty-fourth Annual Report, for the year 1903* (printed 1904), pp. 215-320.

An analysis chiefly statistical, of the early history, and of the condition of Negroes in Massachusetts around 1900, their population, occupations, vital statistics education, ownership of farms and homes, pauperism and crime, churches and social organizations Discusses place of birth of Negroes, showing migration to Massachusetts, pp. 238, 249-53, 258.

M20 Matthews, V. E. (Mrs.)

(a) "Dangers Confronting Southern Girls in the North," *Hampton Negro Conference Annual Report* (1898), 62-69.

A description of the moral dangers surrounding ignorant Negro girls coming north for domestic service. *See also* H6(a).

M21 Mays, Robert L.

(a) "White Workers and Black," *World Tomorrow*, VI, 141-43 (May, 1923).

A short discussion of the relation of Negroes to organized labor.

M22 Melden, Charles M.

(a) *From Slave to Citizen.* New York, Methodist Book Concern (1921), 271 pp.

A very general sympathetic, impressionistic discussion of the problem of race relationships. Pp. 150-63 consider migration as a "silent protest" against the South's ill treatment of the Negro.

Mercier, W. B. *see* U3(26a).

Merriam, William, *see* U3(27a).

M23 Merritt, D.

(a) "Charles Plummer, Radical," *Outlook*, CXXXVIII, 126-28 (September 24, 1924).

A popular account of one Negro's opinion of the benefits of migration.

M24(a) *Messenger.* Vols. for 1917-24.

An irregular publication of radical labor movements Articles scattered throughout give interesting sidelights on the Negro's relations to labor organizations.

M25 Metropolitan Life Insurance Company

(a) *Broadening the Life Span of the American Negro*, Metropolitan Life Insurance Company Statistical Bulletin, Vol. IV, No. 9 (September, 1923), pp. 1-3.

A brief discussion of mortality statistics among Negroes.

(b) *Suicide among Negroes in the United States*, Metropolitan Life Insurance Company Statistical Bulletin, Vol. XI, 4-5 (September, 1930).

A comparison of suicide rates for Negroes and for whites; for rural as compared with urban Negroes; and for Negroes insured in the Metropolitan Life Insurance Company with those for the country as a whole Discusses causes for the high rate among insured Negroes as due to urban living and migration to the North Shows the effect of migration on health in general and on suicide

——— For other works by the same author, *see* D17(f), D17(h), D17(j).

M26(a) "Migrating Negro," *Crisis*, XXI, 267 (April, 1921).

A news item concerning the migration to cities because of unemployment and the consequent dependence of the Negro on charity

M27(a) "Migration," *Opportunity*, I, 224 (July, 1923).
An editorial on labor conditions in the South and the efforts of the South to prevent migration.

M28(a) "Migration," *Opportunity*, II, 218 (July, 1924).
A quotation from an Oklahoma paper on the extent and probable benefits of the present migration.

M29(a) "Migration," *Opportunity*, IV, 399 (December, 1926); V 32, 62, 95 (January, February and March, 1927).
Short comments under the Survey of the Month department, stating briefly contemporary facts concerning recent movements The articles deal with (1) Movements from Georgia and South Carolina to Florida; (2) Movements to Texas and St. Louis, and out of St. Paul; (3) Movements to Brooklyn, to Chicago, to Hot Springs; (4) to St. Louis, Jackson, Chicago, New York City and Brooklyn and from Detroit.

M30(a) "Migration Continues," *Crisis*, XXV, 278 (April, 1923).
Quotations from three newspapers on the causes and extent of migration.

M31(a) "Migration of Colored Workers from the South," *Monthly Labor Review*, XVI, 495 (February, 1923).
A short statement of the effect of the boll weevil on Negro tenant labor; is a statement taken from the report of the Federal Reserve Bank of Richmond *See also* F5(a).

M32(a) "Migration of Negroes," *Crisis*, XXVI 81-83 (June, 1923).
Quotations from newspapers concerning labor conditions, North and South and race relations

M33(a) "Migration of Negroes from Southern to Northern States in Year Ending August 3, 1923," *Economic World*, n.s., XXVI, 626 (November 3, 1923).
A brief summary of the United States Department of Labor release on the extent of migration during the year. *See also* Z55(a), Z55(b).

M34(a) "Migration of Negroes to Northern Industrial Centers," *Monthly Labor Review*, XII, 201-3 January, 1921).
A utilization of census material showing the white and Negro populations in certain northern cities, 1910 and 1920.

M35(a) "Migration of the Negro to Northern States," *Commercial and Financial Chronicle*, CXVII, 160-62 (July 14, 1923).
A collection of quotations from prominent newspapers on the migration, its causes, nature and effects

M36(a) "Migration, The Macon Telegraph," *Crisis*, XIX, 109-10 (January, 1920).
An answer to the charges of the *Macon Daily Telegraph* that Du Bois is

responsible for stirring up unrest among the Negroes Gives some of the reasons for this unrest

M37 **(a)** "Migration to Philadelphia," *Opportunity*, I, 19-20 (May, 1923).

An editorial on the extent and type of migration in

M38 Miller, E. E.

(a) "Cotton, a National Crop," *Review of Reviews*, LXXIV, 70-73 (July, 1926).

Discusses the evils incident to the production of cotton, such as low wages and cheap colored labor, and shows how the situation cao be improved by better utilization of soils, better marketing, etc One sentence asserts that the north ward migration of Negroes improved the chances for industrial development in the South

M39 Miller, Kelly

(a) "The Causes of Segregation," *Current History*, XXV, 827-31 (March, 1927).

Deals with the causes and results of residential segregation and shows the effect of migration during the World War on the housing situation in the North

(b) "The City Negro: Distribution," *Southern Workman*, XXXI, 217-22 (April, 1902).

On the basis of the 1900 Census figures discusses the increase and proportion of Negroes in various cities Contains a brief statement of the causes of the movement to cities

(c) "Darkest America," *New England Magazine*, XXX, 14-21 (April, 1904).

A very general treatment of the movements of the Negro, particularly to the Southwest with inferences as to the Negro's future

(d) "Economic Handicap of the Negro in the North," *Annals*, XXVII 543-50 (May, 1906).

Discusses the causes of migration around 1900, the economic status of the Negro in northern cities, and means of improving his industrial condition. Deals with the characteristics of northern movements and the nature of the occupations into which Negroes go in the North showing the serious limitations of their economic opportunities in northern cities

(e) "Education of the Negro in the North," *Educational Review*, LXII, 232-38 (October, 1921).

A discussion of the educational problems in the North aroused by recent Negro migrations

(f) "Enumeration Errors in Negro Population," *Scientific Monthly*, XIV, 168-77 (February, 1922).

A careful analysis of census figures to show the probability of error in the 1920 Census Merely mentions the effect of migration on the problems of census taking and of birth rates. *See also* B10(a).

(g) *The Everlasting Stain.* Washington, D.C., Associated Publishers (1924), 352 pp.

A collection of essays on various phases of Negro Life and problems, some of which have appeared in periodicals. Chap. xiii is a reprint of M39(f), and Chap. viii deals with the relation of migration to educational problems in the North

(h) "Expansion of the Negro Population," *Forum*, XXXII, 671-79 (February, 1902).

A good discussion of the four principal Negro migrations of the 19th century Interesting for the view held in 1902 as to the future habitat of the Negro.

(i) "The Farm the Negro's Best Chance," *Manufacturers Record*, XC, 96-97 (August 5, 1926).

After discussing the Negro's economic status in cities of the North and South shows why he believes the Negro is better off on the farms.

(j) "Forty Years of Negro Education," *Educational Review*, XXXVI 484-98 (December, 1908).

Describes the work of missionaries and of the Freedmen's Bureau after the Civil War, the rise of Negro colleges, need of differentiating types of schools for various sections etc

(k) "Harvest of Race Prejudice," *Survey*, LIII, 682-83 (March, 1925).

Presents some of the mass effects of race prejudice, emphasizing the practice of segregation which in turn, leads to increased race consciousness among the Negroes and thus influences their reactions in politics business, activities of welfare agencies etc

(l) "Is the Color Line Crumbling?" *Opportunity*, VII 282-85 (September, 1929).

In criticizing V2(a) the author discusses race relations in the North and South and gives instances of an increasing color line in each section

(m) "The Negro as a Working Man," *American Mercury*, VI, 310-13 (November, 1925).

Discusses the Negro's relation to capital on the one hand and to the labor element on the other, and the effect of migration on the Negro's choice between the two.

(n) "Negro in New England," *Harvard Graduate Magazine*, XXXIV 538-49 June, 1926).

A general discussion of the social and economic status of the Negro in New England with a brief summary of New England s historical interest in Negro problems. Mentions migration as not affecting this section to any great extent

(o) *Race Adjustment*: Essays on the Negro in America. New York, Neale Publishing Co. (1908), 306 pp.

A collection of essays dealing sympathetically with many of the Negro's difficulties and problems, such as race relations, progress in industry and in the professions Discusses rates of increase and conditions of Negroes in cities (pp. 118-32) and the nature of interstate migration (pp. 154-67).

(p) *A Review of Hoffman's Race Traits and Tendencies*. American Negro Academy, Occasional Papers No. 1. Washington, The Academy (1897), 36 pp.

An exhaustive review of H32(b), with criticisms of Hoffman's conclusions.

— – For other works by the same author, *see* A13(a), M40(a).

M40 ——— and Herbert J. Seligmann

(a) "Separate Communities for Negrocs: Two Points of View," *Current History*, XXV, 827-33 (March, 1927).

I The Causes of Segregation, pp. 827-31. Discusses the facts of residential segregation and its inevitability, and some of the housing problems resulting from migration.

II. The Negro Protest Against Ghetto Conditions, pp. 831-33. A refutation of Miller's accompanying article, maintaining the necessity of fighting against segregation.

M41 Miller, Loren

(a) "The Negro Faces the Machine," *Opportunity*, VIII, 297-99 (October, 1930).

A critical appraisal of the major efforts being put forward to solve the Negroes' employment problems. Points out the weaknesses of each movement Urban League, National Negro Business League and the Chicago Movement

M42 Miller, Wallace Eldan

(a) *The Peopling of Kansas*. Columbus, Press of Fred J. Herr (1906), 134 pp.

A description of the topography, climate and resources of Kansas and an account of the various population groups that have contributed to the making of the population of the state Chap. vi discusses the movements of Negroes to Kansas up through the 1900 Census and the principal causes of such movements

M43 Mims, Edwin

(a) *A Handbook for Interracial Committees.* Atlanta, Interracial Commission (1920), 32 pp.

A consideration of some of the conditions among Negroes in the South showing how such conditions have led to migration and describing briefly what has been done to improve them.

(b) *Law and Order in Tennessee.* Atlanta, Interracial Commission (1919), 21 pp.

An account of the founding and activities of the Law and Order Commission in Tennessee in the attempt to suppress lynching.

M44(a) *Mississippi and the Mob.* Jackson, Mississippi, Jackson Printing Co. (1926), 78 pp.

A collection of opinions of state officials, officers and members of the State Bar Association, condemning mob violence The first part discusses the history and record of lynching in Mississippi.

M45 Missouri Bureau of Labor Statistics

(a) *Annual Reports, 1920-26,* Jefferson City, State Printing Office.

These reports contain statistics on various phases of the social and economic life of Missouri

(b) *Missouri Red Book, 1921-22.* Jefferson City, 421-24.

Discusses briefly Negro Migration as Shown by Census of 1920," giving tables and statistics of growth of Negro population in Missouri

M46 Missouri Negro Industrial Commission

(a) *Biennial Report for 1921-22.* Jefferson City, Hughs Stephens Press, 84 pp.

Contains material, mainly from the feder l census, on Negro farm labor, health, migration to cities, and the Negro's general industrial situation.

(b) *Biennial Report for 1923-24.* Jefferson City, Hughs Stephens Press, 71 pp.

General report on the industrial, social and educational conditions, and problems of the Negroes in Missouri. Pages 28-32 contain a discussion of migration with statistical tables. *See also* R13(a).

(c) *Fourth Biennial Report: 1925-26.* Jefferson City, The Commission, 80 pp.

A report on the status of the Negro in industry recreation, education and health in the state, and race relations. Shows the effect of migration on these conditions. *See also* W46(a).

(**d**) Second *Report, December, 1920.* Jefferson City, The Commission, 25 pp.

Discusses the beginning of the Negro Industrial Commission in October, 1920. Gives a report of conditions among Negroes in schools and the extent of Negro population in rural communities Mentions migration and congestion in cities

(**e**) *Semi-Annual Report, January 1-July 1, 1921.* Jefferson City, The Commission (1921), 56 pp.

A report of the Commission's activities in surveying conditions of labor, farming, housing, health and sanitation among the Negroes of the state. Shows migration from the South and its effects. For Part 2, *see* C30(a).

M47(a) "Modern Housing for Negroes Brings Gratifying Results," *American City*, XLIII, 151 (November, 1930).

A brief article on the success of the Michigan Boulevard Garden Apartments Corporation of Chicago in providing decent homes for Negroes a demonstration of housing by Rosenwald

M48 Moffat, Adeline

(**a**) "New Problems Caused by the Importation of Colored Labor into the North," *National Federation of Settlements Proceedings* (1918), 18-20.

A brief address on the problems created by the migration of Negroes to the North, and on the Negro's need for help in adjusting to new situations

M49 Moffat, R. Burnham

(**a**) "The Disfranchisement of the Negro, From a Lawyer's Point of View," *Journal of Social Science*, XLII, 31-62 (1904).

An exhaustive analysis of the provisions of the constitutions adopted by various southern states in order to disfranchise Negroes

M50 Moffett, L. W.

(**a**) "Careful Selection of Negroes Urged," *Iron Age*, CXII, 892-93 (October 4, 1923).

Urges the necessity for vocational selection.

M51 Moore, Fred R.

(**a**) "Letting Him into the Labor Unions," *World Outlook* V 28 (October, 1919).

A discussion of the A. F. of L.'s proposal to admit Negroes and reasons for the interest of organized labor in the colored workers, giving migration as one reason.

Moore, John M., *see* H39(a).

M52 Moore, John R., and Austin P. Foster

(a) *Tennessee, The Volunteer State, 1769-1923.* Nashville, S J Clarke Publishing Co. (1923), 982 pp.
A detailed history of Tennessee from its early days. Gives an account of political troubles of Reconstruction Days.

M53 Morton, Richard L.

(a) *The Negro in Virginia Politics, 1865-1902.* Charlottesville, University of Virginia Press (1919), 199 pp. Phelps-Stokes Fellowship Papers No. 4.
An analysis of the political troubles of Reconstruction and an account of the part the Negroes played in the political life of the state until their elimination from politics by the Constitution of 1902.

M54 Moses, Kingsley

(a) "The Negro Comes North," *Forum*, LVIII, 181-90 (August, 1917).
A popularly written article on the migration with little factual material.

M55 Moss, R. Maurice

(a) "American Cities — Grand Rapids," *Opportunity*, VII, 12-15 (January, 1929).
A report of an investigation made in Grand Rapids by the National Urban League, discussing the increase of Negroes, housing conditions and segregation, nature of occupations, professional and business concerns, wages, recreational facilities educational problems (including the effect of migrants upon the extent of retardation), conditions of health crime and juvenile delinquency, and conditions among churches and social agencies dealing with Negroes. *See also* Z35(t).

M56 Mossell, Sadie T

(a) "The Standard of Living among One Hundred Migrant Families in Philadelphia," *Annals*, XCVIII, 173-218 (November, 1921).
An analysis of occupations, incomes and sources of incomes of migrant families in Philadelphia to determine the success of the migrants' adaptation to their new environment An excellent study of the effects of migration on the social and economic life of the Negroes. *See also* N54(a), N68(a).

(b) *The Standard of Living among One Hundred Negro Migrant Families in Philadelphia.* Ph.D. Thesis, University of Pennsylvania (1921).
Reprint of M56(a).

(c) *A Study of the Negro Tuberculosis Problem in Philadelphia.* Philadelphia, Henry Phipps Institute (1923), 31 pp.

An exhaustive survey of the problem of tuberculosis among Negroes in Philadelphia, including a study of the extent of the Negro population in the city the prevalence of tuberculosis and institutional facilities for diagnosis and treatment of Negroes in Philadelphia in 1921.

M57 Moton, Robert R.

(a) "The Duty of Southern Labor during the War," *Southern Sociological Congress: Democracy in Earnest* (1918), 219-28.

A discussion of labor conditions in the South showing the need for increased efficiency of Negro labor because of the war-time demands, and means of preventing migration. Gives a summary of the causes of migration.

(b) "Hampton, Tuskegee and Points North," *Survey*, LIV, 15-18 (April 1, 1925).

A rational discussion of the Negro's problem of adjustment to northern conditions and of the part Hampton and Tuskegee have played in this adjustment by training their students in self reliance

(c) "Migration of Negroes from the Southern to the Northern States and Its Economic Effects," *Economic World*, n.s., XXV, 688-91 (May 19, 1923).

An excellent account of the 1923 migration and of the economic and social effects North and South, of the movement of Negroes

(d) "Organized Negro Effort for Racial Progress," *Annals*, CXL, 257-63 (November, 1928).

An account of various colored organizations which are working toward betterment of conditions among Negroes

(e) "The South and the Lynching Evil," *South Atlantic Quarterly*, XVIII, 191-96 (July, 1919).

Discusses the extent of lynching of Negroes in the South and the factors bringing about a decrease in the number of lynchings. Contends that lynching is the chief cause of unrest and the reason for migration to the North

(f) *What the Negro Thinks.* New York Doubleday Doran (1929), 267 pp.

A thoughtful attempt of a Negro leader to show the Negro's inner reaction to some of the social situations in American life and why these experences lead to race friction. Discusses segregation, disfranchisement etc Shows the inter relationship of migration and social and economic problems.

M58(a) "Mr. B. Weevil," *Crisis*, XXVII, 104 (January, 1924).

An ironical editorial satirizing southern newspaper comments on the causes of migration.

M59 Murchison, Carl A.

(a) *Criminal Intelligence.* Worcester, Massachusetts, Clark University (1926), 291 pp.
In general the book deals with the application of intelligence tests to various classifications of criminals showing the relation of intelligence to the geographical situation types of crime, recidivism, literacy, age, and industrial occupations of the criminals. Part IV Negro Men Criminals" (pp. 199-274) considers the intelligence of Negro criminals as it was measured in state institutions in Ohio, Illinois, Maryland and New Jersey Deals with the relation of intelligence of Negro criminals to the factors mentioned Same material appeared in *Pedagogical Seminary*, Vol. XXXII March December, 1925.

N1 Nash, Roy

(a) "North and South," *Survey*, XXXVII, 362 (December 30, 1916).
A brief statement of the work of the National Association for the Advancement of Colored People in aiding migrants and protecting the interests of the Negroes

N2 National Association for the Advancement of Colored People

(a) *Annual Reports* (1910-30), First to the Twenty-first, New York The Association.
Each report summarizes the activities of the Association during that year, discussing such topics as discrimination, lynching, segregation, etc. *See also* S17(f).

N3 National Commission on Law Observance and Enforcement

(a) *Report on the Cause of Crime* June 26, 1913), 2 vols. (Mimeographed.)
A general and exhaustive discussion of the factors determining crime.
Vol. I (pp. 221-55, on the Negro's relation to work and law observance discusses Negroes in Sing Sing, the charges brought, nativity residence and causes of crime.
Vol. II (pp. 81-82, 95, 105) discusses delinquency among Negro children

N4(a) *National Conference of Colored Men of the United States — Proceedings, Nashville, Tennessee, 1879.* Washington, R. H. Darby, 107 pp.
Daily reports of a conference of colored men whose main consideration was the exodus to Kansas. Contains an account of the various resolutions with discussions thereof and several papers and reports of committees Appendix N Report of the Committee on Migration," presents, particularly, the Negro's view of the causes and remedies of migration. Interesting contemporary material.

N5(a) "National Conference on Negro Migration," *Nation*, CIV, 149 (February 8, 1917).
An editorial comment on the Conference and some of the causes of migration.

National League on Urban Conditions, *see* National Urban League.

N6 National Negro Business League

(a) *Report of the Survey of Negro Business Conditions* (1928), 19 pp.
Gives a picture of the nature of Negro businesses, age of establishments, kind of organization, nature of neighborhood, advertising methods, etc. *See also* N27(a).

N7(a) *National Negro Conference Proceedings* (1909).
Pages 89-98 contain a discussion by W L Bulkley of the economic chances of Negroes, North and South, and of the loss to the South of the best Negroes by migration.

N8 National Urban League

(a) *Bulletin No. 4.* Vol. VI (November, 1916).
Contains a statement that the League supplied several New England indus tries with Negro labor.

(b) *A Challenge to Democracy*: The Migration of a Race. Annual Report (1916-17); National Urban League Bulletin No. 1, Vol. VII (November, 1917), 35 pp.
Contains a report of the work done by the Urban League during 1916-17, furnishing a first-hand account of the influence of the migration upon the activities of social agencies Discusses briefly the migration in that year, the efforts of the League to establish branches in northern cities in order to care for the migrants and some of the problems created by the migration.

(c) *Housing Conditions among Negroes in Harlem, New York City.* National Urban League Bulletin No. 2, Vol. IV (January, 1915), 29 pp.
Contains the report of an investigation of housing conditions, rent, lodgers, etc, among Harlem Negroes

(d) *How Unemployment Affects Negroes.* New York, National Urban League (March, 1931), 41 pp. (Mimeographed.)
A statement on the unemployment situation among Negroes based upon the reports of persons in constant contact with employment problems in the principal cities of the nation. Presents the percentage of Negroes unemployed the percentage of Negroes in the total population and in charity cases Gives information for cities in both South and North and mentions the effect of unemployment upon migration

(e) *Negro Membership in American Labor Unions.* (Ira de A. Reid, Director) New York, National Urban League (1930), 175 pp.

Discusses the extent and nature of Negro membership in labor unions. Contains a summary of the industrial status of the Negro, and discussions of those unions which prohibit colored membership, those which include Negroes colored unions directly affiliated with the A F. of L., and independent Negro organizations, giving for each the type of union, its attitude toward Negroes, and the approximate number of Negro members. The relation of organized labor to Negroes in selected cities is also presented, and the personal experience of some Negroes with unions. *See also* P29(a).

(f) *Negro Workers: A Drama of 5,000,000 American Wage Earners.* New York, National Urban League (1930), 15 pp.

A summarization of the economic status of the Negro as shown by investigations of the National Urban League Sets forth briefly the nature of occupations of colored workers their handicaps, wages and relation to organized labor. *See also* N8(g).

(g) *Negro Workers: A Drama of 5,000,000 American Wage Earners.* New York, National Urban League, revised 1931 edition (April, 1931), 12 pp.

Survey of the status of Negroes in the labor world unemployment replacement by whites relation to unions and communism, occupations, need for vocational guidance etc. *See also* N8(f), N79(a).

(h) *A Study of the Social Welfare Status of the Negroes in Houston, Texas.* (Jesse O Thomas, Director) Houston, Webster, Richardson Publishing Co. (May, 1929), 107 pp.

A discussion of population increase, employment, health, delinquency education, business churches recreation, race relations etc

(i) *Unemployment Status of Negroes.* New York (December, 1931), 56 pp.

A compilation of facts and figures respecting unemployment among Negroes in 106 cities

——— For *Annual Reports, see* J16(k).

——— For other works by the League, *see* H29(a), H29(e), H29(h), J4(k), J4(m), J4(n), J16(b), M55(a), N30(a), R12(a), R12(e), R12(f), T10(a), W9(h), Z35(a-bb).

N9 Nearing, Scott

(a) *Black America.* New York, Vanguard Press (1929), 275 pp.

A somewhat journalistic treatment of economic and social conditions among Negroes in the North and South synthesizing many of the best known surveys of such conditions. Deals with the Negro as an oppressed race, economically exploited by the whites

N10(a) "Negro and Immigrant Labor," *Opportunity*, V, 320-21 (November, 1927).
An editorial on the relation between Negro migration and foreign immigration, with a significant chart

N11(a) "Negro and the Northern Public Schools," *Crisis*, XXV 205-8, 262-65 (March and April, 1923).
A discussion of the problems involved in segregated as compared with mixed schools in the North using the experience of New York City as an illustration. Describes the attitude displayed at Manhattan Trade School, and in de tail the work of Mrs. McDougald as vocational adviser

N12(a) "Negro and the Unions," *Nation*, XCI, 515-16 (December 1, 1910).
An unsigned article on the attitude of Gompers and the A. F. of L. toward Negroes

N13(a) "Negro Apparently Not Wanted in Philadelphia," *Manufacturers Record*, XCII, 52-53 (November 24, 1927).
A discussion of the problem of increased crime in northern cities due to migration of Negroes, quoting an address of Judge Lewis of Philadelphia, and concluding with a comparison of the treatment of Negro law breakers in the North and in the South Maintains that Southerners understand the Negro characteristics and are really more lenient

N14(a) "Negro Common School: Georgia," *Crisis*, XXXII, 248-64 (September, 1926).
Report of an investigation sponsored by the American Fund for Public Ser vice, giving the history of Negro schools in Georgia, laws relating to Negro schools, state expenditures for them, and the condition of schools in specific counties

N15(a) "Negro Common School: Mississippi," *Crisis*, XXXIII 102 (December, 1926).
Discusses the status of schools in Mississippi and describes the equipment etc

N16(a) "Negro Common School: North Carolina," *Crisis*, XXXIV 79-80, 117-18 (May and June, 1927).
Discusses the status of schools in North Carolina and describes the equipment, etc. *See also* S4t(a).

N17(a) "Negro Crime Rate," *Opportunity*, V, 160 (June, 1927).
An editorial comment on the method of handling criminal cases in Columbus Ohio, mentioning the effect of migration in increasing crime and showing how the problem was met in Columbus

N18(a) "Negro Exodus," *New International Encyclopedia.* New York, Dodd, Mead and Co. (1916). Vol. XVI

An article on the causes and nature of the migration of 1879.

N19(a) "Negro Exodus — White Population in South Carolina Exceeds That of Colored for First Time in over One Hundred Years," *Commercial and Financial Chronicle,* CXVII, 160 (July 14, 1923).

A comparison of population figures for whites and Negroes in South Carolina.

N20(a) "Negro Farm Owner," *Southern Workman,* LVII, 1067 (March, 1928).

An editorial comment on the continued exodus from the old cotton states, 1920-25 and after showing the character and extent of the migration.

N21(a) "Negro Governments in the North," *Review of Reviews,* XXXVIII, 471-72 (October, 1908).

Summary of W49(e).

N22(a) "Negro Housing in an American City," *Opportunity,* IV 335-36 (November, 1926).

An editorial on the housing conflicts which have occurred sporadically in Kansas City Missouri since the beginning of the war-time migration.

N23(a) "Negro Housing Situation in Baltimore," *Monthly Labor Review,* XIX, 898 (October, 1924).

A brief statement that the increasing Negro population is, on the whole, adequately housed

N24(a) "Negro Housing Study," *Buffalo Foundation Forum,* IV 8-11 (May, 1921).

A brief report on occupations and conditions of housing among Negroes in Buffalo.

N25(a) "Negro in a White Man's World," *New Republic,* LXIV 59-60 (September 3, 1930).

Editorial summary of J4(b).

N26(a) "Negro in Detroit," *Southern Workman,* LVI, 250-51 (June, 1927).

Brief summary of D8(a).

N27(a) "Negro in Industry and Business," *Monthly Labor Review,* XXIX, 66-69 (July, 1929).

The first part is a summary of the issue of *Opportunity* for May, 1929, which reported addresses delivered at the National Urban League Conference at Louisville Kentucky, April 9-12, 1929. The discussion was concerned with the movement of Negroes to *southern* cities and the effect of this migration upon the nature of occupations in which colored workers were found The second section summarizes the report of the National Negro Business League and gives the nature of business concerns in which Negroes are found. *See also* N6(a).

N28(a) "Negro in Richmond V rginia," *Monthly Labor Review*, XXXI, 313-14 (August, 1930).
Summary of R18(a).

N29(a) "Negro in the Cities of the North," *Charities*, XV, No. 1 (October 7, 1905), 96 pp.
A special number devoted to the subject of the status of the Negro in the North Also printed in pamphlet form. For summary see N31(a). Articles of value for migration are listed separately under authors: B14(a), B33(a), D2(b), D18(a), H45(a), J18(c), K1(a), K2(c), O6(b), P6(b), W6(b), W7(d), W29(a), W49(i).

N30(a) "Negro in the Industrial Department," *Monthly Labor Review*, XXXII, 1326-28 (June, 1931).
Report of a survey made by the Industrial Relations Department of the National Urban League concerning the extent of unemployment and general economic conditions

N31(a) "Negro in the North," *Nation*, LXXXI, 273-74 (October 5, 1905).
Summary of N29(a).

N32(a) "Negro in the North," *Southern Workman*, LVII, 254-56 (July, 1928).
An editorial, largely a quotation from the *Chicago Tribune*, on the serious housing situation in Chicago due to the migration of Negroes to that city

N33(a) "Negro in West Virginia," *Monthly Labor Review*, XXIX 818-20 (October, 1929).
Summary of W14(d).

N34(a) "Negro Labor and Communism," *Opportunity*, III, 354 (December, 1925).
An editorial in answer to the A F. of L.'s warning against exhortations of Communists Shows Negroes not seriously affected

N35(a) "Negro Labor and the Cotton Industry," *Statist*, CI, 493 (March 31, 1923).
An English view of the extent of migration and its probable effect on the cotton market

N36(a) "Negro Labor during and after the War," *Monthly Labor Review*, XII, 835-38 (April, 1921).
A summary of U3(19a).

N37(a) "Negro Labor, Past and Present," *Opportunity*, V (May, 1927).

An editorial comment on W13(a), showing the similarity in the present economic situation of the Negro and that of seventy years ago.

N38(a) "Negro Laborers," *Opportunity*, I, 379-80 (December, 1923).

A brief editorial quoting a Wisconsin paper on the migration of the skilled Negro laborer

N39(a) "Negro Migrant," *Opportunity*, II, 250 (August, 1924).

A quotation from a St Louis paper on the problem of the Negro's adjustment to a new environment

N40(a) "Negro Migrant in Pittsburgh," *Monthly Labor Review*, VI, 155-57 (February, 1918).

A summary of E19(a).

N41(a) "Negro Migrants in Philadelphia in 1923," *Monthly Labor Review*, XIX, 998-99 (November, 1924).

A summary of the 1923 Report of P14(a).

N42(a) "Negro Migration," *Monthly Labor Review*, XVI, 1186-87 (June, 1923).

A very brief statement of the extent of migration in 1923 and the causes of the movement.

N43(a) "Negro Migration," *New Republic*, VII, 213-14 July 1, 1916).

An editorial discussing the War as an opportunity for Negro industrial advancement, and suggesting the probable effects of a migration. Interesting as a forecast.

N44(a) "Negro Migration," *Opportunity*, I, 254-55 (August, 1923).

Quotations from several newspapers concerning the causes and extent of migration.

N45(a) "Negro Migration and the Immigration Quota," *Opportunity*, I, 18-19 (April, 1923).

An intelligent, cautious statement concerning labor shortage as a cause of the migration in 1923.

N46(a) "Negro Migration as the South Sees it," *Survey*, XXXVIII 428 (August 11, 1917).

A résumé of speeches on race relations given at the Southern Sociological Congress held at Ashville dealing particularly with causes of the movement

N47(a) "Negro Migration Conference," *Southern Workman*, XLVI 72-73; 133-35 (February and March, 1917).

Editorials commenting on a conference held in New York by the National Urban League, giving summaries of speeches and resolutions

N48(a) "Negro Migration Ebbs," *Iron Trade Review*, LXI, 1248 (December 13, 1917).

A brief editorial asserting that the extent of migration has been exaggerated and its significance is lessening, and that the Negroes are returning South

N49(a) "Negro Migration from Georgia," *Monthly Labor Review*, XVIII, 32-35 (January, 1924).

Discusses two conferences on Negro migration — one of whites and the other of Negroes. Gives a summary from each point of view of the causes extent and remedies of the migration

N50(a) "Negro Migration in 1923," *Monthly Labor Review*, XVIII, 64-66 (April, 1924).

A good concise statement of the characteristics of migration in 1923.

N51(a) "Negro Migration Problems," *Missionary Review of the World*, XLVII, 481 (June, 1924).

A brief statement of the problems created in Philadelphia by the influx of Negroes aod a description of the union of welfare agencies to aid in solving these problems.

N52(a) "Negro Migration Question Viewed from Different Angles," *Manufacturers Record*, LXXXV, 68 (April 17, 1924).

An excellent editorial commenting on several current articles, E7(a) and W36(a), and stating the attitude of the *Manufacturers Record* toward the results to be hoped for from the migration.

N53(a) "Negro Migrations," *Forum*, LXXII, 853-57 (December, 1924).

A discussion of the causes and effects of migration through a summary of letters from prominent men and women

N54(a) "Negro Migrations and Migrants," *Monthly Labor Review*, XIV, 42-48 (January, 1922).

An excellent summary of M56(a) and W41(e).

N55(a) "Negro Miners," *Independent*, DXIII, 1790 (July 6, 1899).

An editorial comment on fighting between strikers and Negroes who had been imported to man the mines in Illinois during a strike

N56(a) "Negro Miners in the Coal Strike," *Opportunity*, III, 195 (July, 1925).

An editorial on the situation of the Negro coal miners with a brief estimate of the extent of the migration to West Virginia.

N57(a) "Negro Moves," *Crisis*, XXV, 133-34 (January, 1923).
Quotations from newspapers concerning the general movements of Negroes and the resulting problems.

N58(a) "Negro Segregation in Cities," *Chautauqua*, LXII, 11-13 (March, 1911).
An editorial paragraph on a segregation ordinance in Baltimore and its evidence of an undesirable tendency

N59(a) "Negro, South and North," (The Negro, North and South, Title varies) *Coal Age*, XI, 925, 1091: XII, 26, 168, 291-92, 337-38, 507-8, 691-92 (May 26, June 23, July 7, July 28, August 18, August 25, September 22, and October 20, 1917).
A series of letters provoked by E33(a) dealing with the causes of migration.

N60(a) "Negro to Negroes on Voting," *Literary Digest*, CIX, 24 (April 25, 1931).
Comments of a Negro on the political situation among Negroes and the necessity of their proving that they are capable of using the ballot; claims th t so far they have not so shown themselves in the North

N61(a) "Negro Vote," *Opportunity*, IX, 202-3 (July, 1931).
An editorial on the potential strength of Negroes in Louisville Mentions increasing political power as a result of migration to cities

N62(a) "Negro Wage Earners," *American Federationist*, XXXII 878-79, No. 10 (October, 1925).
An editorial condemning leaders who prey on the ignorance of Negroes in urging them to become Communists. Contends that the A F. of L. offers Negroes protection and experience in organized coöperation.

N63(a) "Negro Welfare," *Buffalo Foundation Forum*, No. 3 (April 1921).
A brief report on welf re work among the colored people of Buffalo.

N64(a) "Negro Welfare Workers in Pittsburgh," *Survey*, XL, 513 (August 3, 1918).
Describes the various attempts of large concerns employing Negroes to improve conditions of Negro laborers in Pittsburgh.

N65(a) "Negro Woman Worker," *Southern Workman*, LIX, 375-76 (August, 1930).
A summary of P17(a).

N66(a) "Negro Women in Industry," *Monthly Labor Review*, XV 116-18 (July, 1922).
An excellent summary of U3 (32a).

N67(a) "Negro Women in Industry," *Monthly Labor Review*, XXIX, 554-56 (September, 1929).
Summary of U3(33a).

N68(a) "Negro Worker in the Wor d" *Crisis*, XXVII, 30 (November, 1923).
Brief quotations from M56(a).

N69 *Negro Year Book*. Negro Year Book Publishing Company, Tuskegee Institute, Alabama.
For full references on migrations consult indexes of the several volumes.

(a) *1918-19*: Brief summary of the main phases of migration, its causes, extent, effects, and the attitudc of the North and South, pp. 8-16. Gives population statistics showing migration, pp. 435-36.

(b) *1921-22*: Tables showing changes in population and movement of Negroes, and summary of census figures, pp. 321-23, 383-94.

(c) *1925-26*: Summary of the causes of migration, pp. 5-10; and discussion of census figures showing the movement of Negroes, pp. 437-40. Material on causes is the same as that for W44(d).

(d) *1931-32*: Contains 1930 census figures, showing increase of colored population by states, and a gencral description of conditions in agriculture, industry, business, education, religion, etc.

N70(a) "Negroes and Organized Labor," *Survey*, XXXIX, 527-28 (February 9, 1918).
Reports a discussion by a National Urban League Council of the Unions' dis crimination against Negroes

N71(a) "Negroes and the Coal Mines," *Monthly Labor Review*, XXV, 252-53 (August, 1927).
A summary of W14(c).

N72(a) "Negroes as Workers," *Opportunity*, IV, 90 (March, 1926).
A page of letters from industrial firms employing Negroes stating the suc cess of colored workers in their firms.

N73(a) "Negroes at the North," *Harpers Weekly*, DI, 436 (March 31, 1906).
A good summary of the Kelsey and Brandt articles in the *Charities* volume. *See also* B33(a), K2(c).

N74(a) "Negroes Can Organize is Conference Feature," *Brookwood Review*, V, No. 5 (June-July, 1927).
Report of the chief subjects discussed at a conference on the Negro in indus-

try held May 19-20, 1927, at Brookwood, showing the Negro's status in northern industry aod his relation to unions

N75(a) "Negroes in Industry," *Survey*, XLII, 900 (September 27, 1919).

A short unsigned article on growing race friction in industry since the Armistice and increasing competition for jobs Discusses the work of the Negro Division of the New York State Industrial Commission in trying to overcome some of the prejudice and handicaps faced by Negroes

N76(a) "Negroes in New England," *Survey*, XLVII, 782 (February 18, 1922).

An editorial on the increase of Negroes in New England and on the type of industries they are entering.

N77(a) "Negroes in the Urban Movement," *Outlook*, CI, 457-58 (June 29, 1912).

Editorial comment on the causes and effects of the urban movement of Negroes within the South.

N78(a) "Negroes of Johnstown, Pa.," *Survey*, LI, 74-75 (October 15, 1923).

An editorial criticizing the attitude of the Mayor of Johnstown toward Negroes, aod his demand that the Negroes leave the town

N79(a) "Negroes out of Work," *Nation*, CXXXII, 441-42 (April 22, 1931).

An editorial on the Urban League unemployment report discussing the extent of unemployment among Negroes in 1931. *See also* N8(g).

N80(a) "Negroes Who Go North," *Southern Workman*, LVII, 431-32 (October, 1928).

A short item quoted from *The Raleigh Times* stating that in spite of increased migration to Massachusetts the number of Negroes has not shown an increase in state institutions for insane and paupers

N81(a) "Negro's Brighter Outlook," *Nation*, CV, 627-28 (December 6, 1917).

An editorial on some of the effects of migration.

N82(a) "Negro's Health Progress during the Last Twenty-Five Years," *New York City Department of Health Weekly Bulletin*, XV 93-94 (June 12, 1926).

A brief summary of the decrease in deaths among Negroes from certain di seases, 1920 to 1925, in New York City

N83(a) "Negro's Northward Exodus," *Literary Digest*, CX, 4 (August 29, 1931).

Current newspaper comments on figures of the 1930 Census showing the northward movement of Negroes, with brief summary of the c uses

N84(a) *New Day for the Colored Woman Worker*: A Study of Colored Women in Industry in New York City. Joint Committee for the Study of the Colored Woman, Nellie Swartz, Chairman (March 1, 1919), 39 pp.

An investigation by Jessie Clark and Gertrude McDougald of the general background of colored women workers their schooling, industrial training, age, marital condition the nature of their occupations, working conditions, hours, wages, success, race relations in industry etc

N85(a) "New Exodus," *Outlook*, CXXXIII, 878 (May 16, 1923).

An opinion statement of the causes of the migration and its economic effects in the South

N86 New Jersey Board of Agriculture

(a) "Menace to Rural Homes on Account of Tramps: Migration of Negroes from the South," In *New Jersey Board of Agriculture, 32nd Annual Report* (1904-05), pp. 109-11.

A statement of the necessity for a farmers' organization to protect rural dis tricts from tramps, especially Negroes

N87 New Jersey Bureau of Labor and Industries

(a) "The Negro in Manufacturing and Mechanical Industries," In *Bureau of Industrial Statistics, 26th Annual Report* (1902-03), Part 2, pp. 163-215.

A statistical study of the Negro in New Jersey, mainly of his place and suc cess in the manual training schools and in the industries and unions

N88(a) "New Negro Migration," *Survey*, XLV, 752 (February 26, 1921).

An editorial comment on the movement of Negroes due to unemployment

N89(a) "New Northward Migration," *Survey*, L, 297-98 (June 1, 1923)

An editorial on the renewed migration caused by the returning industrial prosperity of the North

N90 New York Association for Improving the Condition of the Poor

(a) *Health Work for Mothers and Children in a Colored Community.* Publications No. 131 (1924), 15 pp.

A discussion of health work for Negroes in the Columbus Hill District

N91 New York State Department of Labor

(a) *Unemployment in Buffalo, November, 1929*, by F. C. and F. E.

Croxton. New York State Department of Labor, Special Bulletin 163 (1930), 48 pp.

An original, house-to-house investigation of the employment status of 15,164 persons over 18 years of age who were usually gainfully employed For this group is given color, nativity, nature of industry, per cent employed full time, part time or idle

N92 New York Urban League

(a) *Annual Report, 1923.*

Contains a brief article with important illustrative maps dealing with the increase of Harlem population from 1913 to 1924.

(b) *A Challenge to New York. Annual Report, 1927*, 20 pp.

A very general statement of reforms needed to meet the abnormal conditions created by migration to New York City

(c) *Convalescent Need for Negroes in New York.* New York Urban League, 1931, 14 pp.

A statistical presentation of hospital facilities for Negroes in New York City, showing the effect on the health problems of the increase in colored population.

N93 Newbold, N. C.

(a) "Common Schools for Negroes in the South," *Annals*, CXL, 209-23 (November, 1928).

Summarizes expenditures and work of various agencies and states in promoting Negro education in the South

(b) "North Carolina's Adventure in Good Will," *High School Journal*, XIII, 119-23 (March, 1930).

An account of what North Carolina is doing to build up a modern high standard school system for Negroes

N94 Newman, Bernard J

(a) "The Housing of Negro Immigrants in Pennsylvania," *Opportunity*, II, 46-48 (February, 1924).

Discusses the housing situation of the Negro migrants

(b) *Housing of the City Negro.* Philadelphia, Whittier Center, Paper No. 2, 8 pp. (No date, but *c.* 1914.)

A survey of housing conditions among Philadelphia Negroes, particularly of those wishing to improve their living conditions

For other works by this author, *see* P14(a).

N95(a) Nichols, F. O
"Health Measures as They Relate to the Negro Race," *Annals*, CXL, 294-98 (November, 1928).
A description of ways in which various organizations are trying to educate Negroes in the care of health, and in the prevention and control of disease

N96(a) Noble, Stuart G.
Forty Years of Public Schools in Mississippi, with Special Reference to the Education of the Negro. New York, Teachers College, Columbia University (1918), 141 pp.
A study of the educational situation in Mississippi during Reconstruction, under southern rule 1876-86, and since 1886. Studies equipment status of teachers distribution of school funds the influence of education on the life of the Negro as seen in effect on home ownership, agricultural progress crime, etc

N97 North Carolina State Board of Charities and Public Welfare

(a) *Biennial Report, 1926-28.* Raleigh, The Board
The Division of Work among Negroes, pp. 98-110, reports the movement of Negroes to cities and the resulting increase of activities of the social agencies and states some of the work for Negroes. Refers to N97(b).

(b) *Capital Punishment in North Carolina.* Raleigh, The Board (1929), 173 pp. Special Bulletin No. 10.
A history of capital punishment in North Carolina, giving statistics of capital convictions including such factors as type of crime; educational, marital, occupational and age status of prisoners statistics of prison population 1908-27; reports of electrocutions, lynchings and mob violence Largely a study of crime among Negroes since Negroes form over half of those convicted of capital offenses.

(c) *North Carolina's Social Welfare Program for Negroes.* Special Bulletin 8 (1926), 44 pp.
Presents the program of the Board for its work among Negroes and shows what has been accomplished Page 13 mentions migration to North Carolina and resulting problems of crime and dependency

——— For other works concerning this Board, *see* O7(a), O7(b), O7(c), O7(d).

N98(a) "Northern Shift of Negro Labor," *Monthly Labor Review*, XVI, 681 (March, 1923).
A brief statement of the specific industries which Negroes are entering in the northern cities

N99(a) "Northward Migration," *Crisis*, II, 56 June, 1911).
Quotations from various newspapers concerning the changing proportion of

Negroes in southern states and the attitude of the North and Canada toward the migrants

N100(a) "Note on Disfranchisement," *Michigan Law Review*, XXIII, 279-84 (January, 1925).

A discussion of the legality of forbidding Negroes to vote in the primaries

N101(a) "Note on Negro Vital Statistics," *Opportunity*, VI, 195-97 (July, 1928).

An editorial discussing trends in mortality r tes and the effect of specific diseases among Negroes.

O1 Odell, George T

(a) "The Northern Migration of the Negro," *Trade Winds* (January, 1924), pp. 20-22.

A popular superficial account of the extent, causes and results of the migration.

O2 Odum, Howard W.

(a) "Negro Children in the Public Schools of Philadelphia," *Annals*, XLIX, 186-208 September, 1913).

An analysis of the school records of Negro children in Philadelphia. Dis cusses retardation, attendance records, grades etc Mentions migration as one cause of retardation. Also discusses intelligence tests of comparative abilities of white and colored children.

(b) *Rainbow Round My Shoulder*: The Blue Trail of Black Ulysses. Indianapolis, Bobbs-Merrill Co. (1928), 323 pp.

A synthesis of the wanderings and experiences of a migratory Negro, told in the first person.

(c) *Social and Mental Traits of the Negro*. New York, Columbia University Press (1910), 302 pp. Columbia University Studies in History, Economics and Public Law No. 99.

A discussion of various personality traits of the Negro and of factors which influence them. Chap. i deals with school facilities for Negroes in the South around 1900; Chap. v with the Negro offender the high rate of crime among Negroes and the nature of their offenses Contains no discussion of migration but describes conditions of education and crime in the South

O3(a) "On Southern Farms," *Opportunity*, II, 29-30 (January, 1924).

A quotation from a southern newspaper dealing with means of keeping Negroes on the farms, thus showing causes of migration

O4(a) *Opportunity*, VII, 69-100 (March, 1929).

The entire number deals with conditions among Negroes in Chicago. Articles of value for migration are listed separately under individual authors. *See also* B8(a), B56(d), F18(a), F21(b), K9(a), M5(a), W37(a).

O5(a) "'Our Own Subject Race' Rebels," *Literary Digest*, LXII 25 (August 2, 1919).

Summary of newspaper accounts of the race riot in Washington, D C

O6 Ovington, Mary White

(a) *Half A Man*. New York, Longmans, Green and Co. (1911), 236 pp.

A study of the Negro in New York City before 1915—his living conditions, occupations, death rates juvenile delinquency etc

(b) "The Negro Home in New York," *Charities*, XV, 25-30 October 7, 1905).

Deals mainly with conditions found in Negro homes in New York.

(c) "The Negro in the Trades Unions in New York," *Annals*, XXVII 551-58 (May, 1906).

Describes the type of unions in which Negroes were found in New York City the approximate colored membership, the attitude of organized labor toward the Negroes, and the nature of the occupations of colored workers

O7 Oxley, Lawrence A.

(a) "The North Carolina Negro," *Welfare Magazine*, XVIII, 1484-94 (November, 1927).

Describes the purpose of founding the Division of Work Among Negroes of the State Board of Charities the functions, aims and accomplishments of this division.

(b) "North Carolina's State Wide Welfare Program for Negroes," *Survey*, LVII, 511-14 (January 15, 1927).

Same material as N97(a), N97(c), O7(c).

(c) "North Carolina's Venture in Negro Welfare," *Southern Workman*, LX, 348-51 (August, 1931).

A brief history of the work of North Carolina's public welfare program for Negroes and what it has accomplished

(d) "North Carolina's Welfare Program for Negroes," *Southern Workman*, LVI, 16-25 (January, 1927).

An account of the work of the North Carolina State Board of Charities and Public Welfare. One paragraph mentions migration from other states to North Carolina and the effect of this influx on the increase of crime. *See also* N97(a), N97(c).

Parker, S. L., *see* H36(a).

P1 Parker, Thomas F.

(a) "Recreation for Colored Citizens," *Playground*, XIX, 651-52 (March, 1926).

A description of how Greenville, South Carolina, became interested in recreational opportunities for colored people because of the migration, and what is being done to provide leisure time facilities for the Negroes

P2 Patterson, J. Stahl

(a) "Negroes of the South: Increase and Movement of the Colored Population," *Popular Science Monthly*, XIX 784-90 (October, 1881).

An interesting contemporary view discussing the census figures for 1880, which show the increase of the colored population, and dealing with causes of Negro movements

P3 Payne, E. George

(a) "Negroes in the Public Elementary Schools of the North," *Annals*, CXL, 224-33 (November, 1928).

Shows some of the educational problems that have arisen as a result of the migration of Negroes to northern cities, and discusses the problems of segregation, retardation and the rate of attendance

P4 Pearson, Elizabeth W.

(a) *Letters from Port Royal*, Written at the Time of the Civil War, 1862-68. Boston, W. B. Clarke Co. (1906), 345 pp.

One chapter, (pp. 325-34) contains letters written during 1866, 1867 and 1868, mentioning difficulties of raising crops.

P5 Peckstein, L. A.

(a) "Problem of Negro Education in Northern and Border Cities," *Elementary School Journal*, XXX, 192-99 (November, 1929).

Presents the results of various surveys of mixed and segregated schools for Negroes; the laws and actual situations in northern states regarding segregation in schools Touches on the results of migration.

P6 Pendleton, Helen B.

(a) "Cotton Pickers in Northern Cities," *Survey*, XXXVII, 569-71 (February 17, 1917).

An interesting portrayal of social conditions created by the migration to the North, particularly to New Jersey

(b) "Negro Dependence in Baltimore," *Charities*, XV, 50-58 (October 7, 1905).

Discusses charity cases and poverty among Negroes. Merely mentions Negroes flocking to cities

P7 Pennsylvania Bureau of Industrial Statistics

(a) "Study of the Industrial Conditions of the Negro Population of Pennsylvania and Especially of the Cities of Philadelphia and Pittsburgh," by R. R. Wright. *40th Annual Report*, 1912, pp. 21-195, Harrisburg, Pennsylvania.

A careful and exhaustive statistical study of the Negro in Philadelphia and Pittsburgh industries types of labor, age and conjugal condition of colored workers; and their relation to the unions. Specific references to migration on pp. 27-30, 37-43.

P8 Pennsylvania: Consumers League of Eastern Pennsylvania

(a) *Colored Women as Industrial Workers in Philadelphia.* Philadelphia (1920), 49 pp.

A detailed study of local Negro women in industry—types of employment, wages, conditions of work, etc. For summaries, *see* C10(a), C23(a).

P9 Pennsylvania Department of Public Welfare

(a) *Negro Survey of Pennsylvania.* Harrisburg, Pennsylvania (1927), 97 pp.

A very valuable survey of economic and social conditions among Negroes of Pennsylvania in 1924-25, made under the direction of Forrester B Washington in the ninety-one towns and cities containing over one hundred Negroes each, and including about 95 per cent of the Negroes in Pennsylvania. Discusses economic opportunity, housing, health education, recreation and race relations

P10 Pepper, John

(a) "American Negro Problems," *Communist*, VII, 628-38 October, 1928).

A discussion of Negro problems as part of the proletarian revolution against capitalism, showing that the Communist Party must champion the Negro.

P11 Peters, Robert J.

(a) "Industrial Employment of Negroes in Pennsylvania," *Labor and Industry*, XIII, 18-26 (January, 1926).

Presents the results of questionnaires on extent of Negro employment January 1, 1923-September, 1925; the degree of dependability and similar facts.

P12 Peterson, Joseph, and Lyle H. Lanie

(a) *Studies in the Comparative Abilities of Whites and Negroes.* Mental Measurement Monographs, Serial No. 5 (February, 1929).

Part 1 describes the tests used, and analyzes the results secured in comparing twelve-year old white and Negro children in Nashville Chicago and New

York City The migration to the North and its effects on the retardation of school children are mentioned in pp. 13, 16, 18, 96.

Pettit, Walter W., *see* L13(a).

—— Phelps-Stokes Fellowship Papers, *see* B20(a), B47(a), C13(a), F1(a), H30(a), I6(a), J11(a), K15(a), L25(a), M53(a), P20(a), R11(b), S6(a), W38(a), W41(i), Z41(a).

P13 Philadelphia. Armstrong Association

(a) *The Negro in Business in Philadelphia.* Philadelphia, The Association (1917), 14 pp.

A report of a first-hand survey of the character of Negro concerns in Philadelphia, showing type of business, state of birth of proprietors, length of residence in Philadelphia, length of time conducting the business size of building, etc

(b) *Study of Living Conditions among Colored People in Towns in the Outer Part of Philadelphia and Other Suburbs Both in Pennsylvania and New Jersey.* Philadelphia, The Association (1915), 57 pp.

Contains a general discussion of housing conditions of Negroes in these towns giving a brief summary of the conditions the conclusions drawn, and a detailed outline by towns of the situation found in each Concludes that most of the Negro men were employed in unskilled labor and the women in domestic service

P14 Philadelphia Housing Association

(a) *Housing in Philadelphia.* Annual Reports of the Philadelphia Association (1916-17, 1921-30). Directed by Bernard J. Newman.

Housing conditions among Negroes are mentioned as follows: *1916*: pp. 9-11; *1917*: pp. 6-9; *1921*: pp. 23-28; *1922*: pp. 16, 17, 24 comment on the difficulty of supplying the steadily increasing colored population with houses; *1923*: pp. 8, 17, 22, 24-25, 27, 29; *1924*: pp. 23, 25, 28, 34; *1925*: pp. 24, 26-27; *1926*: See index; *1927*: pp. 11, 25, 27-28; *1928*: pp. 29-30, 32; *1929*: p. 28; *1930*: pp. 31-34. *See also* N41(a), N94(a), N94(b).

P15 Philadelphia Municipal Court

(a) *Report for 1929,* 190 pp.

A statistical analysis of work done in this Court References to Negroes are found on pp. 64, 66-67, 126-27, 131, 173.

P16(a) "Phyllis Wheatley Association," *Southern Workman,* LX, 374 (September, 1931).

An editorial on the work of the Association, particularly in Cleveland showing how it has aided in handling the educational problems that arose because of migration to Cleveland

P17 Phyllis Wheatley Branch of the Y.W.C.A.

(a) *Negro Women in the Industries of Indianapolis, Indiana, A Survey and Report, 1929.* Indianapolis (1929), 27 pp.

A first-hand survey of the nature of occupations, wages, working conditions, age, marital status recreation, etc., of Negro women in Indianapolis. *See also* N65(a).

P18(a) "Physical Impairment among Negro Factory Workers in Cincinnati," *Monthly Labor Review*, XXXIII, 298-99 (August, 1931).

Summary of A8(a), A8(b).

P19(a) Pickens, William

"Jim Crow in Texas," *Nation*, CXVII, 155-56 (August 15, 1923).

A vivid account of experiences in Jim Crow cars.

——— For other works by this author, *see* F17(a).

P20(a) Pinchbeck, Raymond

The Virginia Negro Artisan and Tradesman. University of V rginia (1926), 146 pp. Phelps-Stokes Fellowship Papers, No. 7.

Gives the history of the Negro artisan and tradesman in Virginia from carliest seventeenth century days up to the present The only descriptions of migration are on pp. 68-69, 80-81.

P21 Pittsburgh Council of the Churches of Christ

(a) *The New Negro Population, Report on the Recent Influx of Negroes to Pittsburgh.* Pittsburgh (February, 1918). (Unpaged pamphlet.)

A brief discussion of the extent and causes of migration and the problems arising therefrom, together with recommendations as to what the churches can do to aid the Negroes

P22 Pittsburgh Housing Association

(a) *Annual Reports* (1929-31).

Annual reports of housing conditions in Pittsburgh, to date containing little information on the Negro.

P23(a) *Pittsburgh Survey: Findings of the.* New York Russell Sage Foundation (1914), 6 vols.

The only significant material on the Negro is contained in the volume on "Wage Earning Pittsburgh" and is listed under separate authors. *See also* T28(b), W49(n).

P24(a) "Plan for the Southern Migrant," *Crisis*, XIV, 217-18 (September, 1917).

A letter advising Negro migrants to settle in rural districts of the North rather than in northern cities

P25(a) "Play for Negroes," *Survey*, XXVIII, 641-42 (August 17, 1912).
Summary of H6(h).

P26(a) "Population Shift and the Future of the Negro," *Opportunity*, I, 22-23 (June, 1923).
A brief editorial on the probable effect of migration on the future rate of increase of the colored race

P27 Porter, Kirk H.

(a) *A History of Suffrage in the United States.* Chicago, University of Chicago Press (1918), 260 pp.
An account of the struggle for suffrage by various groups in the United States emphasizing the problem of Negro suffrage, how it was acquired used and lost. Chap. viii describes the measures by which the South disfranchised Negroes

P28 Powell, Rachel H.

(a) "Looking in on Harlem Youth," *Southern Workman*, LVII 89 (February, 1928).
A useful summary of J15(a).

P29(a) *Preliminary Survey of the Industrial Distribution and Union Status of Negroes in New York City.* Prepared by The Labor Bureau, Inc., for the New York Urban League, 12 pp. (No date.)
An analysis of the extent of union membership among Negroes in New York City, names of locals types of organizations status of Negro members etc *See also* N8(e).

P30 Price, Joseph S

(a) *The Negro Elementary School Teacher in West Virginia.* The West Virginia Collegiate Institute Bulletin, Series 11, No. 3 (September, 1924), 100 pp.
A statistical study through the questionnaire method, of the status of Negro elementary school teachers in West Virginia. Deals with composition, training, appointments tenure, salary, supervision, etc

Priest, Madge H., *see* W43(a).

P31(a) "Problem of the Negro Laborer," *Iron Trade Review*, LX, 836-37 (April 12, 1917).
Discusses briefly several factors that make Negro labor in the North unsatisfactory

P32(a) "Proceedings of a Mississippi Migration Convention in 1879," *Journal of Negro History*, IV, 51-54 (January, 1919).

Report of a committee of white planters on causes of the 1879 exodus and resolutions adopted in order to improve conditions. Reprint of an article in the *Vicksburg Commercial Daily Advertiser* for May 5, 1879.

P33 Proctor, H. H.

(a) "The Atlanta Plan of Interracial Coöperation," *Southern Workman*, XLIX, 9-12 (January, 1920).

A brief report of the purpose, method of organization, and some of the achievements of the Atlanta Interracial Committee

P34(a) "Professor Moton of Tuskegee on Negro Migration," *Manufacturers Record*, LXXXIII, 53 (May 31, 1923).

An editorial quoting a letter from a Negro leader approving the stand in H50(a).

P35(a) "Propaganda and Common Sense," *Opportunity*, I, 354 (December, 1923).

An editorial showing how the South used false news items in an attempt to frighten Negroes away from the North

P36 Puryear, Thomas L.

(a) "Negro Welfare in Newark," *New Jersey Conference of Social Work Bulletin*, I, 7-11 (May, 1930).

An account of the work of welfare agencies among Negroes in Newark.

Q1 Quillin, Frank U

(a) *The Color Line in Ohio*: A History of Race Prejudice in a Typical Northern State. University of Michigan Historical Studies (1913), 178 pp.

Part 1 gives an historical account of the political and social status of the Negro in Ohio. Part 2 shows his status, at the time of writing, in each of the larger Ohio towns, giving instances of discrimination and antagonism. Evidences of increasing prejudice due to migration and larger numbers are given on pp. 131-132, 139, 142, 145, 150.

(b) "Negro in Cincinnati," *Independent*, LXVIII, 399-403 (February 24, 1910).

A description of discriminations against Negroes and of race prejudice in Cincinnati.

(c) "The Negro in Cleveland Ohio," *Independent*, LXXII, 518-20 (March 7, 1912).

An account of race prejudice in Cleveland.

(d) "Race Prejudice in a Northern Town," *Independent*, LIX, 139-42 (July 20, 1905).
An account of race prejudice in Syracuse Ohio.

R1(a) "Race Conflicts," *Public*, XX, 666-67 (July 13, 1917).
An editorial on the East St Louis riot.

R2(a) "Race Prejudice in the North," *Christian Century*, XLIV 583-84 (May 12, 1927).
Summary of D8(a).

R3(a) "Race Riots in Ohio," *Outlook*, LXXXII, 536 (March 10, 1906).
An editorial paragraph on the Springfield riot, describing the riot and blaming the political situation.

R4(a) "Racial Tension and Race Riots," *Outlook*, CXXII, 532-34 (August 6, 1919).
A good description of the Washington riot.

R5 Ragland, J. Marshall

(a) "The Negro in Detroit," *Southern Workman*, LII, 533-40 (November, 1923).
Discusses the coming of the Negroes to Detroit and some of their present economic and social conditions as these have been affected by migration.

R6 Ramsdell, C. W.

(a) *Reconstruction in Texas.* New York, Columbia University Press (1910), 324 pp. Columbia Studies in History, Economics and Public Law No. 95.
Chiefly a description of political troubles of Reconstruction Days in Texas.

R7 Randolph, A. Philip

(a) "The Economic Crisis of the Negro," *Opportunity*, IX, 145-49 (May, 1931).
Discusses various kinds of unemployment among Negroes during the depression.

(b) "The Truth about the Brotherhood of Sleeping Car Porters," *Messenger*, VII, 37-38 (February, 1926).
An account of the founding of the porters union, how and when it was accomplished and reasons for such an organization.

R8(a) "Reasons Why Negroes Go North," *Survey*, XXXVIII, 226-27 (June 2, 1917).
A summary of D18(f).

R9(a) "Recreation Facilities for the Negro," *Playground*, XXIII 168-69 (June, 1929).
A digest of W9(g).

R10(a) "Redistribution of the American Negro," *Review of Reviews*, LXV, 95-96 (January, 1922).
A summary, with copious quotations, of a newspaper article published by A S. Van de Graaff on the migration of Negroes as shown by the census returns for 1920.

R11 Reed, Ruth

(a) *Negro Illegitimacy in New York City*. New York, Columbia University Press (1926), 136 pp. Studies in History, Economics and Public Law No. 277.
A statistical study of illegitimacy in New York City A few casual references to migration in the discussion of the state of birth of the unmarried mothers (pp. 50-51) and in some of the case histories

(b) *Negro Women of Gainesville, Georgia*. Athens, University of Georgia Bulletin, Vol. XXII, No. 1 (1921), 61 pp. Phelps-Stokes Fellowship Studies No. 6.
A statistical study of the home life education, labor and the general status of Negro women. Slight references to the migration of whites and Negroes in accounting for the growth of population

R12 Reid, Ira de A.

(a) "American Cities—Albany, N. Y.," *Opportunity*, VII (June, 1929).
A report of a careful survey made by the National Urban League, showing birthplace of the Negro population and increase of colored people, housing conditions rents health birth and death rates nature of occupations and wages, relation to unions, crime and juvenile delinquency recreational facilities, place in schools, status of social agencies and churches. *See also* A4(a), Z35(g).

(b) "Let Us Prey," *Opportunity*, IV, 274-78 September, 1926).
An investigation of religious and pseudo-religious organizations in Harlem, showing how many of them exploit the Negroes

(c) "Lily White Labor," *Opportunity*, VIII, 170-73 June, 1930).
Deals with the attitude of the A. F. of L. toward Negro workers

(d) "Mirrors of Harlem," *Social Forces*, V, 628-34 (June, 1927).
A sane discussion of some of the problems of Harlem, such as the adjustment necessitated by diverse population elements, and problems of employment, business, politics the church health and housing.

(e) "Negro Life on the Western Front (Denver, Colorado)," *Opportunity*, VII, 275-81 (September, 1929).

A report of an investigation made by the Urban League dealing with housing conditions, rents, nature of occupations, wages, health, birth and death rates crime and juvenile delinquency, place in schools, recreational facilities churches and social agencies. *See also* R12(f), Z35(b).

(f) *The Negro Population of Denver, Colorado*, Denver Interracial Commission (1929), 46 pp.

An amplification in pamphlet form of R12(e), Z35(b).

(g) *Social Conditions of the Negro in the Hill District of Pittsburgh*. Pittsburgh, General Committee on the Hill Survey (1930), 117 pp.

The report of a survey made in 1929 covering the conditions among Negroes in the Hill District Deals with the composition of the population, housing conditions, health, employment, crime, recreation, education, community organizations, etc Shows the e fect of migration on the problem of adjustment of Negroes to city life

(h) "Some Problems Attending Negro-White Relations in the United States of America," *Student World*, XXIII, 358-65 (October, 1930).

A sane discussion of the problem of race relations in the United States, especially as it is related to industrial problems, including migration.

(i) "A Study of 200 Negro Prisoners in the Western Penitentiary of Pennsylvania," *Opportunity*, III, 168-70 (June, 1925).

A presentation of various characteristics of Negro prisoners Discusses mentality education, age and occupational status. *See also* R24(a).

For other works by this author, *see* N8 (e).

R13(a) "Report of Negro Industrial Commission of Missouri," *Monthly Labor Review*, XX, 988-89 (May, 1925).

Summary of M46(b).

R14(a) *Report of the Committee on Negro Housing of the President's Conference on Home Building and Home Ownership* (1931), Mimeographed; paging not consecutive.

A valuable collection of extracts from numerous surveys and discussions, showing problems of Negro housing in cities North and South, ownership, segregation, etc

R15(a) "Return to the Farm" *Opportunity*, IX, 7 (January, 1931).

An editorial showing the inadvisability of urging Negroes to return to farms, and discussing causes of Negro migration from the rural areas.

R16 Reuter, Edward B.

(a) *The American Race Problem.* New York, T Y Crowell Co. (1927), 448 pp.

An excellent general discussion of the problems and status of the Negro in the United States. For migration see index under migration and population. Gives a brief, impartial discussion of 1920 census figures and general tendencies of Negro movements The discussion of economic, political and social conditions forms a good background for an understanding of the causes and results of migration.

(b) *The Mulatto in the United States.* Boston, Richard C. Badger (1918), 417 pp.

A careful study of mixed blood races in the United States and other countries with emphasis upon the extent and nature of race intermixture in the United States Discusses the rôle of the mulatto in the economic and social life of our country and on race relations Mentions migration pp. 114, 120.

R17 Reynolds, J. S

(a) *Reconstruction in South Carolina, 1865-77.* Columbia, South Carolina, The State Co. (1905), 522 pp.

A minute account of political trials and tribulations of Reconstruction Days in South Carolina devoting much space to showing evils of Negro rule and the inferiority of Negroes Seems partisan in choice of material.

R18 Richmond Council of Social Agencies

(a) *The Negro in Richmond, Virginia*: Report of the Negro Welfare Survey Committee. Richmond Council of Social Agencies (1929), 136 pp.

A report of an intensive study of the status of the Negroes of Richmond, their number, economic situation, housing, health, etc Mentions migration briefly in discussing the proportion of Negroes in the total population of the city References to migration on pp. 5, 67.) Is significant as showing conditions in a locality from which migration has taken place. *See also* G23(a), N28(a), V3(a).

R19 Ridley, Florida R.

(a) "The Negro in Boston," *Our Boston*, II, 15-20 (January, 1927).

A general survey of the status of the Negro historically and at present in Boston. Discusses in general terms his economic opportunities business, social and religious life

R20(a) "Rising T de of Prejudice," *Nation*, CXXII, 247 (March 10, 1926).

An editorial on the increasing attempt of the South to prevent the industrial training and experience of Negroes, and giving evidence of race prejudice

R21 Robinson, J. H.

(a) "Cincinnati Negro Survey and Program," *National Conference of Social Work Proceedings* (1919), 524-31.
Gives briefly the results of a survey of Negroes in Cincinnati discussing the incursion from the South and describing the occupational characteristics of Negroes Original report not available in most libraries

(b) "Negro Migration," *Social Service News*, I, 100-1 (July, 1917).
A general description of migration to Cincinnati, giving the causes extent and resulting problems.

Robinson, J. W., *see* W14(d).

Rochester, Anna, *see* U3(40a).

R22 Rockwood, H. L.

(a) "Effect of Negro Migration on Community Health in Cleveland," *National Conference of Social Work Proceedings* (1926), 238-44.
An unprejudiced intelligent discussion of the relation between migration and the high death rate of Negroes.

R23 Roland John

(a) "Cotton Hands That Stay," *Country Gentleman*, LXXXII, 2004-5; 2061 ff. (December 22, December 29, 1917).
A popularly written account of how four Mississippi plantation owners held their tenants

R24 Root, William T., Jr

(a) *A Psychological and Educational Survey of 1916 Prisoners in the Western Penitentiary of Pennsylvania.* Published by the Board of Trustees of the Western Penitentiary, (*c.* 1927), 246 pp.
An exhaustive statistical analysis of the psychological and educational composition of the prison population in this penitentiary, with the analysis made for various racial and nationality groups. Is very valuable for its study of the crime rate among Negroes, their offenses characteristics, and the effect of migration on crime. Contains detailed tables. *See also* R12(i).

R25 Rose, J. C.

(a) "The Census and the Colored Population," *Nation*, LII, 232-33 (March 19, 1891).
A magazine article discussing census figures from 1860 to 1890.

(b) "Movements of Negro Population as Shown by Census of 1910," *American Economic Review*, IV, 281-92 (June, 1914).
Discusses changes in the proportion of Negroes and whites in southern st tes

R26 Ross, Frank Alexander

(a) "Urbanization and the Negro," *Proceedings of the American Sociological Society* (1932), 115-28.

Discusses the trend of urbanization since the opening of the century and the increasingly important part played by Negroes.

— — For other works by this author, *see* U3(41a).

R27 ——— and Andrew G. Truxal

(a) "Primary and Secondary Aspects of Interstate Migrations," *American Journal of Sociology*, XXXVII, 435-44 (October, 1931).

A discussion of, and a statistical technique for, measuring the nature of primary and secondary migrations, showing the importance of secondary movements Illustrated with Negro material.

Rossiter, William S., *see* U3(42a).

R28 Ruark, Bryant W.

(a) *Some Phases of Reconstruction in Wilmington and the County of New Hanover.* Duke University, Trinity College Historical Society Papers, Series 11, pp. 79-112.

A detailed account of Reconstruction Days in New Hanover County North Carolina, especially in regard to the court system, social, economic, educational and political conditions.

R29 Runnion, J. B.

(a) "Negro Exodus (1879)," *Atlantic Monthly*, XLIV, 222-30 (August, 1879).

An unbiased thoughtful discussion of the causes of the exodus with suggestions for improving the condition of the Negro.

R30 Ryder, Walter S

(a) "The Negro in St. Paul," *Opportunity*, IX, 170-73 (June, 1931).

A description of economic and social conditions among Negroes in St Paul, based on a survey made by the Department of Sociology of Macalister College. Presents the situation in a northern city in which there is not a large Negro population

S1 Sandburg, Carl

(a) *The Chicago Race Riots, July, 1919.* New York, Harcourt, Brace and Howe (1919), 71 pp.

A reprinting in a single volume of a series of newspaper articles giving brief journalistic discussions of the Chicago Race Riot, Negro migration and its causes industrial opportunities relation of the Negro to unions, etc

S2 Sanford, R. G.

(a) "The Economic Condition of the Negroes of Knoxville," *Minutes of the University Commission on Southern Race Questions 1914-17*, 69-72.

A brief summary of conditions of saving, home ownership, poverty and de pendence among Negroes of Knoxville, and nature of occupations of Negroes in Tennessee as a whole indirectly showing causes of migration

S3 Sargent, H. O

(a) "Progress in Training Negro Farmers," *Southern Workman*, LVII, 9-12 (January, 1928).

A general discussion of what is being done to train Negro farmers One paragraph contains a casual reference to migration from the farms because of agricultural conditions.

S4 Satterthwait, Linton

(a) "The Color Line in New Jersey," *Arena*, XXXV, 394-400 (April, 1906).

An account of specific cases of discrimination in a New Jersey town, showing evasion of the law by excluding colored children from white schools

S5 Saunders, W. O

(a) "Where Shall Jim Crow Live," *Colliers*, LXXIII, 16 (January 19, 1924).

In showing why the Negroes migrate, discusses what the colored e le really want — justice and equal opportunities for decent living.

(b) "Why Jim Crow Is Flying North," *Colliers*, LXXII, 15-16 (December 8, 1923).

A popular sympathetic account of the causes and results of the recent migration.

S6 Scarborough, Donald Dewey

(a) *An Economic Study of Negro Farmers as Owners, Tenants, and Croppers*. Bulletin of the University of Georgia, Vol. XXV, No. 2a September, 1924), 37 pp. Phelps-Stokes Fellowship Studies No. 7.

A careful statistical study of the condition of the Negro farmers in four Georgia counties. Mentions some of the causes of migration (pp. 8, 9) and remedies (p. 35).

S7 Scarborough, William S

(a) "The Negro Farmer in the South," *Current History*, XXI, 565-69 (January, 1925).

A sensible discussion of the progress of the Negro farmer; considers some of the results of migration to the North in trying to show that the Negro is probably better off in the South

(b) "The Negro Farmer's Progress in V rginia," *Current History*, XXV, 384-87 (December, 1926).

Shows the progress of Negro farmers in Virginia in their accumulation of wealth, coöperative marketing, education, etc Mentions migration in one sentence as accounting for decrease of Negro farmers, 1910-20.

——— For other works by this author, *see* U3(43a).

S8 Schaffter, Dorothy

(a) "The Iowa Civil Rights Act," *Iowa Law Review*, XIV, 63-76 (December, 1928).

A summary of the Civil Rights Act in Iowa as it applies to Negroes and of the judicial interpretation of its meaning and explanation A review of cases that have come up under this act in the efforts of Negroes to combat discrimination against them.

S9 Schmidlapp, J. G.

(a) "Cincinnati's Answer—Philanthropy at 5 Per Cent," *World Outlook*, V, 15 (October, 1919).

An account of an attempt in Cincinnati to provide decent homes for colored wage earners

Schurz, Carl, *see* U3(9a).

S10 Schuyler, George S.

(a) "From Job to Job," *World Tomorrow*, VI, 147-48 (May, 1923).

A personal narrative of the difficulties of obtaining employment in the North

(b) "Keeping the Negro in His Place," *American Mercury*, XVII 469-76 (August, 1929).

A popular account of discrimination against Negroes in recreational and public places

(c) "Traveling Jim Crow," *American Mercury*, XX, 423-32 (August, 1930).

An account of discriminations and discomforts faced by Negroes when traveling both in the North and South, giving many illustrative anecdotes.

S11 Scott, Emmett J.

(a) "Brightening up the Rural South," *Outlook*, CXIX, 412-14 (July 10, 1918).

A description of the work of the Rosenwald Fund and its influence in keeping Negroes in the South

(b) "The Migration: A Northern View," *Opportunity*, II, 184-85 (June, 1924).

A brief discussion of the Negro as an available source of labor.

(c) *Negro Migration during the War*. New York, Oxford University Press (1920), 189 pp.

One of the most important volumes on the war-time migration Discusses the causes and immediate consequences and is important for its detailed description of the psychological propulsive forces and for its wealth of contemporary local material. *See also* Z33(a). Quoted at length in J3(a).

S12 Scott, J. H.

(a) "Uzziah Goes North," *The Messenger*, VI, 180-82 (June, 1924).

A short story with a plot which brings out some of the causes of migration.

S13 Scroggs, W. O

(a) "Interstate Migration of Negro Population," *Journal of Political Economy*, XXV, 1034-43 (December, 1917).

An excellent discussion of the migratory movements of the Negro with a brief statement of the causes of each prominent movement since the Civil War.

S14 Segal, Alfred

(a) "Black is a Perfectly Beautiful Shade," *World Outlook* V, 10-11 (October, 1919).

A story of the work of the Harriet Beecher Stowe Public School in Cincinnati showing what it is doing for colored children

S15(a) "Segregation," *Opportunity*, VI, 384 (December, 1928).

A brief report of the outcome of strikes of school children in Gary and Chi cago in efforts to secure segregation.

S16(a) "Segregation of Negro Children at Toms River, New Jersey," *School and Society*, XXV, 365 (March 26, 1927).

An editorial on an attempt to segregate Negro children in a New Jersey town

S17 Seligmann, Herbert Jacob

(a) "Democracy and Jim-Crowism" *New Republic*, XX, 151-52 (September 3, 1919).

A brief discussion of race relations in the North and in the South as they have been affected by the War and migration.

(b) "The Menace of Race Hatred," *Harpers*, CXL, 537-43 (March, 1920).

A discussion of the race riot in Washington, D. C., the increasing menace of race prejudice in this country, and the necessity for more intelligent efforts to understand and improve race relations

(c) *The Negro Faces America*. New York, Harper and Bros. (1920), 318 pp.

Scattered references to migration in a general discussion of various phases of race relationships resulting from the contact of whites and Negroes socially and industrially

(d) "The Negro Protest against Ghetto Conditions," *Current History*, XXV, 831-33 (March, 1927).

See also M40(a), Section II

(e) "The Negro's Influence as a Voter," *Current History*, XXVIII, 230-31 (May, 1928).

A brief discussion of the Negro's trend toward more independent voting in the North

(f) "Twenty Years of Negro Progress," *Current History*, XXIX 614-21 (January, 1929).

An account of events which led to the formation of the National Association for the Advancement of Colored People and a discussion of its functions and accomplishments. *See also* N2(a).

——— For other works by this author, *see* J10(a), M40(a).

S18 Sellin, Thorsten

(a) "The Negro Criminal," *Annals*, CXL, 52-64 (November, 1928).

A discussion of ways in which statements of crime rates among Negroes may be exaggerated Includes statistics of arrests, convictions and sentences

S19(a) "Senate Report on the Exodus of 1879," *Journal of Negro History*, IV, 57-92 (January, 1919).

A reprint of portions of U3(38a).

S20 Sewall, J. L.

(a) "Industrial Revolution and the Negro," *Scribners*, LXIX, 334-42 (March, 1921).

A thoughtful consideration of the causes of migration, the successes and failures of the Negro in industry, and the means of increasing the Negro's contribution to our economic life

S21 Shaffer, E. T. H.

(a) "A New South: The Boll-Weevil Era," *Atlantic Monthly*, CXXIX, 116-23 (January, 1922).

A popular discussion of the agricultural situation in the South with emphasis on the blessings resulting from the boll-weevil invasion.

(b) "A New South: The Negro Migration," *Atlantic Monthly*, CXXXII, 403-9 (September, 1923).

A popularly written article on the causes and effects of migration.

S22 Shannon, Alexander H.

(a) *Negro in Washington.* New York, Walter Neale (1930), 322 pp.
A one-sided discussion of the status of the mulatto in Washington, D. C., as evidence of the amalgamation of the races, and an attempt to show the dangers of this amalgamation.

S23 Sheerin, Charles W.

(a) "In Defense of Richmond," *Opportunity*, IX 282 (September, 1931).
An article in answer to H29(l), mentioning some of the things Richmond is doing for Negroes

Shields, E. L., *see* U3(32a).

S24(a) "Shifting Black Belt," *Crisis*, XVIII, 94-95 (June, 1919).
Quotations of newspaper comment on the United States Department of Labor report on the migration of 1916-17. Gives a brief statement of the causes and results of the migration. *See also* U3(30a).

S25(a) "Shoving of the South," *Nation*, CXVII, 131 (August 8, 1923).
A short news item relating incidents which show why Negroes leave the South.

S26 S bley, Elbr dge

(a) *Differential Mortality in Tennessee*: A Statistical Study. Conducted jointly by Tennessee State Department of Public Health and Fisk University. Nashville, Fisk University Press (1930), 153 pp.
An exhaustive statistical analysis of the mortality rates by specific diseases for whites and Negroes in Tennessee from 1917 to 1928, with emphasis upon the difference in such rates for the two races and for rural as contrasted with urban groups.

S27 Siegfried, André

(a) *America Comes of Age.* New York, Harcourt, Brace and Co. (1928), 358 pp.
A popular and exaggerated treatment of causes and effects of recent migrations may be found in Chap. vi

S28 Simpson, Gordon H.

(a) "A Note on Negro Industrial Problems," *Opportunity*, II, 182-83 (June, 1924).
A brief note on the work of the Urban League in aiding migrants in the problem of adjustment to the specialized industrial life of the North.

S29 Slattery, J. R.

(a) "Negroes in Baltimore," *Catholic World*, LXVI, 519-27 (January, 1898).
A general account of the growth of Negro population in Baltimore and the resulting social and religious conditions

S30 Slesinger, Tess

(a) "White on Black," *American Mercury*, XXI, 470-76 (December, 1930).
A story of two colored children in a private school in New York City and the growing race discrimination that faced them. Told by a white member of the same class

S31 Smith, James L.

(a) *Autobiography*. Norwich, Press of the Bulletin Co. (1881), 150 pp.
The life history of a former slave, popularly told The last few pages contain comments on the causes of the 1879 exodus, impressionistic and prejudiced

S32 Smith, Llewellyn

(a) "North Caring for Negroes of the Great Migration," *Dearborn Independent*, XXIV, 10 (December 15, 1923).
A popularly written account of the extent of migration, the work of the Urban League in trying to solve the problems created by the migration, and the place of the Negro in northern industry

S33 Smith, S. L.

(a) "Negro Public Schools in the South," *Southern Workman*, LVI, 315-24 (July, 1927).
Good as supplementing T7(a), U3(23a) and U3(46a) with data for 1925-26.

(b) "Negro Public Schools in the South," *Southern Workman*, LVII 448-61 (November, 1928).
Same. Data for 1926-27, 1927-28.

S34 Smith, William Roy

(a) "Negro Suffrage in the South," *Studies in Southern History and Politics*. New York, Columbia University Press (1914), pp. 231-56.
Discusses the history of Negro suffrage from 1619 to 1914 in four periods: 1619-1787; 1787-1865; 1865-90; and since 1890. Includes material on disfranchisement.

Snavely, T. R., *see* U3(30a).

S35 Snyder, Howard

(a) "Negro Migration and the Cotton Crop," *North American Review*, CCXIX, 21-29 (January, 1924).
A general, rather exaggerated discussion of the causes of the migration and the status of the Negro in the South. *See also* M7(a), S64(a).

(b) "Why the Negro Is Moving North," *Plain Talk*, II, 353-58 (March, 1928).
A popular article on the causes of migration

S36(a) "Social Settlement for Colored People in Detroit," *Survey*, XLII, 637-38 (July 26, 1919).
A brief account of the establishment of a social settlement

S37(a) *Sociological Survey of the Negro Population of Springfield, Massachusetts.* Springfield, Published by St. Johns Institutional Activities (1922), 22 pp.
A survey of the social and economic conditions among the Negroes in Springfield

S38 Somers, Robert

(a) *The Southern States since the War: 1870-71.* New York Macmillan Co. (1871), 286 pp.
Report of a tour of the southern states with occasional mention of the scarcity of labor caused by the migration of Negroes.

S39(a) "South and the Negro," *Manufacturers Record*, LXXXIII 87-88 (June 7, 1923).
A letter written by the editor of the *Manufacturers Record* on the social and economic conditions that should result from the migration.

S40(a) "South Calling Negroes Back," *Literary Digest*, LIV, 1914 (June 23, 1917).
An editorial on the attempt of the South to prevent migration.

S41(a) "South Carolina Negro Common Schools," *Crisis*, XXXIV 330-32 (December, 1927).
One of the Garland Fund studies of southern education. Gives the history of Negro schools in South Carolina, picturing conditions, giving statistics for 1924-25, and comparing colored and white schools. *See also* N14(a), N15(a), N16(a).

S42(a) "South Must Protect and Safeguard the Negro in Every Way," *Manufacturers Record*, LXXXIII, 59-60 (February 8, 1923).
An editorial quoting three letters which show the necessity for better treatment of Negroes.

S43(a) "South Studies the Migrant in the North," *Opportunity*, II, 163 (June, 1924).
An editorial comment on W36(a).

S44(a) "Southern Colored Girls in the North," *Charities*, XIII, 584-85 (March 18, 1906).
A brief discussion of the need of protecting and aiding southern girls who come North

S45(a) "Southern Negro in Cleveland Industries," *Monthly Labor Review*, XIX, 41-44 (July, 1924).
Summary of A1(a)

S46(a) "Southern Negroes Again Moving," *Opportunity*, I, 19, (January, 1923).
An editorial on the probable increase of migration with returning industrial prosperity

S47(a) "Southern Negroes Moving North," *World's Work*, XXXIV 135 (June, 1917).
An editorial emphasizing the economic causes of migration and suggesting some of the possible results

S48(a) "Southern Negro's Place in the Sun," *Coal Age*, XI, 364 (February 24, 1917).
An editorial on the migration of Negroes from the Birmingham coal mines and the necessity for better treatment of Negroes if they are to be retained

Southern Sociological Congress, *see* G8(a), M57(a), N46(a), W44(b), W44(g).

S49 Sozinsky, T S

(a) "Medical Aspects of Negro Exodus," *Penn Monthly*, X, 529-38 (July, 1879).
An article trying to prove that the Negro is able to endure the northern climate of Kansas.

S50 Speed, J. G.

(a) "Negro in New York," *Harper's Weekly*, XLIV, 1249-50 (December 22, 1900).
A discussion of the economic opportunities of the Negro in New York City

S51 Spero, Sterling D., and Abram L. Harris

(a) *The Black Worker*: A Study of the Negro and the Labor Movement. New York, Columbia University Press (1931), 509 pp.
A valuable and exhaustive analysis of the past and present status of the Negro in such organizations as the A. F. of L., the I W. W., Communist and

Socialist Parties, and the attitudes and practices of labor organizations in regard to colored workers Discusses the part played by the Negro in specific industries such as longshore work, coal mines stock yards steel and railroads and his relation to the unions in these industries

S52 Stabler, H. S.

(a) "Draining the South of Labor," *Country Gentleman*, LXXXII 1371 ff. (September 8, 1917).

A popular impressionistic account of the migration and its effect on the labor situation in the South

S53 Stemons, James S

(a) "The Industrial Color Line in the North," *Century*, LX, 477-78 (July, 1900).

A short note on the discrimination of unions against Negroes in the North

S54 Stephenson, Gilbert T

(a) "Education and Crime among Negroes," *South Atlantic Quarterly*, XVI, 14-20 (January, 1917).

A discussion of crime rates for Negroes in the country as a whole, correlated with amount and kind of education. *See also* E8(a).

(b) *Race Distinctions in American Law*. New York, D. Appleton and Co. (1910), 388 pp.

A valuable summary and discussion of laws in the United States dealing with race distinctions in transportation civil rights, intermarriage, schools, suffrage and the procedure of law courts

(c) "Racial Distinctions in Southern Law," *American Political Science Review*, I, 44-61 (November, 1906).

A preliminary treatment of portions of S54(b).

(d) "Separation of the Races in Public Conveyances," *American Political Science Review*, III, 180-204, May 1909.

Same as S54(b).

S55 Stern, A. K.

(a) "Decent Housing for Negroes," *American City*, XL, 102-3 (March, 1929).

An account of the efforts being made in Chicago to provide decent houses for Negroes

S56 Stevens, George E.

(a) "The Negro Church m the City," *Missionary Review*, XLIX 435-39 (June, 1926).

An article showing how the Negro churches of St Louis are aiding in the solution of the educational, housing and employment problems of the Negro.

S57 Steward, Gustavus A.

(a) "Elizabeth Goes to School," *Nation*, CXV, 601-4 (December 6, 1922).

A colored man's account of his daughter s experience with race prejudice in schools in Columbus Ohio.

S58 Stone, Alfred Holt

(a) "The Italian Cotton Grower: The Negro's Problem," *South Atlantic Quarterly*, IV, 42-47 (January, 1905).

Deals with the competition of Italian laborers with Negroes.

(b) "Negro Labor and the Boll Weevil," *Annals*, XXXIII, 391-98 (March, 1909).

A sane discussion of the probable effect of the boll weevil on Negro and white labor. Mentions the migratory habits of the Negro.

(c) "A Plantation Experiment," *Quarterly Journal of Economics*, XIX 270-87 (June, 1905).

An account of an attempt to keep the Negroes on the farms by improving the conditions of tenancy

(d) *Studies in the American Race Problem.* New York, Doubleday, Page and Co. (1908), 555 pp.

An early treatise on the race problem based upon personal experience and treating in detail the economic and political status of the Negro in the South from an impartial standpoint Worth while for a picture of conditions in the South prior to the World War. Contains appendixes by Walter F Willcox *See also* W28(d).

S59 Stone, Percy H.

(a) "Negro Migration," *Outlook*, CXVI, 520-21 (August 1, 1917).

An educated Negro's view of the migration.

S60 Sullenger, T. Earl, and J. Harvey Kerns

(a) *The Negro in Omaha*: A Social Study of Negro Development. University of Omaha and Omaha Urban League (1931), 36 pp.

A survey of the economic status, health, education, church life, race relations, etc. of the Negroes in Omaha.

S61(a) "Superfluous Negro," *New Republic*, VII, 187-88 June 24, 1916).

A discussion of the relation of the European immigrant to the Negroes, showing how immigrant labor made the Negro superfluous in the North, and maintaining that the World War will increase the colored man's economic opportunities because of lessened immigration.

S62 Surface, G. T

(a) "Negro Mine Laborer: Central Appalachian Coal Field," *Annals*, XXXIII, 338-52 (March, 1909).

Chiefly a discussion of the status and efficiency of the Negro laborer

S63(a) *Survey Graphic*, "Harlem, Mecca of the New Negro," *Survey*, LIII, 622-724 (March, 1925).

The entire issue is devoted to Negro problems. Articles of value for migration are listed separately under authors. *See also* E6(a), F11(a), H8(a), H19(b), J4(c), J9(d), L4(a), L24(a), M39(k). For amplification see L24(b).

S64(a) "Survey of Negro Migration," *Crisis*, XXVII, 225-26 (March, 1924).

Quotations from S35(a).

Sydenstricker, Edgar, *see* U3(16a).

T1 Tannenbaum, Frank

(a) *Darker Phases of the South*. New York, G. P. Putnam's Sons (1924), 203 pp.

A popularly written discussion of the psychological background of some of the racial problems in the South

(b) "A Shortage of Scapegoats: Does the South Need More Trouble?" *Century*, CVII, 210-19 (December, 1923).

Deals w th the attitude of the South toward the Negro and the wisdom of migration.

T2 Taylor, Alrutheus Ambush

(a) *The Negro in South Carolina during the Reconstruction*. Washington, D. C., Association for The Study of Negro Life and History (1924), 341 pp.

A study of the economic, social and political problems faced by Negroes, giving the Negroes' point of view Chap. i shows briefly the movements of population from 1870 to 1880. Migration to the southwest during Reconstruction is mentioned on p. 38.

(b) *Negro in the Reconstruction of Virginia*. Washington, D. C., Association for The Study of Negro Life and History (1926), 300 pp.

A careful analysis of the position of the Negro in Virginia during the days of Reconstruction. Chap. v discusses the causes, conditions and general couse quences of the migration of Negroes to other states during that period.
Also in *Journal of Negro History*, XI, 243-415 (April, 1926).

T3 Taylor, Alva W.

(a) "When the Negro Comes North," *Christian Century*, XL, 691-92 (May 31, 1923).

A short article on the problems aroused by the migration of Negroes, with a plea for equality of opportunity

Taylor, D. B., *see* M15(a).

T4 Taylor, Graham R.

(a) "Chicago in the Nation's Race Strife," *Survey*, XLII, 695-97 (August 9, 1919).

An account of the Chicago Riot.

(b) "Public Opinion in Problems of Race and Nationality," *National Conference of Social Work Proceedings* (1923), 492-97.

Largely a summary of C11(a).

(c) "Race Relations and Public Opinion," *Opportunity*, I, 197-200 (July, 1923).

Same as T4(b).

T5 Taylor, Paul S

(a) *Mexican Labor in the United States*. University of California, Publications in Economics, Vol. VI, Nos. 1-5 (1928-30), 457 pp.

An interesting and valuable document facilitating comparisons with the Negro's chief recent competitor, particul rly in California and Texas.

T6(a) "Ten Thousand, Five Hundred Migrants to Philadelphia," *Opportunity*, I, 256 (August, 1923).

A brief discussion of the extent and nature of the migration to Philadelphia.

T7(a) *Texas Educational Survey Report* (L. M. Favrot, Ed.) Texas Educational Survey Commission (1925), 7 vols.

Chap. 16 of Vol. 1 (pp. 246-302, on Negro Education) modernizes U3(23a). *See also* F3(c), S33(a), S33(b), U3(46a).

T8(a) "There Goesthe China!" *Survey*, XLII, 571 July 12, 1919).

An editorial on the work of the National Urban League in training women migrants to become efficient domestic helpers

Thom, W. T., *see* U3 (47a), U3(47b).

T9 Thomas, David Y

(a) "Tenancy as Related to the Negro Problem," *Manufacturers Record*, LXXVII, 127-28 (June 17, 1920).

An intelligent discussion of the evils of the current forms of tenancy and their remedy Mentions these evils as one of the causes of migration.

T10 Thomas, Jesse O

(a) "American Cities — Tulsa," *Opportunity*, VII, 54-56 (February, 1929).

A report of a survey made by the National Urban League dealing particularly with the increase of Negro population, housing conditions, place in politics recreational facilities, and educational problems. *See also* Z35(a).

(b) "Effect of Changing Economic Conditions upon the Living Standards of Negroes," *National Conference of Social Work Proceedings* (1928), 455-66.

An address dealing with the new political and industrial conditions in the South and their relation to race contacts and the Negroes standard of living. Completed by W9(b).

(c) "A Social Program to Help the Migrant," *Opportunity*, II, 71-73 (March, 1924).

An excellent discussion of types of migrants and ways in which migrants can be aided in the process of adjustment to new conditions

For other works by this author, *see* N8(h),

T11 Thomas, William Hannibal

(a) *The American Negro; What He Was, What He Is, and What He May Become.* New York, Macmillan Co. (1901), 440 pp.

A very general, pessimistic discussion written by a Negro, of the Negro's economic status and of his social, moral and intellectual traits, and the possibility of assimilation in our civilization, with casual references to early migration

T12 Thomasson, Maurice E.

(a) "The Negro Migration," *Southern Workman*, XLVI, 379-82 (July, 1917).

A discussion of the causes and probable effects of migration from a colored man s point of view

T13 Thompson, Anna J

(a) "A Survey of Crime among Negroes in Philadelphia," *Opportunity*, IV, 217-19, 251-54, 285-86 (July-September, 1926).

A survey of the nature of arrests and sentences during the first six months of 1924.

T14 Thompson, Clara M.

(a) *Reconstruction in Georgia; Economic, Social, Political, 1865-1872.* New York, Columbia University Press (1915), 418 pp. Columbia University Studies in History, Economics and Public Law No. 154.

An account of the economic, social and political problems which prevailed in Georgia during the days of Reconstruction and adjustment to a new order Deals with such subjects as the break up of large plantations, free labor, schools, churches, relations of southern whites with northern whites and with the freedmen, mob violence and the political turmoil.

T15 Thompson, Holland

(a) *The New South: A Chronicle of Social and Industrial Revolution.* Vol. XLII of The Chronicles of America. New Haven, Yale University Press (1921), 250 pp.

Contains some allusions to migration and certain background material necessary for its interpretation.

(b) "Some Newer Aspects of the Negro Problem," *American Historical Association, Report for 1922*, I, 327-28.

An abstract of a paper dealing with the development of race consciousness among Negroes, mentioning migration as a means of increasing this consciousness.

T16 Thompson, Warren S.

(a) *Population Problems.* New York, McGraw-Hill Book Co. (1930), 462 pp.

Chap. x on Negroes in the United States deals with their movements and ratios to whites, migration to cities and to the North (and the effect of this on birth rates), the composition of Negro groups as affected by migration, health, occupations and economic status

(b) "Recent Changes in the Birth Rate and Their S gnificance for Child Welfare," *Annals*, CLI, 25-31 (September, 1930).

A statistical comparison of birth rates, 1919-29, discussing reasons for the falling rate. Mentions Negro birth rates in the North and South

For other works by this author, *see* U3(48a).

T17 Thorpe, Francis N.

(a) *The Federal and State Constitutions, Colonial Charters and Other Organic Laws of the States, Territories, and Colonies Now or Heretofore Forming the United States of America.* Government Printing Office (1909), 7 vols.

A compendium of various constitutions for each state and for the Federal Government Contains constitutions of southern states showing disfranchisement laws

T18 Tindley, Charles A.

(a) "The Church That Welcomed 10,000 Strangers," *World Outlook*, V, 5-6 (October, 1919).

A minister s account of what his church in Philadelphia did to help the migrants and what it wants to do.

T19 Tobey, James A.

(a) "The Death Rate among American Negrocs," *Current History*, XXV, 217-20 (November, 1926).

Presents some of the chief health problems of Negroes, the general decrease in death rates among them, and the effect of health conditions among Negroes upon the health of whites Mentions migration to the North since the World War and its effect upon the health problems of northern cities

T20 Tobias, C. H.

(a) "The Work of the Young Men's and Young Women's Christian Associations with Negro Youth," *Annals*, CXL, 283-86 (November, 1928).

The history of the development and activities of the Y.M.C.A. and the Y.W. C.A., with particular reference to work among Negroes

T21(a) "Toledo," *Opportunity*, II, 28 (January, 1924).

An extract from the *Toledo Times* summarizing briefly the extent of the increase of Negro population in that city and the nature of the colored man's occupations

T22 Tourgée, Albion Winegar

(a) *An Appeal to Caesar*. New York, Fords, Howard and Hulbert (1884), 422 pp.

A very general discussion by a contemporary white of the characteristics and possible future of the Negro.

T23 Towns, George A.

(a) "The Negro Farmer, His Problems and His Prospects," *World Tomorrow*, VI, 143-45 (May, 1923).

A discussion of farming conditions among Negroes in the South showing effects of migration on farms.

T24(a) "Trade Union Program of Action for Negro Workers, *Communist*, IX, 42-47 (January, 1930).

A program issued by the International Trade Union Committee of Negro Workers of R.I.L.U., stating what they wish to accomplish for the Negroes

T25 Trask, John W.

(a) "The Significance of the Mortality Rates of the Colored Population of the United States," *American Journal of Public Health*, VI 254-64 (March, 1916).

A general discussion of death rates among Negroes in the North and South particularly in cities

For other works by this author, *see* U3 (49a).

T26(a) "Troubles of a Black Policeman," *Literary Digest*, XLIV 177-79 (January 27, 1912).

An account of one policeman s struggle against race prejudice in New York City

T27 Truesdell, Leon E.

(a) "Rural-Urban Migration," *National Conference of Social Work Proceedings* (1928), 514-24.

In a general treatment of the urban movement discusses Negro migration to cities of the South and North Worth while for its explanation of the place of the Negro movements in the general urban trend

——— For other works by this author, *see* U3 (15a).

Truxal, Andrew G., *see* R27(a).

T28 Tucker, Helen A.

(a) "Negro Craftsmen in New York," *Southern Workman*, XXXVI 545-51, 613-15 (October and November, 1907).

An original survey of industrial opportunities among Negroes in New York City showing occupations and wages Gives birthplace and age of migrants to New York

(b) "The Negroes of Pittsburgh, 1907-1908," In *Pittsburgh Survey*, volume on "Wage Earning Pittsburgh," pp. 424-36.

Discusses the extent and source of migration of Negroes to Pittsburgh, accent ting their social and industrial status. *See also* P23(a).

(c) "Negroes of Pittsburgh," *Charities*, XXI, 599-608 (January 2, 1909).

A brief description similar to T28(b) and using the same material.

T29 Turner, W. S

(a) "The Negro and the Changing South," *Social Forces*, VII, 115-19 (September, 1928).

A general discussion of the effect of migration on the social, political and economic relations of whites and blacks in the South

T30 Tyler, Ralph W.

(a) "Negro Migration," *Pearsons Magazine*, XXXVIII, 226 (November, 1917).

A brief, popular and generalized discussion of labor agents as a primary cause of the movements of Negroes to the North

Tyson, F. D., *see* U3(30a).

U1(a) "Unemployment," *Opportunity*, VIII 103 (April, 1930).

An editorial on the present unemployment crisis, showing that it is particularly serious for the colored workers because of their recent entrance into industry and because of the restrictions and discriminations against them.

U2(a) "Unemployment among Negroes," *World Tommorow*, XIV, 135-36 (May, 1931).

An editorial summarizing the state of unemployment among Negroes.

U3 UNITED STATES GOVERNMENT DOCUMENTS

(1) *Agriculture Yearbook, Department of*

(a) *1921*: Contains a good description of the boll weevil and its ravages (pp. 349-55).

(b) *1922*: Contains casual references to the boll weevil.

(c) *1923*: Gives a brief discussion of migration to cities and a map of Negro migration, and contains material on the tenancy system (pp. 10-11, 593).

(d) *1924-30*: Contain casual references to the boll weevil.

(2) Best, Ethel L., and Ethel Erickson

(a) *A Survey of Laundries and their Women Workers in Twenty-three Cities.* Women's Bureau Bulletin 78 (1930), 166 pp.

A careful survey of working conditions, hours, wages and such factors as nativity and race, age, marital status, reasons for working, etc., of women laundry workers Gives information for colored women.

(3a) *Births, Stillbirths, and Infant Mortality*: Statistics for the Birth Registration Area of the United States, 1928, Bureau of the Census (1930), 319 pp.

Has tables giving births and deaths, and infant mortality rates for states and counties in by color

(4) Blose, David T

(a) *Statistics of Education of the Negro Race.* Bureau of Education Bulletin 19 (1928), 42 pp.

Contains tables giving enrollment, total and by grades, of colored children for specified states; average attendance value, receipts, etc of teacher training institutions; number of students, professors etc in colored universities

(5) Boeger, E. A., and E. A. Goldenweiser

(a) *A Study of the Tenant System of Farming in the Yazoo-Mississipp Delta.* Agriculture Bulletin 337 (1916), 18 pp.

A first-hand study of the tenancy system in this region.

(6) Brannen, C. O.

(a) *Relation of Land Tenure to Plantation Organization.* Agriculture Bulletin 1269 (October 18, 1924), 77 pp.

See also later edition B34(a).

(7) Channing, Alice

(a) *Child Labor on Maryland Truck Farms.* Children's Bureau Bulletin 123 (1923), 52 pp.

An investigation of conditions surrounding the work of children on truck farms. Deals with the kind of work done by the children type of family, length of working day, and the effect of this work on their schooling. Negro children are included and there is also a discussion of the migratory family both white and black. Illustrates seasonal and family migration of Negroes

(8a) *Condition of the Negro in Various Cities.* Labor Bulletin 10, Vol. II, 257-369 (May, 1897).

Contains a statistical analysis of sickness deaths, household conditions and occupations of Negroes in various cities Deals with southern cities and makes no mention of migration.

(9a) *Condition of the South.* Senate Executive Document 2, 39th Congress, 1st Session (1865), 108 pp.

The report of Carl Schurz to President Johnson after his tour of the South to investigate conditions. Deals with the attitude of the whites toward the Union, with political status of the Negroes and of the whites Mentions removing Negroes for labor, and their vagrancy (pp. 15, 29-30).

(10a) *Condition of the South.* House Report 261, 43rd Congress, 2nd Session, 3 parts.

Report of a committee which investigated political conditions in the South from 1865 to 1875. Tells of violence in the South and intimidation of colored voters

(11a) Decennial Reports of the Bureau of the Census.

Official statistics for Negroes are given in practically every section — as Population, Agriculture etc. For each census the volumes on Population contain basic data dealing with internal migration, showing volume and direction of movements (e.g., tables giving state of birth for residents of each state, as in the Fourteenth Census, Vol. 2, Chap. v); age, sex and marital composition, occupations, etc

(12) Du Bois, W. E. Burghardt

(a) *Negro in the Black Belt — Some Social Sketches.* Labor Bulletin 22, Vol. IV, 401-17 (May, 1899).

A brief social survey of selected country districts villages and towns Incidental mention of migration from country to towns

(b) *Negro Landholder of Georgia.* Labor Bulletin 35, pp. 647-777 (July, 1901).

An exhaustive statistical analysis of property v lues and increases of land ownership by Negroes in Georgia since the first records available Mentions migration to towns and the causes for it (pp. 676-77). Among the causes lists the difficulty of making a living on farms, the tenancy system, poor schools and the social lure of the city

(c) *Negroes of Farmville, Virginia — A Social Study.* Labor Bulletin 14, Vol. III, 1-38 (January, 1898).

A valuable, unbiased, early statistical survey of Negro life in one community Refers to city and northward migration in discussing the composition and economic life of the group.

(13a) *East St. Louis Riots.* House Document 1231, Serial No. 7444, 65th Congress, 2nd Session (July 15, 1918), 24 pp.

The full report of a committee which investigated the riot in East St Louis and the political corruption so largely responsible for the disgraceful occurrences. Though it has little mention of migration, it portrays the effects of the movement out of the South

(14a) *Geographic Distribution of Population.* Census Bureau Bulletin 1 (1903), 24 pp.

Contains tables, based on 1880, 1890 and 1900 census figures showing the distribution of the Negro population by drainage basins, altitude, physiographic regions, temperature etc

(15) Goldenweiser, E. A., and Leon E. Truesdell

(a) *Farm Tenancy in the United States.* Census Monograph IV (1924), 247 pp.

A study of the growth of farm tenancy the nature of various types of tenancy etc Chap. viii R ce and Nativity of Tenants" gives increases of colored farm tenants and owners from 1910 to 1920.

(16) Gover, Mary, and Edgar Sydenstricker

(a) *Mortality among Negroes in the United States.* Public Health Bulletin 174 (1928), 63 pp.

Discusses the distribution of Negroes within the United States, birth rates, death rates, causes of death and trends in mortality, all as compared with those of whites

(17) Hager, John M.

(a) *Commercial Survey of the Southeast.* Domestic Commerce Series 19 (1927).

A statistical survey of economic conditions in the southeastern states, including an analysis of conditions in agriculture, mining, forests industries, manufactures, etc Mentions movements of Negroes (pp. 22-24). Useful for up-to-date background

(18) Harmon, G. E., and G. E. Whitman

(a) "Absenteeism among White and Negro School Children in Cleveland, 1922-1923," *Public Health Reports*, XXXIX, 559-67 (March 21, 1924).

A comparative statistical study of the amount of time lost by Negro and white children on account of illness, causes other than illness etc in Cleveland schools

(19) Haynes, George E.

(a) *Negro at Work during the World War and Reconstruction.* Division of Negro Economics (1921), 144 pp.

An impartial statistical survey of the status of Negro labor with recommendations for the lessening of race friction; gives a short summary of causes and effects of migration discusses the work of the Division of Negro Economics in dealing with the problems of Negro labor arising from the migration; and also has a chapter on the work of colored women during the War. *See also* N36(a).

(20) Hill, Joseph A.

(a) *Women in Gainful Occupations, 1870-1920.* Census Monograph IX (1929), 416 pp.

Chap. xiii, on "Negro Women in Gainful Occupations," discusses the nature of the occupations of Negro women in both North and South and in northern cities

(21) Hunter, W. D., and B. R. Coad

(a) *The Boll Weevil Problem.* Farmers Bulletin 1329 (June, 1923).

A discussion of the boll weevil, its origin spread, and damage, its life history, and methods of combating and controlling it. Latest edition of previous bulletins

(22a) *Industrial Commission Report.* Vols. X XI XII (1901).

These volumes contain interesting contemporary opinions on the migratory tendency of Negroes and probable results of their movements The first gives verbatim testimony on the causes, advisability and results of migration of Negroes; the second contains a brief report on the causes of the movement to cities while the last presents testimony that colored labor was brought into the mines

(23) Jones, Thomas Jesse

(a) *Negro Education, A Study of the Private and Higher Schools for Colored People in the United States.* Bureau of Education Bulletins 38 and 39 (1916), 724 pp.

These Bulletins contain a report of an investigation of schools for colored people in the South The first describes the general facilities, standards and financial support of Negro schools, the status of secondary, rural and industrial schools, and educational funds and associations assisting in the work of Negro education. The second deals mainly with statistics and evaluations of specific schools in each of the southern states Useful as background material. *See also* S33(a), S33(b), T7(a), U3(46a).

(b) *Recent Progress in Education.* Bureau of Education Bulletin 27 (1919), 16 pp. Also in *Biennial Survey of Education in the United States 1916-1918.*

A discussion of the status of Negro education in the southern states since 1916, maintaining that migration has brought the problem of educational facilities for colored children to the attention of the South, as the lack of such facilities was one of the important causes of migration. *See also* U3(23a).

(24) Laws, J. B.

(a) *Negroes of Cinclaire Central Factory and Calumet Plantation, Louisiana.* Labor Bulletin 38 (January, 1902), pp. 95-120.

An impartial, statistical survey of the social and economic life of the Negroes in this district Brief references to migration to these plantations

(25a) "Living Conditions of Small Wage Earners in Chicago," *Handbook of Labor Statistics, 1924-1926.* Labor Miscellaneous Series 439, pp. 187-91.

Summarizes the chief points of H55(a).

(26) Mercier, W. B.

(a) *Extension Work among Negroes, 1920.* Department of Agriculture Circular No. 190 (1921), 24 pp.

A discussion of the agricultural extension work among Negroes Contains a brief paragraph on the movement to cities

(27) Merriam, William

(a) *Population by Sex, General Nativity, and Color for States and*

Territories: 1900. Census Bulletin 103 of the Twelfth Census (October 10, 1901), 32 pp.
A summary of the 1900 census figures on population by states and color, with increase of Negroes by states from 1890 to 1900. Summarizes and compares figures given in previous bulletins. *See also* B25(a).

(28a) "Negro Farmers Moving North," *Weather, Crops and Markets*, Vol. III, No. 17 (April 28, 1923).
A brief editorial statement of the movement of Negro farmers to the North during 1922-23. Gives the percentage of colored farm hands who have left by states.

(29a) "Negro in Industry," *Handbook of Labor Statistics, 1924-1926* Labor Miscellaneous Series 439, pp. 395-412.
Merely a summary of A1(a), H28(b), U3(30a).

(30a) *Negro Migration in 1916-17*. Reports of an investigation by R. H. Leavell, T. R. Snavely, T. J. Woofter, Jr., W. T. B. Williams and F. D. Tyson, Division of Negro Economics (1919), 158 pp.
One of the principal authentic sources of information on the recent migration Contains reports on migration in general, and specifically from Mississippi, Alabama, North Carolina, and Georgia, with additional information on the condition of the Negro in the North Excellent material on the causes and effects of the migration and the status of the Negro in industry. *See also* S24(a), U3(29a).

(31a) *Negro Population in the United States, 1790-1915*. Bureau of the Census (1918), 844 pp.
A careful detailed analysis of statistics concerning Negro population, presenting statistics on migration by divisions states, counties urban and rural districts

(32a) *Negro Women in Industry* (E. L. Shields, Director). Women's Bureau Bulletin 20 (1922), 65 pp.
A study of the occupations, hours wages and conditions of labor of Negro women Merely mentions the fact of the migration of women, p. 8. Summarized in H25(a), N66(a).

(33a) *Negro Women in Industry in Fifteen States*. Labor Bulletin 70 (1929), 74 pp.
Summarizes for Negroes the reports of various state investigations made in the South and the North, 1919-25. Discusses the nature of occupations in which Negro women are found in these fifteen states their occupational distribution by industries and the nature of the tasks in each the changes in occupations from 1910 to 1920, hours, wages, age and marital status of workers etc The summary is for entire fifteen states and not by individual states. For the sit nation in the several states see the respective bulletins in this series. *See also* N67(a).

(34a) *Negroes in the United States.* Census Bureau Bulletin 8 (1904), 333 pp.

A statistical analysis of the Negro population based on the 1900 Census Contains no real discussion of migration, though the tables of state population show increase and decrease of Negroes by census periods. *See also* J18(c).

(35a) *Negroes in the United States.* Census Bureau Bulletin 129 (1915), 207 pp.

An advance, abbreviated edition of U3(31a).

(36a) *Prisoners, 1923*: Crime Conditions in the United States as Reflected in Census Statistics of Imprisoned Offenders. Bureau of the Census (1926), 363 pp.

A statistical analysis of the prison population in 1923 with information concerning place of commitment, offenses sex color or race and nativity, age, marital status state of birth sentences, prior commitments etc Mentions Negro migration in accounting for the high rate of Negro criminals in the North

(37a) *Prisoners in State and Federal Prisons and Reformatories, 1926.* Bureau of the Census (1929), 139 pp.

Statistics for prisoners received and discharged during the year 1926 for state and federal penal institutions. Information for Negroes given (pp. 31-32, 38-41, 80, 86).

(38a) *Removal of Negroes from Southern States.* Report and Testimony of Select Committee to Investigate. Senate Document 693, Parts 1, 2, 3, Serial Nos. 1899, 1900, 46th Congress, 2nd Session (1880), 558 pp. (Parts 1 and 2), 448 pp. (Part 3).

Contains the report of the committee which investigated the nature and causes of the movement of Negroes to Kansas and Indiana in 1879. Is divided into the majority report, which holds that the exodus was caused by northern politicians; and the minority report, which opposes the majority report and describes the miserable condition of the Negroes which caused the exodus The document also contains the verbatim testimony rece ved by the committee during fifty-three days of investigation Interesting for its contemporary account of conditions leading to the exodus. *See also* L2(a), S19(a), W39(a).

(39a) *Report of the Assistant Commissioners of the Freedmen's Bureau from December 1, 1865 to March 1, 1866.* Senate Executive Document 27, 39th Congress, 1st Session (March 5, 1866), 166 pp.

Contains circulars, letters and reports showing the work of the Bureau Discusses what is being done to aid Negroes in their adjustment to new conditions, and their problems and status in education, labor, health, etc Describes mob violence of the period Mentions transporting Negroes to fill the demand for labor in other sections of the South, as on p. 37.

(40) Rochester, Anna

(a) *Infant Mortality*: Results of a Field Study in Baltimore, Maryland, Based on Births of One Year. Children's Bureau Publication 119 (1923), 400 pp.

An exhaustive analysis of conditions surrounding infant mortality in Baltimore — home conditions, father s occupation nationality of parents, housing, age and causes of death, and social and economic factors involved Gives material for colored children showing the social and economic reasons for a high rate

(41) Ross, Frank Alexander

(a) *School Attendance in the United States, 1920.* Census Monograph V, (1924), 285 pp.

Discusses the school attendance figures of the 1910 and 1920 Censuses for the country as a whole, for the several states and for localities Deals with the trends of the several population elements including the Negro.

(42) Rossiter, William S

(a) *Increase of Population in the United States, 1910-1920.* Census Mongraph I (1922), xi, 255 pp.

Chap. xi discusses the population statistics of the Negro, giving a clear, definite but brief treatment of the causes of migration to cities and the North Has maps showing increases of colored population by states. *See also* W15(a).

(43) Scarborough, William S

(a) *Tenancy and Ownership among Negro Farmers in Southampton, Virginia.* Agricultural Bulletin 1404 (1926), 27 pp.

A careful study of one section of Virginia with reference to changes in agricultural organization, credit systems, accumulation of wealth and standards of living. Mentions migration to the North and to cities, and the local movements of farmers

(44a) *Special Reports*: Supplementary Analyses and Derivative Tables, 1900 Census, Bureau of Census (1906), 1144 pp.

A statistical analysis of 1890 and 1900 census figures

I The section on "Interstate Migration," by Joseph A Hill (pp. 276-327) contains tables showing the increase of Negroes in various cities and geographical divisions, and the distribution of Negroes by state of birth and residence

II. The section on "Negroes" (pp. 185-275) contains information on the bution of the colored population, age, sex, marital status etc

III The chapter on the "Negro Farmer," by W E Burghardt Du Bois (pp. 511-76) deals with the Negro's agricultural status systems of land tenure value of property, acreage, etc

(45a) "Study of Negro Infant Mortality," *Public Health Reports* 45, Vol. XLIV, 2705-31 (November 8, 1929).

An investigation of the causes and trends in mortality rates of Negro infants as compared with those of whites Compares rates for urban and rural North and South, and 4 cities; for other cities gives tables of mortality rates from 1917 to 1927 and the trend for different causes of infant deaths

(46a) *Survey of Negro Colleges and Universities* (1929), 964 pp. Bureau of Education Bulletin 1928, No. 7.

For seventy nine Negro colleges and universities discusses administration, physical plant, preparatory departments educational programs, admission and graduation requirements enrollment, facilities etc. *See also* S33(a), S33(b), T7(a), U3(23a).

(47) Thom, W. T

(a) *Negroes of Litwalton, Virginia—A Social Study of the Oyster Negro.* Labor Bulletin 37, Vol. VI, 1115-70 (November, 1901).

A statistical and general study of the social and economic conditions of Lit walton. Mentions migration briefly in showing some of the effects of migra· tory habits

(47b) *Negroes of Sandy Spring, Maryland.* Labor Bulletin 32, Vol. VI, 43-102 (January, 1901).

A careful statistical study of the economic and social life of the Negroes in Sandy Spring. Brief references to Negro migration to cities and to the North

(48) Thompson, Warren S

(a) *Ratio of Children to Women, 1920*: A Study in the Differential Rate of Natural Increase in the United States. Census Monograph XI (1931), 242 pp.

An exhaustive statistical analysis of the ratio of children to women, by states, in cities and in rural communities Chap. vi contains an analysis of ratios of children to women among Negroes compared with similar ratios for native whites commenting on lowered birth rates after migration to northern cities

(49) Trask, John W.

(a) "Death Rates of the Colored Population," *Public Health Bulletin* 329, Vol. XXXI, 705-11 (March 17, 1916).

Tables and discussion of death rates among Negroes in selected states and cities

(50) Wright, Richard Robert

(a) *Negroes of Xenia, Ohio—A Social Study.* Labor Bulletin 48, Vol. VIII, 1006-44 (September, 1903).

An unbiased statistical study of the social and economic conditions among the

Negroes of Xenia. Scattered references to migration, showing type of person who migrated

U4(a) "Urban League Conference," *Southern Workman*, LVII, 205-6 (May, 1928).

An editorial comment on the work of the Urban League in its efforts to aid in the solution of problems intensified or cre ted by the migration.

U5(a) "Urbanization and Negro Mortality," *Opportunity*, I, 323 (November, 1923).

An editorial attempting to show that migration has not increased the mortality rates

U6 Usher, Roland G.

(a) "Negro Segregation in St. Lo *New Republic*, VI, 176-78 (March 18, 1916).

An article protesting against the St Louis segregation ordinance and discussing its significance for race relations

Van de Graaff, A. S., *see* R10(a).

V1 Vance, Rupert B.

(a) *Human Factors in Cotton Culture*. Chapel Hill, University of North Carolina Press (1929), 346 pp.

Gives the history and the nature of cotton production, an account of the risks involved the effect on living conditions etc Contains a description of the plantation system; discussions of the boll weevil showing its effect on migration, and of the effect of migration on tenants remaining.

V2 Villard, Oswald Garrison

(a) "The Crumbling Color Line," *Harpers*, CLIX, 156-67 (July, 1929).

An optimistic account of present interracial relations in the South, and a discussion of the National Interracial Conference Washington, D. C., in December, 1928. Mentions migration as one of the causes of the South s changed attitude toward Negroes. *See also* M39(l).

V3(a) "Virginia Conference on Race Relations," *Southern Workman*, LX, 5-8 (January, 1931).

Summary of R18(a).

Wagner, M. E., see C4(a).

W1 Wallace, Jesse Thomas

(a) *A History of the Negroes of Mississippi from 1865 to 1890*. Clinton, Mississippi (1927), 188 pp.

Describes the problems of economic, political and social adjustment faced by the Negroes and whites after the Civil War, and the methods used to solve them. Mentions the 1879 exodus and its causes, and the vagrancy of Reconstruction Days.

W2 Waller, Calvin H.

(a) "The Negro Farmer in the Southwest," *Opportunity*, VIII (March, 1930).

A description of the work of the Extension Service and what it has done to improve farming methods and conditions among the Negroes in Texas.

W3 Walrond, Eric D.

(a) "From Cotton, Cane and Rice Fields," *Independent*, CXVII, 260-62 (September 4, 1926).

A general account of the situation leading to migration and of the success of migrants in northern industry

(b) "The Largest Negro Commercial Enterprise in the World" *Forbes Magazine*, XIII, 503-5 (February 2, 1924).

The story of the beginning and success of the Standard Life Insurance Co. of Atlanta.

(c) "The Negro Comes North," *New Republic*, XXXV, 200-1 (July 18, 1923).

A somewhat prejudiced treatment of the causes of Negro migration.

(d) "Negro Exodus from the South," *Current History*, XVIII, 942-44 (September, 1923).

A brief story of the causes and extent of the 1916-17 movement

(e) "On Being Black," *New Republic*, XXXII, 244-46 (November 1, 1922).

Three stories showing discriminations against Negroes in the North

W4 Walton, Lester A.

(a) "The Negro Comes Back to the United States Congress," *Current History*, XXX, 461-63 (June, 1929).

A brief account of the life of Representative Oscar de Priest and of his election to Congress Mentions the effect of migration upon the political life of the chief northern cities

(b) "The Negro in Politics," *Outlook*, CXXXVII, 472-73 July 23, 1924).

Discussion of Negro desertion from the Republican Party, particularly in northern cities

W5(a) "War and Labor," *Crisis*, XIV, 77 June, 1917).

Extracts from newspaper editorials showing the southern attitude toward migration.

W6 Waring, J. H. N.

(a) "Some Baltimore Homes," *Hampton Negro Conference Annual Report* (1906), 60-67.
A description of the deplorable housing conditions among the Negroes of Baltimore

(b) "Some Causes of Criminality among Colored People," *Charities*, XV, 45-49 (October 7, 1905).
A general description of social and economic conditions leading to crime among Negroes

W7 Washington, Booker T

(a) "Census and the Negro," *Independent*, LXXII, 785-86 (April 11, 1912).
A popular interpretation of 1910 census figures

(b) "The Negro and the Labor Unions," *Atlantic Monthly*, CXI, 756-67 (June, 1913).
Presents the attitude of unions toward Negroes and that of Negroes toward organized labor.

(c) "Rural Negro and the South," *National Conference of Social Work Proceedings* (1914), 121-27.
Chiefly a discussion of the extent and importance of Negro farm labor in the South. Contains a brief section on why Negroes move to cities

(d) "Why Should Negro Business Men Go South?" *Charities*, XV 17-19 (October 7, 1905).
Discusses the better opportunities of Negro professional and business men among members of their own race in the South

W8 ——— and W. E. Burghardt Du Bois

(a) *The Negro in the South.* Philadelphia, G. W. Jacobs and Co. (1907), 222 pp.
Casual references to early migration to cities and its c uses on pp. 94, 96, 97, 102-4.

W9 Washington, Forrester B.

(a) "Detroit Newcomers Greeting," *Survey*, XXXVIII, 333-35 (July 14, 1917).
See L15(a), Section II

(b) "Effect of Changed Economic Conditions upon the Living Standards of Negroes," *National Conference of Social Work Proceedings* (1928), 466-68.
An address dealing with problems of health, education, delinquency crime

and family disorganization among Negroes in southern cities. Continuation of T10(b).

(c) "Headway in Social Work" *Southern Workman*, LIX, 3-9 (January, 1930).

A discussion of growing opportunities for Negroes to hold positions in social work, mentioning the effect of migration in increasing such opportunities

(d) "Health Work for Negro Children," *Opportunity*, III (September, 1925).

A discussion of the high mortality rates among Negro children in all parts of the country and of ways of improving the situation.
Same material contained in *National Conference of Social Work Proceedings* (1925), 226-31.

(e) "Program of Work for the Assimilation of Negro Immigrants in Northern Cities," *National Conference of Social Work Proceedings* (1917), 497-503.

Gives the program of the Detroit League on Urban Conditions among Negroes for the assimilation of Negro immigrants, with a discussion of various aspects of migration. Summarized in H24(a). *See also* L15(a).

(f) "Reconstruction and the Colored Woman," *Life and Labor*, IX 3-7 (January, 1919).

Presents the problem of colored women workers in such industri l centers as Chicago, Detroit and Newark States that they entered industry during the World War but are being displaced

(g) "Recreational Facilities for the Negro," *Annals*, CXL, 272-82 (November, 1928).

Discusses the problem of wholesome recreation for Negroes in southern and northern cities Maintains that one cause of migration is the desire for more leisure time, which increases the necessity for providing proper recreation, and holds that segregation adds to the di ficulty. *See also* R9(a).

(h) *Study of Negro Employees of Apartment Houses in New York City*. New York, National Urban League, Reports, Vol. VI, No. 5 (December, 1916), 36 pp.

An investigation of the nativity, percentage of all Negroes employed, age and other personal characteristics of apartment house workers, conditions of apart ment work — duties hours, wages, living conditions, social and leisure time activities

For other works by this author, *see* L15(a), P9(a).

W10 Weatherford, Willis D.

(a) *Lawlessness or Civilization — Which?* Nashville, Williams Printing Co. (1917), 126 pp.

The report of the addresses and discussion connected with the Law and Order Conference held at Blue Ridge, North Carolina, in 1917. Deals with the problem of lynching and the effect on this problem of systems of court procedure the attitude of officials etc., and the relation of lynching to migration. In the discussion of the causes of migration (pp. 3-11, 67-69) lynching is emphasized Other references to migration are given on pp. 33, 97-99.

(b) *The Negro from Africa to America.* New York, George H. Doran Co. (1924), 487 pp.

De ls with the problem of race adjustment showing the effect of African background and of slavery upon the Negro's present economic religious, legal, educational and social status and condition. Chap. x discusses the nature of occupations, relation to unions wages and success in the North Chap. xi discusses migration briefly — the 1879 exodus, other migrations before 1910, the urban movement especially about 1920, and migration during the World War. Pages 282 *et seq.* deal with the causes of recent movements such as the agricultural situation, the activities of labor agents suggestion, discussion, etc Contains a good bibliography, summarized and evaluated

(c) *Present Forces in Negro Progress.* New York Association Press (1912), 191 pp.

A fair-minded discussion of Negro character, race solidarity, population movements Negro farmers and educational and religious work among colored people Chap. iii gives statistics, based on the Census showing migration to cities and to the North

W11 Weber, Adna F.

(a) *The Growth of Cities in the Nineteenth Century.* New York, Columbia University Press (1899), 497 pp. Columbia University Studies in History, Economics and Public Law No. 29.

A comprehensive statistical analysis of the urban trend of the 19th century in both European and American countries its extent characteristics causes and effects Gives an excellent discussion of the causes of concentration of population in general in Chap. iii and a description and analysis of internal migration in Europe and America in Chap. iv Negro migration is mentioned in discussing the urban trend up to 1890 (pp. 310-14). Very valuable as giving background

W12 Wembridge, Eleanor R.

(a) "Negroes in Custody," *American Mercury*, XXI September, 1930).

An account of experiences with Negroes brought before the courts in Cleveland for misdemeanors, with comments on the traits of colored people as thus re-ve led and observed Mentions that most of these Negroes have migrated from the South

W13 Wesley, Charles H.

(a) *Negro Labor in the United States, 1850-1925*: A Study in American Economic History. New York Vanguard Press (1926), 343 pp.

A careful w rth while and det iled account of the development of Negro labor from slavery to modern industry, and of the place of the Negro in the economic life of the United States Consult index for migration and see Chap. x particularly. *See also* N37(a).

W14 West Virginia Bureau of Negro Welfare and Statistics: *Biennial Reports* (1921-28). Charleston, West Virginia.

(a) *First Biennial Report, 1921-22*. "The Negro in West Virginia," by T. Edward Hill, Director. 102 pp.

Survey of economic and social conditions of the Negroes in West Virginia. Contains a description of the founding of the Bureau to meet the problems raised by the migration of Negroes to the state, and a discussion of migration to West Virginia. *See also* E3(a).

(b) *Second Biennial Report, 1923-24*. "The Negro in West Virginia," by T. Edward Hill, Director. 102 pp.

A survey of the health industrial and business status of Negroes in West Virginia, as well as their education, housing, etc. *See also* W47(a).

(c) *Third Biennial Report, 1925-26*. "The Negro in West V rginia," by T. Edward Hill, Director. 147 pp.

A survey of population increases, economic and social conditions among the Negroes of West Virginia. *See also* E4(a), N71(a).

(d) *Fourth Biennial Report, 1927-28*. "The West V rginia Negro," by J. W. Robinson, Director. 74 pp.

A report covering the economic and social conditions among Negroes in the state. *See also* N33(a).

W15(a) "What Ten Years Did to Us," *Literary Digest*, LXXVII 22-23 (June 23, 1923).

Largely a quotation from U3(42a).

W16(a) "When Jim Crow Comes to Church," *Literary Digest*, CIII, 32-36 (October 12, 1929).

A summary of statements and newspaper comments connected with the attempt of an Episcopal minister to discourage Negroes from coming to his church in Brooklyn

W17 Whipple, Katherine Z. W.

(a) "How a Tuberculosis and Health Committee Grew," *Opportunity*, VIII, 106-8 (April, 1930).

An account of the establishment and functioning of the Harlem Tuberculosis and Health Committee

W18 White, Park J.

(a) "The Health of Colored Babies in St. Louis," *The Nation's Health*, VII, 257-59 (April, 1925).

Deals with the high infant mortality among Negroes in St. Louis and the reasons for it

(b) Segregation and the Health of Negroes," *Hospital Social* S XVII, 224-28 (March, 1928).

Shows the effect of segregation upon increasing morbidity and mortality rates among Negroes because it denies them economic opportunity chance for professional medical training, etc

W19 White, R. Clyde

(a) "Cotton and Southern Civilization," *Social Forces*, II, 651-54 (September, 1924).

Considers the relation of cotton culture to illiteracy, to farm tenancy and to the percentage of Negroes in the cotton producing states Mentions migration briefly in considering whether the Negro is essential to the growth of the cotton crop.

W20 White, Walter F.

(a) "The Negro and the Flood," *Nation*, CXXIV, 688-89 (June 22, 1927).

A sympathetic presentation of the Negro labor situation in the flood area, pointing out the injustice of restricting the Negro's freedom to change employers.

(b) "The Negro and the Supreme Court," *Harpers*, CLXII, 238-46 (January, 1931).

A discussion of the rejection by the Senate of John J. Parker as a member of the United States Supreme Court, and its political significance showing the part the Negro played in securing this rejection and dealing with the Negro's growing consciousness of political power

(c) *Philadelphia Race Riots of July 26 to July 31, 1918.* New York, National Association for the Advancement of the Colored People (1918), 7 pp.

An account of the Philadelphia riots.

(d) *Rope and Faggot: A Biography of Judge Lynch.* New York, Alfred A. Knopf (1929), 272 pp.
Presents the results of an exhaustive study of lynching; deals with the psychological, social and economic factors back of the practice and some of the effects of lynching as well as its relation to law.

(e) "The Success of Negro Migration," *Crisis*, IX, 112-18 (January, 1920).
An optimistic account of the Negro's success in northern industry

(f) "The Sweet Trial," *Crisis*, XXXI, 125-29 (January,
A description of the trial resulting from the bombing of Dr Sweets home in Detroit. Infers migration in describing the increase of the colored population in Detroit and the effect of this increase on housing and race relations.

W21(a) "Whites and Blacks in Mississippi," *Nation*, XXVIII, 386 (June 5, 1879).
A letter from a Mississippi man protesting against reports of southern white men's violence in attempts to prevent the exodus of 1879. Includes a brief summary of the agricultural situation in the South in the early days of the tenancy system.

Whitman, G. E., *see* U3(18a).

W22 Whittier Center

(a) *Survey of the Health of Negro Babies Born in 1922.* Philadelphia, Philadelphia Health Council: Tuberculosis Committee (1925), 40 pp.
A survey of the health of Negro children in specific wards in Philadelphia.

W23 Whittle, C. A.

(a) "Negro Migration and the Future of Cotton," *Manufacturers Record*, LXXXIV, 85 (July 19, 1923).
A brief article considering the probable effect of migration on the production of cotton.

W24(a) "Why the Negro Emigrates," *Nation*, CXVII, 490-91 (October 31, 1923).
A l tter from a Negro stating some of the causes of migration as he sees them.

W25(a) "Why the Negroes Go North," *Literary Digest*, LXXVII 13-14 (May 19, 1923).
An editorial summary of the extent, causes and probable efects of recent migration.

W26 Wilcox, E. V

(a) "The Negro Moves North," *Country Gentleman*, LXXXVIII 3-4 (June 9, 1923).
A popular account of migration — the extent, causes and possible remedy

W27(a) "Will the South Lose by the Negro Migration Now under Way?" *Manufacturers Record*, LXXXIII, 67-68 (May 24, 1923).

An editorial on the necessity of improving conditions in order to retain the best Negroes in the South, and on the lessons the South must le rn from the migration.

W28 Willcox, Walter F.

(a) "Census Statistics of the Negro" *Yale Review*, XIII 274-86 (November, 1904).

A summary of the most important 1900 statistics concerning the status of the Negro. Mentions migration in discussing the per cent increase of Negro population in cities and rural districts

(b) "Distribution and Increase of Negroes in the United States," *Eugenics in Race and State*, II, 166-74. Scientific Papers of the Second International Congress of Eugenics, Baltimore, Williams and Wilkins Co. (1923).

Compares the rates of increase of Negroes with those of whites for every decade up to 1920, and shows the distribution of Negroes in various parts of the country Discusses World War migration (p. 170), births and deaths of Negroes in the North, (1915-19), (pp. 171-72).

(c) "Migration of Negroes," *American Statistical Association Publications*, V, 371-72 (December, 1897).

A book review of B41(b), which is rather inaccessible

(d) "Negro Criminality," *Journal of Social Science*, XXXVII (1899).

Deals with the high rate of crime among Negroes and the principal causes of defective family life and training, competition of white labor, race friction and violence. Also printed as Part 5, pp. 443-75, of S58(d).

(e) "The Probable Increase of the Negro Race in the United States," *Quarterly Journal of Economics*, XIX, 545-72 (August, 1905). Digest in *Review of Reviews*, XXXII, 347-48 (September, 1905).

Briefly mentions migration in discussing past census figures as a basis for estimating the probable rate of increase of the Negro population.

W29 Williams, F. B.

(a) "Social Bonds in the 'Black Belt' of Chicago," *Charities*, XV 44 (October 7, 1905).

A discussion of the attempt of Negro organizations to better social conditions among members of their race

W30 Williams, Florence C.

(a) "Health Work among Negroes in North Carolina," *Southern Workman*, XLIX, 405-11 (September, 1920).
Presents the plan of activity of the Health Committees which are working among Negroes in North Carolina.

W31 Williams, G. Croft

(a) *The Negro Offender.* New York, Russell SageFoundation (1922), 11 pp.
A discussion of crime among Negroes in 1920, causes of Negro delinquency and southern treatment of Negro criminals

W32 Williams, George Washington

(a) *History of the Negro Race in America from 1619 to 1880.* New York, G. P. Putnam's Sons, 2 vols. (1882).
Chap. xxviii contains a brief, impressionistic description of the exodus giving an almost c ntemporary view of the movement though b sed largely on U3(38a).

W33 Williams, H. S

(a) "The Development of the Negro Public School System in Missouri," *Journal of Negro History*, V, 137-65 (April, 1920).
An historical account of the development of schools for Negroes in Missouri since 1865. Page 161 mentions migration from farms to cities since 1900, making the educational problem largely a city problem.

W34 Williams, W. T. B.

(a) "The South's Changing Attitude toward Negro Education," *Southern Workman*, LIV, 398-400 (September, 1925).
A discussion of the problems of Negro education, containing a brief mention of the effect of migration upon the educational situation in the South

——— For other works by this author, *see* U3(30a).

W35 Williams, William H.

(a)"The Negro in the District of Columbia during Reconstruction," *Howard Review*, I, 97 148 (June, 1924).
A survey of the political, educational, economic and social conditions of Negroes in Washington during Reconstruction.

W36 Wilmer, S. G.

(a) "Negro Exodus as Viewed in North and West," *Manufacturers Record*, LXXXV, 79-83 (April 17, 1924).
Detailed report of answers to an industrial questionnaire sent by the Georgia Real Estate Association to Chambers of Commerce and Real Estate Boards in

leading cities of the North and West. The answers indicate the varied reactions of the cities toward migration and the success of the Negro in northern industry. For summary, *see* N52 (a), S43(a).

W37 Wilson, Edward E.

(a) "Responsibility for Crime," *Opportunity*, VII 95-97 (March, 1929).

A discussion of the proportion of crimes in Chicago attributed to Negroes, reasons for a high rate and the nature of the offenses committed by Negroes Shows the effect of migration on crime.

W38 Wilson, Ernest B.

(a) *The Water Supply of the Negro.* Bulletin of the University of Georgia, Vol. XXXI, No. 3a (March, 1931), 80 pp. Phelps-Stokes Fellowship Studies No. 10.

A chemical analysis and general description of the water supply of urban and rural communities of Georgia with a sociological interpretation of conditions that were found Mentions migration as probably carrying off most of the enterprising Negroes and hence leading to deplorable living conditions of the sections investigated

W39 Windom, William

(a) "Speech before the Senate, June 14, 1880, presenting views of minority of Committee to Investigate Exodus of 1879," *Congressional Record*, X, 4518-27, Part 5, Government Printing Office.

Speaker s version of S19(a), U3(38a).

W40 Woodson, Carter Godwin

(a) *A Century of Negro Migration.* Washington, D. C., The Association for the Study of Negro Life and History (1918), 221 pp.

An excellent descriptive account of the migratory movements of the Negro from about 1815 to the present time, discussing the causes conditions, attitude of whites and blacks in the North and South, and effects of the migrations. Concerned chiefly with early movements North and West with one chapter on the exodus during the World War. Furnishes a good general background for the study of movements of colored population.

(b) "Insurance Business among Negroes," *Journal of Negro History*, XIV, 202-26 (April, 1929).

A careful account of the history and present status of the Negro insurance business

(c) *The Negro in Our History.* Washington, Associated Publishers (1922), 393 pp.

Discusses the influence of the Negro on the history of the United States and contains an account of the various Negro movements — nature, causes and results. Consult index under migration.

(d) *The Rural Negro.* Washington, The Association for the Study of Negro Life and History (1930), 265 pp.

One of the most recent surveys of the status of the Negro in agriculture in the South describing the tenancy system, industries and trade carried on in rural sections, difficulties involved in making a success of farming, the effect of migration on sections from which migrants have gone, and the general education and social life of Negroes in rural areas.

——— For other works by this author, *see* G20(a).

W41 Woofter, Thomas Jackson, Jr

(a) *The Basis of Racial Adjustment.* New York, Ginn and Co. (1925), 258 pp.

An excellent unbiased discussion of the problem of racial contacts Mentions migration on pp. 41-55, 85-87, 127 ff. and in Chap. vi chiefly discussing its causes and probable effects

(b) *Black Yeomanry.* New York, Henry Holt and Co. (1930), 291 pp.

A first-hand investigation of the economic and social life of Negroes on St Helena Island in the effort to discover such facts as the effect on Negroes of land ownership, possibility of improvement in health, morals, education, etc Chap. iv discusses migration from the Island, its extent, causes, and effects on population remaining and on migrants. *See also* K10(a).

(c) "The Negro and Industrial Peace," *Survey*, XLV, 420-21 (December 18, 1920).

Discusses various aspects of the employment of the Negro and his relation to unions, industrial peace etc Mentions migration as a cause of the present situation

(d) "The Negro and the Farm Crisis," *Social Forces*, VI, 615-20 (June, 1928).

An analysis of some of the fundamental factors underlying the changing economic organization of the South with emphasis on phases of the agricultural depression. Shows how these changes have affected the Negroes Mentions the movement of Negroes from agriculture to the cities and to industry but gives no real discussion of it

(e) *Negro Migration, Changes in Rural Organization and Population of the Cotton Belt.* New York, W. D. Gray (1920), 195 pp.

An excellent, concise statistical treatment of rural life in the South, particularly Georgia, describing land tenure and organization in the cotton belt and how these result in movements of the population. Part 2 deals with various aspects of migration. *See also* N54(a).

(f) "Negro Migration to Cities," *Survey*, LIX, 647-49 (February 15, 1928).

A summary of W41(h).

(g) "The Negro on a S r ke," *Social Forces*, II 84-88 (November, 1923).

An intelligent statement of the causes and effects of the migration.

(h) *Negro Problems in Cities*. New York, Doubleday, Doran and Co. (1928), 284 pp.

An impartial, understanding study of some phases of the adjustment of Negro newcomers to northern and southern cities Deals with the condition of Negro urban neighborhoods, housing, schools and recreation. Chap. ii discusses the migration particularly, and the entire study deals with the situations result ing from migration. *See also* W41(f), Z31(a).

(i) *The Negroes of Athens, Georgia*. Bulletin of the University of Georgia, Vol. XIV, No. 4 (December, 1913), 62 pp. Phelps-Stokes Fellowship Studies No. 1.

A statistical study of social and economic conditions among the Negroes of Athens Slight reference to the movement of the Negroes from the surround ing counties to Athens (pp. 5, 7).

(j) "A Square Deal for Negroes — at the American Rolling Mill Company's Plant in Middletown, Ohio," *Southern Workman*, L, 209-16 (May, 1921).

A description of the welfare work carried on by this Company in its endeavor to secure and keep desirable colored employees Contains casual reference to migration in accounting for the presence of colored laborers and of the social problems which necessitated this welfare work.

(k) *A Study of the Economic Status of the Negro*. Mimeographed Report of Survey made for the Rosenwald Fund (1930), 58 and 56 pp.

Discusses (1) agricultural conditions in the South dealing with changes in numbers of farmers kinds of crop, extent and nature of the credit system, and trends in land tenure showing indirectly the effect of such conditions upon migration; (2) estimates of migration from farms to cities 1920-30; and (3) industrial opportunities in North and South, comparing occupational increases and decreases 1910-20, and trends since 1920 based on community surveys and questionnaires Discusses also the success of Negroes in industry and their relation to unions. *See also* B15(a), E5(a).

——— For other works by this author, *see* H40(a), U3(30a).

W42 ——— and Isaac Fisher

(a) *Coöperation in Southern Communities*: Suggested Activities for

County and City Interracial Committees. Atlanta, Commission on Interracial Coöperation (1921), 66 pp.

A brief picture of conditions of education, press economic justice church coöperation, health and housing, recreation, care of delinquents and dependents etc., as these exist generally in the South, and a description of agencies that can improve these conditions with suggestions for activities and functions of such agencies

W43 ——— and Madge H. Priest

(a) *Negro Housing in Philadelphia.* Philadelphia Housing Association — Whittier Center (1927), 30 pp.

A report of an original investigation of housing conditions among Negroes in Philadelphia. Much of the material is contained in W41(h).

W44 Work, Monroe N.

(a) "Crime among the Negroes of Chicago," *American Journal of Sociology*, VI, 204-23 (September, 1900).

The report of a survey, made in 1897-98, of criminal rates among Negroes in Chicago, and a comparison of such rates with those of whites in that city and in the United States Discusses birth place of Chicago Negroes, occupations, church life criminal statistics and nature of offenses

(b) "Interracial Coöperation and the South's New Economic Conditions," *Southern Sociological Congress: Distinguished Service Citizenship* (1919), 122-29.

A discussion of increased demand for interracial coöperation in the South because of the World War with its calls for greater industrial and agricultural production Discusses ways in which this coöperation is being and can be improved in the fields of educational facilities health conditions, agricultural conditions, justice etc Incidentally discusses causes of migration.

(c) "Negro Criminality in the South," *Annals*, XLIX, 74-80 (September, 1913).

Gives criminal st tistics for Negroes from 1870 to 1904 and discusses some of the principal factors of Negro criminality in the South such as the convict lease system, inequality before the law, etc

(d) "Negro Migration," *Southern Workman*, LIII, 202-12 (May, 1924).

A survey of the causes, nature and effect of Negro movements, 1916-20 and 1922-24. Summarizes the statements issued by two state conferences on the causes of migration Same as N69(c), pp. 5-10.

(e) "Problems of Negro Urban Welfare," *Southern Workman*, LI, 10-16 (January, 1922).

A general discussion of migration to cities — both in the North and South but with emphasis upon the South — and the resulting problems in family life crime, health, education, religion, etc

(f) "The Race Problem in Cross-Section — The Negro in 1923," *Social Forces*, II, 245-52 (January, 1924).

Earlier and briefer version of W44(i).

(g) "Southern Labor as Affected by the War and Migration," *Southern Sociological Congress Proceedings* (1919), 122-29.

A discussion of labor conditions in the South and the means of preventing migration.

(h) "The South's Labor Problem" *South Atlantic Quarterly*, XIX 1-8 (January, 1920).

Discusses the labor shortage in the South and the consequent necessity of improving health conditions, of using more machinery, and of checking migration through giving better wages, better educational facilities and more just treatment

(i) "Taking Stock of the Race Problem" *Opportunity*, II (February, 1924).

An impartial review and interpretation of various statistics for 1923 concerning the Negro. Deals with migration briefly in discussing the increase of Negro population. An amplification of W44(f).

W45(a) "Work for the Migrants," *Opportunity*, II, 355 (December, 1924).

An editorial on unemployment as a cause of migration.

W46(a) "Work of the Negro Industrial Commission of Missouri," *Monthly Labor Review*, XXV, 1083-84 (November, 1927).

Summary of M46(c).

W47(a) "Working and Living Conditions of Negroes of West Virginia," *Monthly Labor Review*, XXI, 256-59 (August, 1925).

Summary of W14(b).

W48 Wright, Blanche

(a) "For the Colored Citizens of New Haven," *Playground*, XVII 217-18 (July, 1923).

A description of plans for a community house for colored people in New Haven

W49 Wright, Richard Robert

(a) "Growth of Northern Negro Population," *Southern Workman*, XLI, 333-44 (June, 1912).

Discusses vital statistics for Negroes in the North and mentions migration as the source of the increase in northern Negro populations

(b) "Housing and Sanitation in Relation to the Mortality of Negroes," *Hampton Negro Conference Annual Report* (1906), 52-60.

A discussion of the high Negro death rates in northern cities and their relation to bad housing conditions, with particular reference to Philadelphia. *See also* H6(e).

(c) "Migration of Negroes to the North," *Annals*, XXVII, 559-78 (May, 1906).

A critical discussion of the extent of the early century Negro migration to the North the reasons for the movement and the social effects on the North the South and the Negro.

(d) "Negro Communities in New Jersey," *Southern Workman*, XXXVII, 385-93 (July, 1908).

A description of some Negro communities in New Jersey

(e) "Negro Governments in the North," *Southern Workman*, XXXVII, 486-98 (September, 1908).

A survey of three types of Negro governments in the North represented by Calvin Michigan Brooklyn Illinois, and Buxton, Iowa. Each of these towns is composed largely of Negroes Deals with general economic and social conditions in each Summarized in N21(a).

(f) "The Negro in Chicago," *Southern Workman*, XXXV, 553-66 (October, 1906).

A study of the economic and social status of the Negro in Chicago. Mentions the sources, causes and results of migration to Chicago.

(g) *The Negro in Pennsylvania*: A Study in Economic History. Philadelphia, A. M. E. Book Concern (1912), 250 pp.

A painstaking, fair-minded study of the economic condition of the Negro in Pennsylvania. Brief discussion of causes of migration and types of migrants (pp. 52-70) and casual references to migrants in discussions of attitudes of employers and property owners, of the formation of social classes, of education, crime, etc

(h) "Negro in Professions in the North," *Southern Workman*, XXXVIII, 237-45 (April, 1909).

Discusses the number of Negroes in various professions. Mentions migration as creating a demand for a professional cl ss in the North

(i) "The Negro in Times of Industrial Unrest," *Charities*, XV (October 7, 1905).

A discussion of the part Negroes played in the Chicago strikes of 1900, 1904 and 1905.

(j) "The Negro in Unskilled Labor," *Annals*, XLIX, 19-27 (September, 1913).

Discusses occupations of Negroes in the North and South on the basis of 1900 census figures Mentions migration to northern cities and discusses the type of work the Negro finds there

(k) "Negro Rural Communities in Indiana," *Southern Workman*, XXXVII, 158-72 (March, 1908).

A history and description of Negro communities in rural Indiana, showing the decrease of population because of migration to cities

(l) "The Negro Skilled Mechanic in the North," *Southern Workman*, XXXVIII, 155-68 (March, 1909).

Studies the number of Negroes in different trades reasons for the scarcity migrants' difficulty in getting work, and the relation of the Negro to the unions.

(m) "Negroes in Business m the North," *Southern Workman*, XXXVIII, 36-44 (January, 1909).

Enumerates the number and kinds of Negro business enterprises in the North with a few individual studies

(n) "One Hundred Negro Steel Workers," In *Pittsburgh Survey*, volume on "Wage Earning Pittsburgh," pp. 97-113.

Describes the status before 1914, of colored workers in Pittsburgh steel industries, dealing with age, length of time in the work, birthplace of workers wages, relation to unions relations with white workers etc. The only real discussion of migration is in a casual discussion of the birthplaces of workers *See also* P23(a).

(o) "Poverty among Northern Negroes," *Southern Workman*, XL, 700-9 (December, 1911).

Discusses causes of poverty and agencies for relief of Negroes in the North

(p) "Recent Improvements in Housing among Negroes in the North," *Southern Workman*, XXXVII, 601-12 (November, 1908).

Merely mentions migration to cities in the North as a cause of the housing shortage.

——— For other works by this author, *see* P7(a), U3(50a).

Y1 Young, Benjamin

(a) "The Boll Weevil Starts North — A Story," *Opportunity*, IV 43 (February, 1926).

A short story with a migrant as the central figure

Y2 Young, P. B.

(a) "Contribution of the Press in the Adjustment of Race Relations," *Southern Workman*, LVII, 147-54 (April, 1928).

A discussion of ways in which the attitude of the southern press has changed in dealing with news of Negroes and of ways in which it has thus improved race relations

Part B

MANUSCRIPTS AND INACCESSIBLE MIMEOGRAPHS

Part B

MANUSCRIPTS AND INACCESSIBLE MIMEOGRAPHS

Alphabetical List by Author and / or Title

This Part lists a store of valuable and pertinent but relatively inaccessible mimeographed or typewritten documents. It is by no means exhaustive, being confined mainly to documents filed in New York City. The compilers have not attempted to locate manuscripts in libraries and organization files in other centers. A mere list would be of little value and at best would be incomplete. Further, digests could not be made with the uniform thoroughness exacted in the case of all works included in the bibliography without lengthy and extremely costly travel by the compilers themselves.

The arrangement, coding and cross referencing within this part are similar to those in Part A, and there is limited cross referencing between the two Parts. The distinction in coding is that the letter "Z," not used in Part A since no authors or titles were found with this initial, precedes all of these. Wherever it appears it is an indication that the original material probably never was printed except in abstract form, that it has had narrow circulation, and that it is relatively inaccessible.

The New York repository of each manuscript is designated in parentheses after each title, except where the agency is obvious, as Columbia University Masters Essays and National Urban League documents. In some instances the material is available in more than one organization. Alternative repositories have not been indicated.

Z1 Baltimore Urban League

(a) *A Survey of Negro Business in Baltimore*, mimeographed, no date or page numbering (National Urban League).

Contains lists of Negro business concerns with some general conclusions as to the status of business among Negroes

Z2 Batchelor, Carey

(a) *What the Tenement Family Has and What It Pays for It*, survey for United Neighborhood Houses and League of Mothers' Clubs, typewritten, 10 pp. (National Urban League).

A study of 1,014 tenement families including some Negroes, in New York City showing income, rents and housing conditions.

Z3 Berry, Theodore M.

(a) *Survey Abstract: "The Status of the Negro in Industry and Occupational Opportunities in Cincinnati"* (1930), mimeographed, 13 pp.
A report of a survey conducted under the Cincinnati Chamber of Commerce and the Department of Public Welfare Deals with the increase of Negro population in Cincinnati industrial status and occupational opportunities success of colored workers relation of white and colored laborers, wages, relation to organized labor, with brief reference to housing and standards of living among Negroes

Z4 Binder, Louis Richard

(a) *The Negro in Paterson, New Jersey*: A Study in Leadership, Columbia University Master's essay (1927), 69 pp.
Gives theoretical discussions of the need for developing the character of leadership, and applies each theory to actual situations found among Paterson Negroes Mentions migration (p. 17) and gives a brief picture of housing conditions and occupations

Z5 Bond, Max

(a) *Fourteen Negro Churches in Pittsburgh*, thesis for sociology course in the University of Pittsburgh (1928), mimeographed, 8 pp. (National Urban League).
Description of fourteen churches their equipment, personnel and activities

Z6 Cleveland Federal Reserve Bank

(a) *Negro Population of the Fourth Federal Reserve District* (1924), typewritten, 24 pp. (Social Science Research Council).
A good synthesis of information on extent, causes and results of migration to this locality

Z7 Clyde, John P.

(a) *The Negro in New York City*, Columbia University Master's essay (1899), 30 pp.
An investigation of the population elements, economic status, vital statistics crime, religion, education, political status and home life of the Negroes in New York City based largely on the 1890 Census Valuable as an early study of census material.

Z8 Covington, Floyd C.

(a) *Occupational Choices in Relation to Economic Opportunities of Negro Youth in Pittsburgh*, Master's thesis for the University of Pittsburgh (1928), typewritten, 103 pp. (National Urban League).
A study of 434 Negro students in the Pittsburgh High Schools — age, sex, oc-

cupational choice, parental occupation in relation to choices of children and in relation to educational and economic opportunities

Z9 Crime Committee of the Cincinnatus Association

(a) *An Analysis of 11,180 Misdemeanor Cases.* Cincinnati Bureau of Governmental Research, Report No. 19 (January, 1930), mimeographed, 21 pp. (National Urban League).

A report on an analysis of misdemeanor arrests by age, color, residence disposition and causes

Curley, C. Benjamin, *see* Z48(a).

Z10 Doles, John T

(a) *The Labor Problem in New York as Affecting Negroes with an Analysis of Union Organization.* Columbia University Master's essay (1928), 68 pp.

An investigation of the history of the Negro's industrial activity in New York his present occupational distribution and his relation to the unions Mentions migration (pp. 14 15), discrimination as the cause of migration from the South (p.21), and the extent of migration to New York before 1915.

Z11 Douthitt, Mildred A., and Adeline Vatz

(a) *The Social and Recreational Opportunities for the Negro in Pittsburgh*, thesis for Social Service Certificate, Pennsylvania College for Women (1927), typewritten, 36 pp. (National Urban League).

Discusses the increase of Negro population due to migration, churches (number and part they play in the Negro's social life), Y.M.C.A. and Y.W.C.A., Boy and Girl Scouts settlements, public and private recreational centers etc

Z12(a) *Employment for Negroes in Harlem* (1926), typewritten, 6 pp. (National Urban League).

General survey of the employment of colored persons in stores and businesses in Harlem.

Z13 Fairclough, Alice Brown

(a) *A Study of Occupational Opportunities for Negro Women in New York City*, New York University Master's essay (1929), (National Urban League).

Deals with the nature of occupations of Negro women in New York City the wages received and the relations of these colored workers to the white employees.

Z14 Forman, Clarke

(a) *The Development of Interracial Coöperation*, Columbia University Master's essay (1927).

Studies the stages in interracial relations: (1) individual aid, (2) religious coöperation, (3) coöperation in education, (4) interracial commission. Contains brief report of the founding of the Interracial Commission.

Z15 Forster, Harvey G.

(a) *Statistics of Negro Population in Manhattan*, Columbia University Master's essay (1920), 52 pp.

Depicts the history of the Negro in Manhattan, the growth of Negro population from 1704 to 1915 and its distribution within the city, the Negro in Harlem, and the foreign-born Negro. Studies the distribution of Negroes within the various districts of Manhattan and the civic problems arising from that segregated distribution Interested chiefly in distribution by assembly districts

Z16 Frazier, E. Franklin

(a) *Negro Longshoremen* (1921), Typewritten, 67 pp. (Russell Sage Foundation Library).

A first-hand survey of the status of the Negro longshoremen in New York City

Printed in nearly complete form in F21(i).

Z17 Gauger, Carolyn

(a) *Negro Migration in South Carolina*, Columbia University Master's essay (1926), 31 pp.

A study of migration from farms to cities and from county to county within South Carolina, and of the social and economic factors influencing these movements The chief factor is given as economic — the desire to improve conditions of living.

Z18 Hardy, Eric West

(a) *The Negro in His Relation to Trade Unionism*, University of Chicago (1911), typewritten (typed excerpts on file at National Urban League).

Discusses the history of the Negroes relation to unionism, the number of Negroes in the A F. of L, causes of exclusion, effects of exclusion, etc

Z19 Harris, Abram

(a) *New Negro Worker in Pittsburgh*, University of Pittsburgh Master's essay (1924), 79 pp. (National Urban League).

A valuable study of the types of occupations of Negroes in Pittsburgh, showing the efect of migration in the increased employment of Negroes in occupations hitherto closed to them. The emphasis is on the nature of occupations and the relation to unions but also discusses housing, health vital statistics crime and interracial relations

(b) *Report of Preliminary Findings in Columbus Hill* (1922) typewritten, 8 pp. (National Urban League).

A summary of economic aod social conditions of the Negroes in the Columbus Hill district

Z20 Holmes, Norma A.

(a) *Preliminary Report of the Survey of Colored Population of Columbus Hill and Vicinity* (1922), mimeographed, 10 pp. (National Urban League).

A briefer report of Z20(b).

(b) *Sociological Survey of the Negro Population of Columbus Hill of New York City* (1922), mimeographed, 27 pp. (National Urban League).

A general study of social and economic conditions.

Z21 Hopper, Ernest J.

(a) *A Northern Negro Group* Columbia University Master's essay (1912), 49 pp.

A study of a group of Negroes in New York City in one assembly district the location of Negroes within the city the history of their spread within New York their present population distribution and demotic composition Mentions birthplaces, and briefly discusses age, occupations, sex and wages

Z22 Hospital Library and Service Bureau

(a) *Report on Informal Study of the Educational Facilities for Colored Nurses and Their Use in Hospitals, Visiting and Public Health Nursing*, Chicago (1925), mimeographed, no page numbering. (National Urban League).

A general survey of the opportunities for colored nurses

Z23 Hunter, Claudia

(a) *A Comparative Study of the Relationships Existing between the White Race and the Negro Race in the State of North Carolina and in the City of New York*, Columbia University Master's essay (1927).

A study based on questionnaires sent to a white and a Negro church congre gation and a white and a Negro college in North Carolina and in New York Gives questionnaires and an analysis of them.

Z24 Jackson, Isaiah, Jr

(a) *Report of Social Survey—Negro Family Life* (May, 1928), typewritten, 3 pp. (National Urban League).

A brief report to the President of the Edward Waters College, submitted by the Department of Sociology and Economics, on the condition of Negro family life in Jacksonville

Z25 Johnson, Charles S.

(a) *Abstract of Reports for Conference of Causes and Trends of Negro Migration and Results*, m meographed, 10 pp. (National Urban League).

Notes on the causes trends and results of Negro migration prepared for the National Urban League Conference of October 15, 1919.

Z26 Johnstone, Robert Z.

(a) *The New Negro in New York*, Columb University Master's essay (1911), 62 pp.

An early study of the social attainments and prospects of the Negro in New York. Part 1 de ls with his home life extent of education, occupations and political activities Part 2 gives a theoretical discussion of psychological and social principles. Pages 1-4 discuss the fact of migration to New York since 1880, and sources of this movement, segregation, rents, housing conditions, congestion, occupations and political life

Z27 Kingsley, Harold M.

(a) *The Negroes of the "Oak Street District,"* a thesis in the senior class of the Yale Divinity School (1911), typewritten, 27 pp. (National Urban League).

A study of occupations, wages religion and educational status living conditions etc., in this district

Z28 Lee, H. G.

(a) *History of the Negroes in Organized Labor to 1872*, University of Wisconsin thesis (excerpts in the National Urban League).

The title explains the subject matter

Z29 Locke, Benjamin H.

(a) *The Community Life of a Harlem Group of Negroes*, Columbia University Master's essay (1913), 36 pp.

A study of the leisure time activities of a group of 35 Harlem Negroes and of the relative effects of the environments of New York and the South upon these activities Includes a brief discussion of economic status

Z30 McDougald, G. Elise

(a) *Report of the School End of the Survey of Occupations in New York City, 1921-1923*, typewritten, 33 pp. (National Urban League).

A survey of the occupations of Negroes with reference to training and vocational guidance

Z31 McGuinn, Henry

(a) *A Study of Commercial Recreation for Negroes in 17 Cities*, Columbia University Master's essay (1927).

A study of municipal attitudes toward recreation for Negroes and the facilities for them, as well as of the race contacts arising from recreation. Same recreation section in W41(h).

Z32 Maxwell, Vashti C.

(a) *Recreation Survey* (1919), typewritten, 58 + 6 pp. (National Urban League).

A survey of how persons in Harlem spend their leisure time, the recreational facilities available and the needs. Contains some reference to occupations and housing.

Z33(a) *Migration.* A collection of typed reports, letters and records made by Scott and Johnson in their studies of Negro migration during the War. (National Urban League).

Collection of scattered notes on the extent, causes and results of World-War migration. *See also* S11(c), Z25(a).

Z34 Moss, R. Maurice

(a) *Survey of the Negro Population of Westchester County, New York* (1924), typewritten, 92 pp. (National Urban League).

A general economic and social survey

Z35 National Urban League

(a) *An Elementary Study of Negro Life in Tulsa* (Jesse O Thomas) (October, 1928), typewritten, no page numbering, but long

A survey of the composition, housing, health recreation, social agencies, employment churches race relations, etc., of the Negroes in Tulsa.
Published in briefer form as T10(a).

(b) *The Housing of the Negro Population of Denver* (Ira de A. Reid), typewritten, 15 pp.

A special report on housing. *See also* R12(e), R12(f).

(c) *How Unemployment Affects Negroes* (March, 1931), mimeographed, 41 pp.

A survey of the status of unemployment shifting of workers from city to city and results upon social agencies etc North and South

(d) *Industrial Survey of Negro Population of Los Angeles, California* (C. S. Johnson) (1926), typewritten, 83 pp.

Deals with the growth of Negro population in Los Angeles, nature of employment, wages and the relation of Negroes to unions. Summarized in J4(m).

(e) *The Negro in Buffalo* (C. S Johnson) (1922), typewritten, 92 pp.
An Urban League investigation of the economic and social status of the colored people in Buffalo. Shows the relation of migration to the composition of the group, housing, church membership, relations with white people and with northern Negroes

(f) *Negro Population in Flushing* (1922), typewritten, 29 + 10 pp.
A general social and economic survey

(g) *The Negro Population of Albany, New York* (Ira de A. Reid) (1928), 71 pp.
Report of an investigation of the Negro population of Albany — age and sex composition, health, housing, occupations, wages, membership in labor unions, crime, education, recreation and religious life Mentions migration in discussing the growth of the colored group. Also published in part as A4(a), R12(a).

(h) *Negro Population of Albany* (Ira de A. Reid) (1928), mimeographed, 45 pp.
A briefer presentation of Z35(g).

(i) *The Negro Population of Austin, Texas*: A Study of the Social Welfare Status (Jesse O Thomas) (April, 1913), typewritten.
An original investigation of the composition of the Negro population of Austin — occupations, housing, health crime, education, recreation etc Mentions competition with Mexicans.

(j) *Negro Population of Elizabeth, New Jersey*: A Survey of the Economic and Social Conditions (Ira de A. Reid) (1930), mimeographed, no page numbering, but large report.
A survey of the Negro population covering housing, employment, health, etc

(k) *Negro Population of Hartford, Connecticut* (1921), typewritten, 150 pp.
A survey of the Negro population, composition, living conditions, rents, occupations, unions, migration to Hartford, etc

(l) *The Negro Population of Warren, Ohio* (Ira de A. Reid) (July, 1929), typewritten, 13 pp.
A brief report of the composition of the colored population, their educational and occupational status housing, health, recreation, churches, organizations, etc with recommendations for a program of work.

(m) *Negro Population of Waterbury, Connecticut* (C. S Johnson), typewritten, 43 pp.
A general social and economic survey
Summarized in J4(k).

(n) *Observations on the Social Condition of the Negro Population of*

Norwalk, Connecticut (Ira de A. Reid) (October, 1929), typewritten, 11 pp.
A brief survey in Norwalk covering occupations, housing, health, schools delinquency recreation, etc

(o) *Report for the National Conference on Migration*. Recent migration of Negroes to Pennsylvania and New Jersey and the status of these in their new environment, illustrated especially by their status in and about Philadelphia (January, 1917), typewritten, 5 pp.
The title is self-explanatory.

(p) *A Study of the Negro Families in the Pinewood Avenue District, Toledo, Ohio*, survey made in 1928, mimeographed, 5 pp.
Discusses population increase due to migration, housing, religious life, occupations, education, etc
Summarized in J6(a).

(q) *A Survey of the Living Conditions among Negroes in White Plains, New York* (R. Maurice Moss) (1929), typewritten, no folios.
A survey of housing and occupations.

(r) *Survey of the Negro Population in Milwaukee, Wisconsin* (1917), typewritten, 93 + 16 pp.
A survey of the colored group in Milwaukee considering such topics as increase of Negroes in the city, age and sex housing, occupations health education, etc

(s) *Survey of the Negro Population of Fort Wayne, Indiana* (C. S Johnson) (1928), typewritten, 75 + pp.
A general social and economic survey dealing with the increase of population by migration and the effect of migration upon various phases of the life of the group.

(t) *Survey of the Negro Population of Grand Rapids, Michigan* (R. Maurice Moss) (1928), typewritten, 128 + pp.
A general social and economic survey
Summarized in M55(a).

(u) *Survey of the Negro Population of Morristown, New Jersey* (Ethel McGhee) (1924), typewritten, 24 pp.
A brief survey of the composition, wages, occupations, education, etc

(v) *A Survey of the Negro Population of Nassau and Suffolk Counties, Long Island, New York* (1919), typewritten, 97 pp.
Discusses the composition of the population, working and living conditions, education, religion, recreation, etc

(w) *A Survey of the Negro Population of Plainfield, New Jersey* (C. S Johnson) (1925), typewritten, no page numbering.
A general survey of social and economic conditions.

(x) *Survey of the Negro Population of Springfield, Illinois* (1927), typewritten, 74 pp.
A survey of the housing, occupational, recre ti n l etc conditions

(y) *Survey of the Negro Population of Trenton* (C. S Johnson) (1924), typewritten, no page numbering.
A survey of the economic, political and social situation of Negroes in Trenton.

(z) *Survey of the Negro Population of Worcester, Massachusetts* (R. Maurice Moss and Joseph S. Jackson, Jr.) (1929), typewritten, 115 pp.
A survey of the Negroes of Worcester their housing, occupations, wages, health education, crime, recreation, religious life etc

(aa) *Trojans of Color:* A Social Survey of the Negro Population of Troy, New York (Ira de A. Reid) (1931), typewritten, 54 pp.
An economic and social survey

(bb) *Unemployment among Negroes* (November, 1930), mimeographed, 14 pp.
A study of the unemployment situation in twenty-five cities Mentions migration of laborers in search of work and the efforts of the Urban League to cope with the situation.

Z36(a) *Negro Papers and Documents.* The Carter G. Woodson Collection of Negro Papers and Documents, Washington, D. C. (Congressional Library).
A collection of letters and documents dealing with various phases of Negro life and problems. Includes the original correspondence from prospective Negro migrants at the time of the 1916-18 and 1922-23 movements Valuable as showing the interest in migration and the conditions which led to the movements Part published as L19(a).

Z37 New York Urban League

(a) *Negro Churches in Harlem* (May, 1926), typewritten, 7 pp.
A survey of the total number of churches in Harlem, denominations, types of building, membership, attitude of ministers etc

(b) *Twenty-Four Hundred Negro Families in Harlem* (May, 1927), 30 pp.
A survey of Negroes in Harlem concerning their housing conditions the composition of the households rentals, number of children, occupations of the men and women total family earnings, lodgers, working mothers broken families etc

Z38 Ogburn, William F.

(a) *The Richmond Negro in New York City, His Social Mind as Seen in His Pleasures*, Columbia University Master's essay (1909), 75 pp.
A study and comparison of the Negro in Richmond and New York, describing the environment in each place and the types of recreation in each city, in order to show the effect of the changed environment on the social mind of the Negroes

Z39 Paul, Seymore

(a) *A Group of Virginia Negroes in New York City*, Columbia University Master's essay (1912), 56 pp.
A study of fourteen migrants, particularly in the use of their leisure time in a new environment Studies their physical, social and economic environment in Richmond and their leisure time activities, contrasting these with conditions in New York

Z40 Peden, Robert W.

(a) *The Status of the Negro in the United States*, Columbia University Master's essay (1920), 70 pp.
A general treatment of various aspects of Negro nature and problems, mentioning migration.

Z41(a) *Phelps-Stokes Papers*: Preliminary Outline on Interracial Organization in Northern Cities (Russell Sage Foundation-Library).
A preliminary report on a survey of the social and economic problems that have arisen from migration, and an account of work being done or that should be done in the way of interracial coöperation in solving these problems.

Z42 Pritchard, Arthur O

(a) *A Study of the Negro Population of Newport, Rhode Island*, Columbia University Master's essay (1903), 58 pp.
A study of the social, economic and political life of the Negro group in New port

Z43 Rast, John M.

(a) *Recent Negro Migrations from the South*, Columbia University Master's essay (1924), 34 pp.
Gives a brief history of the Negro in the United States and shows the extent characteristics and causes of the migration during the World War.

Z44 Reid, Ira de A.

(a) *Mrs. Bailey Pays the Rent*, typewritten, 9 pp. (National Urban League).
A study of rent parties in Harlem.

(b) *The Negro in the Major Industries and the Building Trades of Pittsburgh*, University of Pittsburgh Master's essay (1925), 59 pp. (National Urban League).

Discusses the occupations of Negroes in Pittsburgh, their wages success in industry, and the relation of Negroes to the labor unions

Z45(a) *Report on South Side Survey*, Chicago (April, 1931), typewritten, no page numbermg, but long (National Urban League).

A survey of social agencies working among Negroes, unemployment crises in relation to social service etc

Z46(a) *Report to the Julius Rosenwald Fund of Survey in Birmingham, Alabama, January, 1930, to Determine Vocational Opportunities for Negro Youth* (1930), typewritten, 11 pp. (National Urban League).

Discusses Negro population and the industrial status of Negroes in Birmingham, showing the need for vocational training.

Z47 Ridley, Venola

(a) *Public Opinion and the Negro Press*, Columbia University Master's essay (1928), 97 pp.

An examination of Negro periodicals and a study of their efforts to mold public opinion; nature of these periodicals and opinions they are trying to get across to the public

Z48 Smith, A. Macco, and C. Benjamin Curley

(a) *Economic Survey of Negro Business in Harlem*, typewritten, 8 pp. (National Urban League).

Lists the number of concerns in each kind of business and discusses the general situation.

Z49(a) *Social Science Research Council, Hanover Conference* (August 18-September 1, 1928), mimeographed, 275 pp. (National Urban League).

A minute report of the addresses and speeches at the Hanover Conference in 1928. Pages 194-213 contain abstracts of speeches by W W Alexander Mary van Kleeck and Charles S. Johnson dealing with the activities of the Inter racial Commission and a program for the Interracial Conference

Z50(a) *Study of Paul Lawrence Dunbar High School at Little Rock, Arkansas* (May 22, 1931), typewritten, 7 pp. (National Urban League).

A description of that institution, with recommendations for vocational training and guidance

Z51(a) *Survey of Social Work among the Colored People of Stam-*

ford, Connecticut. Made by the Social Work Council, Stamford Community Chest (1931), mimeographed, no folios (National Urban League).

A general economic and social survey with emphasis on what social agencies are doing and should do.

Z52 Sydnor, Edith G.

(a) *Causes of the Recent Migration of Negroes*, Columbia University Master's essay (1923).

A discussion of the causes of migration, based largely on Scott's *Negro Migration*. *See also* S11 (c).

Z53 Taylor, Paul S.

(a) Unpublished material on employment of Negroes in certain industries from 1910 to 1928 (in the possession of the author at the University of California).

Contains lists showing the number of Negroes employed in specific companies for the period stated

Z54 Truxal, Andrew G.

(a) *The Dispersion of the American Negro — 1860 to 1920*, 38 pp. (in the possession of the author at Dartmouth College).

An analysis of the census statistics showing the characteristics of the dispersion of Negroes within the United States since 1860. Deals with the direction of such movements both to the Southwest and to the North the urban trend particularly in the northern drift the extent of these movements in various decades the sources of migration to selected states; and the distances travelled

Z55 United States Department of Labor

(a) *Inclusion of Negro Workers into Northern Industry*, Press Release (July 9, 1923), Washington.

Report of a survey made by P H Brown on the increase of skilled and unskilled Negro workers in the North

(b) Press Release (October 24, 1923), Washington, mimeographed 1 p.

Report on the extent of migration by states during 1923. *See also* M33(a).

Z56 Van Deusen, John G.

(a) *Negro Migration*, 250 pp. (in the possession of the author at Hobart College).

An exhaustive account from a compilation of historical and census reports of the migrations of Negroes, 1860-1920, by decades Each decade analysis includes the extent of movements for each of the southern and northern states the causes of such migrations where it is possible to discover them, and the possible implications and significance of these migrations

Z57 Van Vleck, Joseph

(a) *A Survey of Witherspoon Young Men's Christian Association of Princeton, New Jersey* (1930), 104 pp.

A study of the colored community of Princeton and of the activities of the Witherspoon Y.M.C.A., in order to make recommendations for more complete functioning of that organization in the future

Vatz, Adeline, *see* Z11 (a).

Z58(a) *Vocational* Survey — *Greenville,* South *Carolina, Negro City School* System, no date, typewritten, 13 pp. (National Urban League).

Discusses occupations in which Negroes were found, to show needs and fields for vocational training.

Z59 Walls, Ellie A.

(a) *The Delinquent Negro Girl in New York*, Columbia University Master's essay (1912).

Discusses the extent of the need for institutional care of the delinquent Negro girl in New York, describing the situation among juvenile delinquents and girls of from eighteen to twenty-one years of age, and giving the subsequent history of girls not sent to institutions; also discusses the adequacy of the institutions, and gives a tentative plan for temporary amelioration.

Z60 White House Conference on Child Health and Protection, Committee on Child Dependency

(a) *The Problem of Child Dependency among Negroes* (1930), mimeographed, 71 + 6 pp. (National Urban League).

A general survey of Negro population, Negro family conditions, health living conditions, occupations, and the problem of dependent children in the North and the South

Z61 Wilson, Agnes E.

(a) *The Facilities for the Care of Dependent, Semi-Delinquent and Delinquent Negro Children in Los Angeles*, Community Welfare Federation (February-March, 1925), mmeographed, 44 pp. (National Urban League).

Discusses Negro migration to Los Angeles causes, types of migrants, distribution of Negro population within the city, facilities for the care of dependent and delinquent Negro children health and recreational facilities

Part C

BIBLIOGRAPHIES

Part C

BIBLIOGRAPHIES

Alphabetically Arranged by Author and / or Title

The few titles * here listed are those of publications whose sole function is bibliographic. They are not coded, and nowhere else enter the present volume. They do not include any bibliographies incidental to text. Many such lists of books, articles, etc., do exist as portions of volumes primarily valuable for their other content. Notable among these are *The Negro Year Book* and the Atlanta University Publications, appearing elsewhere in this Bibliography.

Bailey, M. E., "Some New Books on the Negro," *Bookman*, LII, 301-6, (January, 1921).

Bibliography on the Race Problem. Typewritten, 3 pp. (No date, available in the files of the National Urban League).

"Books about the Negro," *Branch Library Book News* (New York City) II, 131-36, (December, 1925).
A reading list compiled by the One Hundred and Thirty-fifth Street Branch of the New York City Public Library.

* Eaton, Allen, and Shelby Harrison, *Bibliography of Social Surveys.* New York, Russell Sage Foundation (1930), 467 pp.
A bibliography of social surveys arranged by specific subjects. Includes topics connected with surveys among Negroes.

Lindsay, Samuel M., "A Partial List of Books and Pamphlets on the Negro Question in the United States," in *Southern Society for the Promotion of the Study of Race Conditions and Problems in the South, Report of the First Annual Conference, 1900.* Richmond, B. F. Johnson Publishing Co., 224-40.

Murray, Daniel, *Preliminary List of Books and Pamphlets by Negro Authors.* Library of Congress, Washington, D.C., Government Printing Office, (1900), 8 pp.

"The Negro: A Selected Bibliography, 1929," *Branch Library Book News* (New York City) VII, 19-30 (January, 1930).
A revision of "Books about the Negro" compiled by the One Hundred

* Those marked with an asterisk are particularly valuable for Negro Migration.

and Thirty-fifth Street Branch of the New York City Public Library.

"The Negro in Print: A Selected List of Magazines and Books by and about Negroes," *Survey*, LIII, 703-7 (March 1, 1925), Survey Graphic.

Russell Sage Foundation Library, *The Negro*. New York, Foundation Library Bulletin No. 111 (1923), 4 pp.

Russell Sage Foundation Library, *The Negro in Industry*: A Selected Bibliography. New York, Foundation Library Bulletin No. 66, (1924), 4 pp.

* St. Louis Public Library, "American Negro," A Selected List of Books Compiled by Norma Klinge and Georg-Anna Tod. *St. Louis Public Library Monthly Bulletin* (December, 1922), 3-14.
Revised by Margaret McDonald, in *St. Louis Public Library Monthly Bulletin* (August, 1929), 239-54.

Sieg, Vera, *The Negro Problem*: A Bibliography. (Madison) Wisconsin Free Library Commission (November, 1908), 22 pp.

United States Government Publications

"Bibliography of the Negro in America," *United States Commission of Education Report for 1893-1894*, Vol. I, 1038-61.

List of Books on the Negro Question, 1915-1926. Library of Congress (1926), typewritten, 10 pp. Select List of References No. 956.

List of Discussions of the Fourteenth and Fifteenth Amendments with Special Reference to Negro Suffrage. Library of Congress (1906), 18 pp.

* *List of References on Negro Migration*. Library of Congress, Dec. 20 (1923), typewritten, 7 pp. Select List of References No. 793.

* "The Negro: A Selected Bibliography," by H. L. Pier and M. L. Spalding, *Monthly Labor Review*, Vol. XXII, No. 1 (January, 1926), 216-44.

Select List of References on the Negro Question. Library of Congress (1903), 28 pp.
Second Edition, 1906, 61 pp.

* Work, Monroe N., *A Bibliography of the Negro in Africa and America*. New York, H. W. Wilson (1928), 698 pp.

* Those marked with an asterisk are particularly valuable for Negro Migration.

Part D

TEMPORAL AND FUNCTIONAL CLASSIFICATION OF PARTS A AND B

Part D

TEMPORAL AND FUNCTIONAL CLASSIFICATION OF PARTS A AND B

The organization of this part of the Bibliography is an outgrowth of the practical uses to which the original file has been put. It is divided into two general sections: I, that containing references dealing primarily with migration; and II, background material, chiefly descriptive of conditions in the Old South, and general works on Negro education, health, economic status, etc., irrespective of migration. Thus works discussing health as a concomitant of migration are in Section I; those dealing with health of the Negro without regard to migration are in Section II. No attempt has been made to make Section II exhaustive.

The accompanying outline presents the detailed organization of this part. It is mere repetition of the categories, but here affords a needed key to facilitate use of the categories themselves. There are many categories, primarily in Section I under C4, D3 and D4 and in Section II, that seem to duplicate each other. Examples of these are Economic topics, Health, Education, Violence and Discrimination, Housing and Social Maladjustment. The seeming duplication occurs because these topics fall late in the hierarchical order of classification criteria. Their interrelationships are apparent; their distinctions require explanation.

Violence may cause migration; and if the author says so his document has been placed in category 3 of Periods A, B, C or D. Violence may be decreasing in the rural South as a consequence of *loss* of farm hands and the desire to placate those that remain; if so its place is in category 4a under the proper period.[1] Again, race riots have occurred in St. Louis, Chicago, Washington and other localities — South as well as North — *to* which migrants have gone. Descriptions of these have been allocated to the appropriate categories of 4b.[1] Finally, general discussions of violence, neither as cause nor result of migration, but as lists or accounts of lynchings, arguments against mob action, etc., have been placed in section II. Lack of educational facilities, a series of poor crops or disfran-

Period D is the only one having subdivisions of 4a. However the other periods were thought of as having similar subdivisions when the classification was made

chisement may be set forth as causes of movement; they may be presented as results either in the regions losing or in those gaining population; or they may be described or discussed *per se* according to the particular intention of the individual author. In each event they have been allocated to a Cause, Result, or Background category, with occasional overlapping.

In many instances border line cases have been assigned arbitrarily. The tendency has been to imply cause, even though it is not actually stated, if the topic is one usually treated as cause; not to imply results for regions *from* which migrants have come; to imply results in regions *to* which they have gone; and to put only residual or obviously non-migrational material in Background categories.

Attention should be called to the inclusiveness of certain categories. Documents in Category 1 (Inclusive Works) of Section I, Periods A, B, C and D, may include works of specific interest in any subsequent coördinate or subordinate category of the respective period. In Section I under D2a and D3a there may be entries applicable to the other lettered classes of D2 and D3 rubrics. Under Section I, C4b(1), D4a(1) and D4b(1), there may be works bearing on any coördinate or subordinate class. In ID4b(3)(a) there are collected references that belong to several of the later categories (b), (c), (d), (e) and (f). Finally, Section IIA contains items pertinent to subsequent categories and to those of Section I as well.

Under each category there appear code designations for the various works listed therein. These refer to Parts A and B. (See Introductions, pp. 13-14, 177.) The initial letters "A" through "Y" refer to documents in Part A; the letter "Z" to those in Part B. Wherever the "Z's" appear, in Parts D and E, they are preceded by the word "Unpublished." In some [2] instances the grouping of the former is broken into two subgroups designated Important" and "Less Important." These are to be interpreted in terms of importance to the subject Negro Migration.

Exemplification

The particular ultimate categories in the present scheme were adopted, after a considerable amount of experimentation, as being the best from the standpoint of the present-day student of Negro m gration. An infinitude of classificatory systems might have been designed in place of the

[2] The intention of this should be clear to the reader without further explanation. Every attempt has been made to break down each category in this fashion, in most instances unsuccessfully It is obvious that what would be quite unimportant for one user would be of great significance for another

one adopted. Each would satisfy some users and be of little use to others. One interested in the subject of "Negro Child Welfare," "Negro Artistic Achievement," "The Negro in Steel" or similar topics will not find a single category adequate to his needs. Footnotes have been added to many categories, but considerable search will be necessary to locate items pertinent to such topics. A practical illustration may aid users.

Mr. D. wishes to discover what literature exists bearing on "The Negro in Steel." He must from the start realize that the Bibliography does not cover all works either on the Negro or on steel. It is concerned primarily, as far as his problem goes, with descriptions of migration to or from steel areas, with the steel industry as a factor in migration, and with results of migration in steel regions.

He will find no category mentioning steel, but he will in various parts of the classification discover categories that presumably include references pertinent to his quest. Since the Negro's real entrance into the steel industry is fairly recent, there is little [3] to be expected in the temporal clasification before Periods C (1900-1915) and D (1915 to date).

Attention would center in the entries of ID4b(3)(b), (d) and (e). However, as previously explained, no one of (b), (d) or (e) is complete, as (a) includes many works covering all the subtopics into which Economic Conditions has been subdivided, and codes for these have not been repeated in the subclasses thereunder. The same is true for the entries of ID4b(1). Since the writer is concerned with areas *to* which migrants went, he is not interested in any of the categories of ID4a.

It is improbable that he would be interested in the causes of migration. Should he be, he must concern himself with the various classes of ID3. Depending on his interests, he will use or ignore ID2. In any event he will wish to investigate entries in ID1, ignoring if he chooses the "Less Important" and "Unpublished" groups. Under IC, his attention will center in 1 (Inclusive Works) and in 4b(1) and 4b(3).

Mr. D. will find it easy to eliminate a large majority of the lengthy list of possible items as soon as he reads the titles in Parts A and B. Further deletion will come with reading of the abstracts under the several titles. Many works will remain that must be actually referred to before their usefulness can be determined.

If he wishes information regarding the enslaved Negro iron workers who designed and executed the beautiful grilles of Charleston and New Orleans, he might find some mention in the "Industrial" portions of Section II But their efforts fall in a period earlier than this Bibliography covers, and there is no migrational connection

After search of Part D, it will frequently be advantageous to refer to logical localities in Part E (see illustration p. 221).

It should be reiterated here that no pretence is made that this Bibliography covers all works on the Negro or on any economic, social or similar topic. Its sole interest is to aid students of Negro Migration. Many important documents on closely allied fields have been omitted as having too indirect a bearing.

I REFERENCES ON MIGRATION

A. 1865-1875

1. Inclusive Works
2. Mechanics of the Movement
3. and 4. Causes and Results

B. 1875-1900

1. Inclusive Works
2. Mechanics of the Movement
3. Causes
4. Results

C. 1900-1915

1. Inclusive Works
2. Mechanics of the Movement
3. Causes
4. Results
   a. Results in Regions *from* Which Migrants Moved
   b Results in Regions *to* Which Migrants Went
      (1) General Summaries
      (2) Demographic Composition
      (3) Economic Conditions
      (4) Housing, Rent and the Standard of Living
      (5) Health and Vital Statistics
      (6) Social Maladjustment, Including Crime, Juvenile Delinquency, Dependency, Suicide and Insanity
      (7) Recreation and Recreational Facilities
      (8) Activities of Social Agencies Concerned with the Negro
      (9) Education and Educational Institutions
      (10) Political Participation, Affiliation and Influence
      (11) Religious Organizations and Their Activities
      (12) Interracial Relations, Particularly Violence, Discrimination and Other Manifestations of Race Prejudice
      (13) Relations with Foreign-born Groups
      (14) Intra-racial Relations

(15) Psychological Effects on the Migrants
(16) The Negro Family

D. 1915 to Date

1. Inclusive Works
2. Mechanics of the Movement
   a. General Description of the Migration
   b Sources of the Migration
   c. Extent and Direction
   d Return Movement to the South
   e. Types of Migrants and of Migration
3. Causes
   a. Inclusive Works
   b Economic Factors
   c. Social Factors, Primarily Discrimination and Violence
   d Socio-psychological Factors, Including Influence of Leaders, Letters from Migrants, Labor Agents and Agencies
4. Results
   a. Results in Regions *from* Which Migrants Moved
      (1) General Summaries
      (2) Economic Conditions
      (3) Social Conditions, Including Education, Health, Recreation and Living Conditions
      (4) Effect of the Movement on Race Relations, Including Violence, Discrimination and Other Manifestations of Race Prejudice
      (5) Psychological Effects
      (6) Southern Efforts to Retain and Recall
   b Results in Regions *to* Which Migrants Went
      (1) General Summaries
      (2) Demographic Composition
      (3) Economic Conditions
         (a) Inclusive Surveys and General Discussions of Economic Conditions
         (b) Nature of Occupations in Professions, Industry and Business
         (c) Unemployment
         (d) Achievement in Industry, Including Discussions of Reliability and Labor Turnover

(e) Wages and Hours of Labor
(f) Relation to Labor Organizations, Including the Communist Movement

(4) Housing, Rent and the Standard of Living
(5) Health and Vital Statistics
(6) Social Maladjustment, Including Crime, Juvenile Delinquency, Dependency, Suicide and Insanity
(7) Recreation and Recreational Facilities
(8) Activities of Social Agencies Concerned with the Negro
(9) Education and Educational Institutions
(10) Political Participation, Affiliation and Influence
(11) Religious Organizations and Their Activities
(12) Interracial Relations, Particularly Violence, Discrimination and Other Manifestations of Race Prejudice
(13) Relations with Foreign-born Groups
(14) Intra-racial Relations
(15) Psychological Effects on the Migrants
(16) The Negro Family

II. BACKGROUND MATERIAL

A. General Conditions
B. General Economic Conditions
C. Agricultural Situation
D. Occupations
E. Business Enterprises
F. Education and Educational Institutions
G. Political Situation
   1. General Political, Including Disfranchisement and Legal Status
   2. The Reconstruction Period, Emphasizing Political Conditions
H. Discrimination and Violence, Particularly Lynching
I Health
J Social Maladjustment
K. Contemporary Discussions of the Status of the Negro
L. Race Traits and Amalgamation
M. Miscellaneous Social Conditions

I. REFERENCES ON MIGRATION

This is a hierarchical arrangement, hence Inclusive" categories must be consulted as supplements to each specific category.

A. 1865-1875[1]

1. Inclusive Works

Important: B9(a), M2(a), T2(a), T2(b), U3(9a), U3(11a), U3(39a), W1(a), W40(a), W40(c).

Less Important: J4(h), S13(a), W10(b), W13(a).

2. Mechanics of the Movement

Important: B22(a), B35(b), B41(b), L7(a), M39(h), M42(a), R25(a), U3(27a), U3(31a), U3(34a).

Unpublished: Z54(a), Z56(a).

3. and 4. Causes and Results

Important: A15(a), B35(b), B41(b), D12(a), M42(a), S38(a), S51(a), U3(10a), W35(a).

Unpublished: Z28(a), Z56(a).

B. 1875-1900[1]

1. Inclusive Works

Important: A15(b-e), B9(a), D18(i), F12(c), H32(b), I6(a), S13(a), T2(a), T2(b), U3(11a), U3(12a), U3(12c), U3(38a), U3(44a), W13(a), W40(a).

Less Important: B35(a), D18(b), J4(h), U3(22a), W32(a), W40(c).

2. Mechanics of the Movement

Important: B32(a), B33(b), B35(b), B41(b), D15(a), G1(b), I5(a), J18(a), M19(a), M39(b), M39(h), M42(a), P2(a), U3(14a), U3(27a), U3(31a), U3(34a), W1(a), W28(a).

Much valuable supplementary material for these periods is to be found in Section II, Categories A, C, G1 and 2, H and K.

Less Important: B22(a), B25(a), B41(a), D14(b), G9(a), H6(a), N18(a), R25(a), S29(a), W10(b), W28(e), W44(a).

Unpublished: Z54(a), Z56(a).

3. Causes

Important: B35(b), B41(b), D14(a), D18(j), F13(a), G21(a), G22(a), H16(a), H51(a), M42(a), N4(a), N18(a), P32(a), R29(a), S51(a), U3(12b), W1(a).

Less Important: B1(a), F15(a), G12(a), L2(a), M16(a), M39(b), P2(a), S31(a), W21(a).

Unpublished: Z56(a).

4. Results

Important: A20(a), B32(a), B33(b), D18(n), D26(a), F13(a), G1(a), G22(a), I5(a), J9(a), L12(a), S29(a), S51(a), U3(8a), W11(a), W44(a).

Less Important: C22(a), H6(b), H32(c), M20(a), S49(a), S50(a), S53(a), W28(d).

Unpublished: Z7(a).

C. 1900-1915

1. Inclusive Works

Important: B2(a), B9(a), J4(h), U3(11a), W13(a), W40(a), W40(c), W49(c).

2. Mechanics of the Movement

Important: B35(b), D15(a), D22(a), E14(a), H19(g), J18(a), J18(b), M19(a), N69(a), R25(b), S13(a), T28(a), T28(b), U3(31a), W7(a), W10(b), W10(c), W49(a), W49(k), W49(n).

Less Important: B39(b), C35(a), H6(c, f, h), H34(a), I7(a), J14(a), M39(c), M39(d), M39(o), N86(a), N99(a), U3(50a), W7(d), W8(a), W49(f), W49(g).

Unpublished: Z29(a), Z54(a), Z56(a).

3. Causes [2]

Important: A18(a), B35(b), B39(b), G20(a), H6(h), H19(c), H19(h), M39(c), S13(a), S51(a), S58(b), U3(47b).

Valuable material will also be found in Section II, Categories A, B, C, and

Less Important: B14(a), H6(c, g), K2(c), N7(a), N87(a), S2(a), W7(c), W8(a), W49(f), W49(g).

Unpublished: Z56(a).

4. Results

a. Results in Regions *from* Which Migrants Moved

Important: S17(f), W49(k).

b Results in Regions *to* Which Migrants Went

(1) General Summaries

Important: B30(a), B59(a), D2(a), D16(a), E14(a), H19(h), J9(a), J14(a), M17(a), M19(a), O6(a), S2(a), T28(b), U3(24a), U3(47a), U3(50a), W41(i), W49(d), W49(e), W49(f), W49(g), W49(k).

Less Important: E17(a), H19(c), M39(o).

Unpublished: Z26(a), Z27(a), Z42(a).

(2) Demographic Composition

Important: B33(a), M39(d), P7(a), W49(n).

Unpublished: Z21(a).

(3) Economic Conditions[3]

Important: B19(a), B55(a), C35(a), D2(b), D20(a), G20(a), M39(d), N12(a), N87(a), O6(c), P7(a), P13(b), S51(a), S62(a), T28(a), W7(b), W49(h), W49(i), W49(j), W49(l), W49(m), W49(n).

Unpublished: Z18(a), Z21(a), Z29(a), Z39(a).

(4) Housing, Rent and the Standard of Living

Important: A19(a), C28(a), D18(g), G8(a), H45-(a), M39(d), N94(b), O6(b), P13(b), W6(a), W49(h), W49(p).

(5) Health and Vital Statistics[4]

Important: G8(a), W49(a), W49(b).

[3] Supplementary material will be found in Section II, Categories A B D and E; and C4b(13) below

[4] See also Categories A and I of Section II

(6) Social Maladjustment, Including Crime, Juvenile Delinquency, Dependency, Suicide and Insanity [5]

Important: D18(m), H6(d), K1(a), P6(b), S44(a), W6(b), W49(o).

Unpublished: Z59(a).

(7) Recreation and Recreational Facilities

Unpublished: Z29(a), Z38(a), Z39(a).

(8) Activities of Social Agencies Concerned with the Negro

Important: W29(a), W49(o).

(9) Education and Educational Institutions [6]

Important: B26(a), O2(a), W33(a).

(10) Political Participation, Affiliation and Influence [7]

Important: A13(a), D18(a), E12(a), Q1(a).

(11) Religious Organizations and Their Activities

Unpublished: Z29(a).

(12) Interracial Relations, Particularly Violence, Discrimination and other Manifestations of Race Prejudice [8]

Important: B55(a), C16(a), N58(a), Q1(a), Q1(b), Q1(c), Q1(d), R3(a), S4(a), T26(a), W49(n).

(13) Relations with Foreign-Born Groups [9]

Important: C19(a), S58(a).

(14) Intra-racial Relations

Important: W29(a).

(15) Psychological Effects on the Migrants

Unpublished: Z38(a).

(16) The Negro Family

Important: D18(g), O6(b).

[5] See also Categories A and J of Section II

[6] See also Categories A and F of Section II

[7] See also Categories A and G1 of Section II

[8] See also Categories A and H of Section II; and C3 above, and C4b(13) below.

[9] See also C4b(3) and C4b(12) above

D. 1915 to Date

1. Inclusive Works

Important: C13(a), D13(a), D15(a), H19(o), J4(h), K10(a), M57(f), R16(a), S11(c), U3(11a), U3(30a), W10(b), W41(a), W41(b), W41(e).

Less Important: B3(a), B9(a), B35(a), H15(b), H19(j), K7(a), M35(a), N9(a), W25(a), W26(a), W40(a), W40(c), W44(d).

Unpublished: Z25(a), Z33(a).

2. Mechanics of the Movement

a. General Description of the Migration

Important: B35(b), B44(a), C11(a), D8(a), H10(e), H19(i), H28(b), J4(e), K3(a), M12(a), N50(a), T6(a), U3(42a).

Less Important: C18(a), H19(e), N20(a), N83(a), S13(a).

Unpublished: Z17(a), Z43(a), Z54(a), Z56(a), Z61(a).

b Sources of the Migration

Important: A1(a), B54(a), C3(b), C4(a), E33(a), F1(a), G4(a), J6(a), L5(a), L27(a), M56(a), P9(a), P13(a), R12(a).

c. Extent and Direction

Important: A4(a), B10(a), C3(b), C8(a), C17(a), C21(a), D18(f), E7(a), E29(a), F5(a), F25(a), G4(a), G11(a), J12(a), J16(f), K15(a), L21(a), M29(a), M33(a), M39(f), M45(b), M46(a), M55(a), M57(c), N69(a-d), N76(a), N92(a), P9(a), R5(a), R12(a), R12(e), R26(a), T10(a), T16(a), T27(a), U3(28a), W14(a), W14(c).

Less Important: B5(a), B24(a), D18(e), D22(a), D24(a), D27(a), E3(a), G25(a), H1(a), H2(a), H10(d), H29(b), H29(d), H29(e), H49(a), I6(a), J4(a), J4(r), K6(b), L16(a), L18(a), M13(a), M30(a), M34(a), M37(a), M39(n), M46(d), N8(h), N9(a), N19(a), N27(a), N35(a), N42(a), N44(a), N48(a), N49(a), N56(a), N57(a), P21(a), P24(a), R10(a), R12(g), R21(b), S32(a), S51(a), T21(a), U3(1c), W3(d), W44(i).

Unpublished: Z6(a), Z35(d), Z35(r), Z35(s), Z55(a), Z55(b).

d. Return Movement to the South[10]

Important: E7(a), H29(m), H53(a), K6(b), L21(a), L27(a), N48(a), R15(a).

e. Types of Migrants and of Migration[11]

Important: A1(a), H19(q), K12(b), M37(a), N38(a), T8(a), T10(c), U3(7a).

3. Causes

a. Inclusive Works

Important: B35(b), C11(a), D18(f), F14(a), G4(a), H19(n), H22(a), H26(a), H41(a), H50(a), I6(a), J4(e), J4(f), J4(j), J16(f), K3(a), K6(b), N69(a,c), R18(a), S13(a), W10(a), W13(a), W40(d), W41(g).

Less Important: A12(a), A14(a), A16(a), B1(a), B2(b), B17(a), B42(a), B45(a), B50(a), D8(a), D18(h), D27(a), E10(a), E15(a), E20(a), E26(a), E29(a), E31(a), E35(a), F10(a), F17(a), G17(a), H1(a), H19(d), H19(e), H19(q), H29(m), H39(a), J4(i), J8(a), K15(a), L11(a), L16(a), L25(a), M7(a), M22(a), M30(a), M36(a), M54(a), M57(a), M58(a), N5(a), N44(a), N46(a), N47(a), N49(a), N53(a), N59(a), N85(a), P21(a), R15(a), R21(b), S1(a), S5(a), S5(b), S12(a), S20(a), S21(b), S24(a), S25(a), S35(a), S35(b), T12(a), U3(19a), U3(42a), W3(c), W3(d), W24(a), W44(b).

Unpublished: Z6(a), Z17(a), Z36(a), Z43(a), Z52(a), Z56(a), Z61(a).

b Economic Factors[12]

Important: B34(a), D6(a), F1(a), G11(a), G20(a), H10(d), J4(a), J4(q), L21(a), S6(a), S21(a), S51(a), V1(a), W41(d), W41(k).

Less Important: B4(a), B5(a), B8(a), C17(a), E2(a), F5(a), J9(d), L20(a), M31(a), M57(b), N42(a), N45(a), N89(a), O3(a), R23(a), S11(b), S46(a), S47(a), T9(a), U3(1c), W3(a), W44(h), Y1(a).

[10] See also D4a(6) below.

[11] See also D4b(2) below.

[12] See also Categories A, B and C in Section II; and D4a(2) below.

c. Social Factors, Primarily Discrimination and Violence[13]
Important: G14(a), J2(a), L9(a), M13(a), M43(a), M57(e), S17(c), S27(a), U3(23b).
Unpublished: Z10(a).

d Socio-psychological Factors, Including Influence of Leaders, Letters from Migrants, Labor Agents and Agencies
Important: B5(a), B40(a), D10(a), G24(a), H5(a), H12(a), L19(a), M57(b), N8(a), S51(a), T30(a).

4. Results

a. Results in Regions *from* Which Migrants Moved

(1) General Summaries
Important: B45(a), D18(e), H19(d), I1(a), M57(c), R18(a), U3(7a), W40(d), W41(g).
Less Important: B2(b), E7(a), F10(a), H1(a), H19(q), H38(a), H52(a), J1(a), J8(a), K6(a), N53(a), S5(b), S21(a), S21(b), S24(a), S27(a), S39(a), T10(b), T12(a), T29(a), W44(b).

(2) Economic Conditions[14]
Important: A7(b), F5(a), G7(a), G11(a), H29(m), J12(a), L27(a), V1(a), W41(d), W41(k).
Less Important: B4(a), D11(a), E20(a), E26(a), E28(a), E29(a), E32(a), G17(a), K6(b), K8(a), L28(b), M27(a), M32(a), N85(a), S7(b), S52(a), T23(a), W23(a), W44(h).

(3) Social Conditions, Including Education, Health, Recreation and Living Conditions[15]
Important: B29(a), C9(a), F3(b), H3(a), P1(a), U3(23b), W34(a), W38(a).

(4) Effect of the Movement on Race Relations, Including Violence, Discrimination and Other Manifestations of Race Prejudice[16]

[13] See also Categories A, G1 and H in Section II; and D4a(4) and D4b(12) below

[14] See also Categories A B and C in Section II; and D3b above

[15] See also Section II, Categories A, F and I

[16] See also Section II, Categories A, G1 and H; and D3c above, and D4b(12) below

Important: A7(b), C25(a), E11(a), F4(b), J4(b), M43(a), M43(b), M44(a), O7(c), P33(a), R12(h), S17(f), W42(a).

Less Important: C26(a), E11(b), E20(a), E21(a), E21(b), H3(a), H29(l), H39(a), H40(a), J16(g), L32(a), M32(a), M39(l), N69(a), P34(a), S17(a), S42(a), T1(b), V2(a), W5(a), Y2(a).

Unpublished: Z14(a), Z23(a).

(5) Psychological Effects

Important: D1(b), H57(a).

(6) Southern Efforts to Retain and Recall[17]

Important: B4(a), G24(a), H29(m), H50(a), L11(a), L27(a), M27(a), M57(a), O3(a), P35(a), R23(a), S11(a), S40(a), S48(a), U3(26a), W2(a), W20(a), W27(a), W44(g).

b. Results in Regions *to* Which Migrants Went

(1) General Summaries

Important: A4(a), A9(a), B53(a), C3(b), C11(a), D3(a), D8(a), D22(a), E19(a), F4(b), F20(a), F21(b), F21(g), F21(i), H10(e), H19(l), H19(n), H26(a), H42(a), H55(a), J4(k), J6(a), J16(c), J16(e), J16(f), K3(a), L5(a), L18(a), M12(a), M46(a-c), M46(e), M55(a), M56(a), N8(h), P9(a), P17(a), R11(b), R12(a), R12(d), R12(e), R12(g), R18(a), R21(a), R21(b), R30(a), S37(a), S60(a), T10(a), U3(7a), W9(h), W14(a-d), W41(h).

Less Important: A12(a), B2(b), B5(a), B18(a), B23(a), B50(a), E7(a), E15(a), H2(a), H19(g), H19(q), H41(a), H52(a), J4(s), J8(a), J9(a), J16(g), K6(a), L16(a), L28(b), L30(a), M39(n), M48(a), M54(a), M57(b), M57(c), N39(a), N53(a), N57(a), N92(b), P6(a), P21(a), R19(a), S1(a), S5(b), S7(a), S21(b), S24(a), S27(a), T3(a), T10(b), T12(a), T29(a), W9(b), W36(a), W41(g), W44(e).

[17] See also D2d above.

Unpublished Z19(a), Z19(b), Z20(b), Z34(a), Z35(a), Z35(e), Z35(f), Z35(g), Z35(i), Z35(j), Z35(k), Z35(l), Z35(m), Z35(n), Z35(o), Z35(p), Z35(r), Z35(s), Z35(t), Z35(u), Z35(v), Z35(w), Z35(x), Z35(y), Z35(z), Z35(aa), Z37(b), Z41(a), Z51(a), Z57(a).

(2) Demographic Composition[18]

Important: J4(c), N84(a), T16(a).

(3) Economic Conditions[19]

(a) Inclusive Surveys and General Discussions of Economic Conditions

Important: B16(a), C18(b), C18(c), F6(a), G20(a), H1(a), H7(a), H18(b), H29(g), H29(k), I3(a), I4(a), J4(c), J4(d), J4(f), J4(m), J4(n), J16(d), M4(a), P8(a), P11(a), S51(a), U3(2a), U3(19a), U3(32a), U3(33a), W9(f), W13(a), W41(k).

Less Important: G13(a), H19(i), J9(b), S32(a), T16(a).

Unpublished: Z1(a), Z3(a), Z6(a), Z13(a), Z16(a), Z35(d), Z44(b).

(b) Nature of Occupations in Professions, Industry and Business

Important: A1(a), A6(a), B8(a), B52(a), C3(c), D24(a), D27(a), E25(a), F19(a), F21(j), F21(k), G4(a), G15(a), H18(a), H19(d), H28(b), H29(d), H29(e), H29(f), H29(i), H29(j), J4(o), J4(r), K13(a), N27(a), N84(a), P13(a), R5(a), S20(a), U3(20a), U3(40a), W41(c).

Less Important: C4(a), D23(a), E3(a), E18(a), F23(a), F24(a), G15(b), H25(a), H29(a), J9(d), L18(c), M32(a), M39(i), N24(a), N38(a), N74(a), N76(a), N98(a), S17(c), T21(a), W3(a), W9(c).

D2e above

Categories A, B, D and E in Section II; and D4b(13) below.

Unpublished: **Z**4(a), **Z**8(a), **Z**10(a), **Z**12(a), **Z**22(a), **Z**30(a), **Z**32(a), **Z**35(q), **Z**46(a), **Z**48(a), **Z**53(a).

(c) Unemployment

Important: A7(d), D1(a), D1(e), E25(a), H7(b), H12(a), H29(a), H29(b), H29(e), H29(i), H53(a), H54(a), K11(a), L18(c), M26(a), M41(a), N8(d), N8(i), N30(a), N79(a), N88(a), N91(a), R7(a), S10(a), U1(a), U2(a), W45(a).

Unpublished: Z35(c), **Z**35(bb), **Z**45(a).

(d) Achievement in Industry, Including Discussions of Reliability and Labor Turnover

Important: A1(a), C3(c), F2(a), F23(a), H39(a), H48(a), K14(a), M1(a), M3(a), M50(a), N72(a), N84(a), P31(a), S20(a), W3(a), W20(e), W41(c).

(e) Wages and Hours of Labor

Important: A6(a), H18(a), H29(f), K13(a), N84(a).

Unpublished: **Z**2(a).

(f) Relation to Labor Organizations, Including the Communist Movement [20]

Important: A7(c), A11(a), B28(a), C1(a), C6(a), C27(a), D1(c), D1(d), D18(e), D24(a), F22(a), H10(a), H10(b), H10(c), H10(f), H10(g), H19(d), H29(d), H29(e), H29(f), H29(j), H56(a), J4(l), J4(r), L29(a), M21(a), M51(a), N8(e), N34(a), N55(a), N56(a), N62(a), N70(a), N74(a), P10(a), P29(a), R7(b), R12(c), S17(c), T24(a), W41(c).

Unpublished: **Z**10(a).

(4) Housing, Rent and the Standard of Living

Important: B49(a), B49(b), B49(c), C30(a), D21(a),

[20] See also D4a(4) above, and D4b(12) below.

F4(a), J19(a), K15(a), M5(a), M11(a), M39(a), N8(c), N94(a), P14(a), P22(a), R14(a), U3(40a), W20(f), W43(a).

Less Important: B51(a), B58(a), E17(b), E34(a), G13(a), H1(a), H23(a), H43(a), H46(a), H47(a), J4(f), J16(a), L22(a), M40(a), M47(a), N22(a), N23(a), N24(a), N32(a), S9(a), S17(c), S55(a).

Unpublished: Z2(a), Z3(a), Z4(a), Z6(a), Z32(a), Z35(b), Z35(q), Z44(a).

(5) Health and Vital Statistics[21]

Important: A8(a), A8(b), B6(a), D17(a), D17(e), D17(j), G19(a), H11(a), H11(b), H21(a), H28(b), H35(a), H35(b), H36(a), K16(a), L3(a), L3(b), L4(a), M25(a), M25(b), M56(c), N82(a), N90(a), N92(c), N101(a), R22(a), S26(a), T16(a), T16(b), T19(a), U3(40a), U3(45a), U3(48a), W9(d), W18(a), W22(a), W28(b).

Less Important: B54(a), B57(a), D17(d), E16(a), F21(f), H20(a), J4(f), L28(a), M3(a), M14(a), N95(a), P26(a), U3(18a), U5(a), W17(a), W18(b), W30(a).

Unpublished: Z61(a).

(6) Social Maladjustment, Including Crime, Juvenile Delinquency, Dependency, Suicide and Insanity[22]

Important: B11(a), B27(a), B36(a), E23(a), F21(c), F21(f), I2(a), J15(a), L4(a), L28(a), M25(b), M59(a), N3(a), N13(a), N17(a), N80(a), N97(c), O7(d), P15(a), R11(a), R12(i), R24(a), S18(a), T13(a), U3(36a), W12(a), W37(a).

Unpublished: Z9(a), Z61(a).

(7) Recreation and Recreational Facilities[23]

Important: A21(a), J19(b), L8(a), L28(a), W9(e), W9(g).

Unpublished: Z11(a), Z31(a), Z32(a), Z61(a).

[21] See also Categories A and I in Section II

[22] See also Categories A and J in Section II

[23] See also D4a(3) above

(8) Activities of Social Agencies Concerned with the Negro

Important: A7(a), B38(a), B52(a), C18(a), E15(b), E23(a), F18(a), H29(h), H40(a), H54(b), J16(b), J16(j), J16(k), K11(a), L3(b), L13(a), L15(a), L18(b), M14(a), M14(b), M57(d), N8(b), N95(a), N97(a), N97(c), O7(a), O7(d), P36(a), S17(f), T20(a), U3(19a), W9(c), W41(j).

Less Important: B8(a), E6(a), E17(b), F16(a), H49(a), H53(a), K5(a), N1(a), N47(a), N51(a), N63(a), N64(a), N75(a), S23(a), S28(a), S32(a), S36(a), S56(a), T8(a), T10(c), U4(a), W17(a), W30(a), W48(a).

Unpublished: Z11(a), Z35(c), Z35(bb), Z45(a).

(9) Education and Educational Institutions [24]

Important: C32(a), E17(b), G16(a), J16(i), L11(b), M39(e), M39(g), M46(d), N11(a), P3(a), P5(a), P12(a), P16(a), R5(a), S14(a), S16(a), U3(18a), W33(a).

Unpublished: Z6(a), Z46(a), Z50(a), Z58(a).

(10) Political Participation, Affiliation and Influence [25]

Important: B56(a), B56(b), B56(c), B56(d), D18(k), J9(c), N60(a), N61(a), S17(e), W4(a), W4(b), W20(b).

(11) Religious Organizations and Their Activities

Important: C5(a), F21(f), G18(a), H19(a), H19(b), H39(b), K9(a), K9(b), L34(a), R5(a), R12(b), T18(a).

Unpublished: Z5(a), Z11(a), Z37(a).

(12) Interracial Relations, Particularly Violence, Discrimination and Other Manifestations of Race Prejudice [26]

Important: B46(a), B51(a), D1(c), D18(e), F4(b), F18(a), G10(a), H19(p), H40(a), J4(b), J4(f), J4(r), J16(g), K6(b), L15(a), M18(a), M39(m),

[24] See also Categories A and F in Section II; and D4a(3) above.

[25] See also Categories A and G1 in Section II; and D3c above.

[26] See also Categories A, G1 and H in Section II; and D3c, D4a(4) and D4b(3)(f) above, and D4b(13) below

N84(a), R4(a), R5(a), R12(h), S17(b), S51(a), U3(13a), U3(19a), W20(c), W20(f), Y2(a).

Less Important: A2(a), A5(a), B1(b), C7(a), E11(b), G2(a), H19(r), H29(c), H29(l), H47(a), J13(a), J16(a), L1(a), L22(a), M9(a), M32(a), M39(k), M39(l), N69(a), N75(a), N78(a), O5(a), R1(a), S10(b), S15(a), S17(a), S30(a), S57(a), T4(a), U6(a), W3(e), W16(a).

Unpublished: Z3(a), Z13(a), Z23(a).

(13) Relations with Foreign-born Groups[27]

Important: E18(a), G25(a), H19(i), H29(e), J4(a), J4(d), J4(q), J4(r), N10(a), S61(a), T5(a).

Unpublished: Z35(i).

(14) Intra-racial Relations

Important: B46(a), D18(e), F21(a), N69(a).

(15) Psychological Effects on the Migrants

Important: D18(l), F11(a), F21(k), H8(a), H15(a), H19(d), J4(c), L10(a), L24(a), M39(k), S51(a), T15(b).

(16) The Negro Family

Important: F21(a), F21(c), F21(d), F21(e), F21(f), F21(h), F21(l), G15(a), G15(b), M6(a).

Unpublished: Z24(a).

II. BACKGROUND MATERIAL

A. General Conditions

A10(a), A10(d), E24(a), H30(a), J4(p), L24(b), N69(a-d), R16(a), S58(d), T1(a), T15(a), U3(31a), W10(c) W40(d), W41(a).

B. General Economic Conditions[1]

B43(a), B47(a), D1(a), D18(c), D18(d), H31(a), K2(a), U3(17a).

[27] See also D4b(3) and D4b(12) above.

[1] See also C3, C4b(3), D3b, D4a(2) and D4b(3) of Section I.

C. Agricultural Situation [2]

B7(a), B13(a), B20(a), B21(a), B34(a), B39(a), B47(a), E9(a), E22(a), G6(a), H4(a), H31(a), K2(b), M38(a), S58(c), U3(1a), U3(5a), U3(15a), U3(21a), U3(43a).

D. Occupations [3]

A10(b), B43(a), D20(a), N8(f), N8(g), P20(a), U3(20a).

E. Business Enterprises [3]

H9(a), H37(a), H37(b), H37(c), L23(a), N6(a), W3(b), W40(b).

F. Education and Educational Institutions [4]

A17(a), B12(a), B47(a), C31(a), C31(b), D19(a), F3(a), F3(c), F3(d), J11(a), J17(a), M15(a), M39(j), N14(a), N15(a), N16(a), N93(a), N93(b), N96(a), O2(c), P30(a), S33(a), S33(b), S41(a), S54(a), T7(a), U3(4a), U3(23a), U3(41a), U3(46a).

G. Political Situation

1. General Political, Including Disfranchisement and Legal Status [5]

   C2(a), H13(a), J7(a), J9(e), J10(a), K4(a), M49(a), M53(a), N2(a), N100(a), P27(a), S34(a), S54(b), T17(a).

2. The Reconstruction Period, Emphasizing Political Conditions [6]

   C20(a), C29(a), C33(a), D4(a), D7(a), D25(a), E1(a), F8(a), F9(a), F12(a), F12(b), G3(a), H33(a), J5(a), L7(a), L14(a), L26(a), L31(a), M52(a), M53(a), R6(a), R17(a), R28(a), T14(a).

H. Discrimination and Violence, Particularly Lynching [7]

C25(b), C36(a), H14(a), L33(a), N2(a), P19(a), R20(a), S8(a), S10(c), W20(d).

See all subdivisions of Periods A and B, and also C3, D3b and D4a(2) of Section I

[3] See also C4b(3) and D4b(3) of Section I.

[4] See also C4b(9), D4a(3) and D4b(9) of Section I.

[5] See all subdivisions of Periods A and B, and also C3, C4b(10), D3(c), D4a(4), D4b(10) and D4b(12) of Section I

See also Periods A and B, all subdivisions, Section I.

[7] See all subdivisions of Periods A and B, and also C4b(12), D3c, D4a(4) and D4b(12) of Section I

I. Health[8]

D17(c), D17(d), D17(g), D17(h), H32(a), H36(a), J4(g), T25(a), U3(3a), U3(16a), U3(45a), U3(49a).

J Social Maladjustment[9]

C3(a), K1(b), N97(b), O2(c), S54(a), W31(a), W44(c). Unpublished: Z60(a).

K. Contemporary Discussions of the Status of the Negro[10]

B48(a), H17(a), M8(a), P4(a), T11(a), T22(a).

L. Race Traits and Amalgamation

F7(a), H27(a), K12(a), K12(b), R16(b).

M. Miscellaneous Social Conditions

D18(g), E13(a), N2(a), W11(a).

[8] See also C4b(5), D4a(3) and D4b(5) of Section I.

[9] See also C4b(6) and D4b(6) of Section I

[10] See also Periods A and B, all subdivisions, Section I

Part E

GEOGRAPHICAL CLASSIFICATION OF PARTS A AND B

Part E

GEOGRAPHICAL CLASSIFICATION OF PARTS A AND B

General and by States and by Localities

As its title implies, this section is a geographical arrangement of the materials listed in Parts A and B, cutting across the categories of Part D. It includes only those items that have definite geographical significance. The code symbols refer (as in Part D) to the items of Parts A and B.

The first class comprises works containing material either for the country as a whole or for so many specific states and localities as to make listing under the several states and localities too redundant. The next order of classes covers states. The area, New England, is treated as a state, as is Washington, D.C. Subordinate under each state are categories for localities, *i.e.*, cities, counties and plantations or similar units. The entries under these subordinate local classes do not include works that deal with several other localities in the same state. Such are listed under State Generally.

An example (see introduction to Part D) will aid the reader. Mr. D., interested in "The Negro in Steel," will find it to his advantage to search the list under Pittsburgh, Pennsylvania; Gary, Indiana; and Birmingham, Alabama. In addition to these local categories, he should look under State Generally under Pennsylvania, Indiana and Alabama. Finally, he should search the items of Geographical Classification, General.

It should be noted that some of the most valuable material from a geographic point of view is to be found in the unpublished material.

1. Geographical Classification, General

A20(a), B2(a), B36(a), B41(b), B56(a), B56(c), C3(a), C25(b), D18(m), D19(a), D20(a), D22(a), F3(c), F3(d), F4(a), F4(b), F21(j), G1(a), G1(b), G19(a), G20(a), H29(f), H32(b), I4(a), J4(h), J7(a), J16(k), K3(a), K11(a), L13(a), M29(a), N8(d), N8(e), N8(f), N8(g), N8(i), N9(a), P3(a), P5(a), R14(a), S11(c), S51(a), S54(b), T10(b), T17(a), U3(2a), U3(3a), U3(4a), U3(8a), U3(11a), U3(14a), U3(16a), U3(17a), U3(19a), U3(20a), U3(23a), U3(27a), U3(28a), U3(30a),

U3(31a), U3(33a), U3(34a), U3(36a), U3(38a), U3(41a), U3(42a), U3(44a), U3(45a), U3(46a), U3(48a), U3(49a), W9(b), W9(g), W13(a), W36(a), W40(d), W41(h) W41(k).
Unpublished: Z31 (a), Z35(c), Z35(bb), Z55(a), Z55(b), Z60(a).

By States and by Localities

2. ALABAMA

a. State Generally
A10(b), B12(a), C26(a), F12(a), H26(a), U3(12a).

b. Birmingham
E33(a), K5(a), S48(a).
Unpublished: Z46(a).

c. Montgomery
H37(a).

3. ARKANSAS

a. State Generally
A17(a), C20(a), W20(a).

b Little Rock
Unpublished: Z50(a).

4. CALIFORNIA

a. State Generally
T5(a).

b. Imperial Valley
B31(a).

c. Los Angeles
J4(m).
Unpublished: Z35(d), Z61(a).

5. COLORADO

a. State Generally (none)

b Denver
J16(c), R12(e), R12(f).
Unpublished: Z35(b).

6. CONNECTICUT

a. State Generally (none)

b. Hartford
Unpublished: Z35(k).

c. New Haven
A19(a), B59(a), W48(a).
Unpublished: Z27(a).

d. Norwalk
Unpublished: Z35(n).

e. Stamford
Unpublished: Z51(a).

f Waterbury
J4(k).
Unpublished: Z35(m).

7. DELAWARE

a. State Generally
C32(a), W4(b).

8. FLORIDA

a. State Generally
D7(a).

b Jacksonville
K10(a).
Unpublished: Z24(a).

9. GEORGIA

a. State Generally
B7(a), B39(a), B39(b), B45(a), C9(a), D18(d), D18(m), E29(a), F1(a), G7(a), G14(a), G17(a), H14(a), L14(a), N14(a), N49(a), S6(a), T14(a), U3(12a), U3(12b), W38(a), W41(e).

b. Athens
W41(i).

c. Atlanta
A7(a), P33(a).

d. Clarke County
H30(a), J11(a), L25(a).

e. Gainesville
R11(b).

f. Oglethorpe
G6(a).

g. Savannah
K10(a).

10. ILLINOIS

a. State Generally
M59(a), N55(a).

b. Brooklyn
W49(e).

c. Chicago
B8(a), B18(a), B30(a), B56(b), B56(d), B57(a), B58(a), C11(a), C28(a), D16(a), D21(a), E12(a), E25(a), F18(a), F21(b), F21(c), F21(g), G13(a), G15(a), G15(b), H6(a), H11(a), H11(b), H42(a), H55(a), J4(c), K9(a), K9(b), M5(a), M47(a), N32(a), P12(a), S1(a), S15(a), S55(a), T4(a), W4(a), W4(b), W9(f), W29(a), W37(a), W44(a), W49(f), W49(i).
Unpublished: Z45(a).

d. East St. Louis
L15(a), R1(a), U3(13a).

e. Springfield
Unpublished: Z35(x).

INDIANA

a. State Generally
A15(c), W49(k).

b. Fort Wayne
Unpublished: Z35(s).

c. Gary
S15(a).

d. Indianapolis
P17(a).

12. IOWA

a. State Generally
S8(a).

b Buxton
W49(e).

13. KANSAS

a. State Generally
A15(c), F13(a), G22(a), M42(a).

KENTUCKY

a. State Generally
C29(a), C33(a), J5(a).

b. Louisville
H29(l), H53(a), N61(a).

LOUISIANA

a. State Generally
A15(c), F3(a), F9(a), L26(a), L27(a), W20(a).

b. Cinclaire Factory and Calumet Plantation
U3(24a).

16. MARYLAND

a. State Generally
B32(a), M18(a), M59(a), N58(a), U3(7a), W4(b).

b. Baltimore
B6(a), B32(a), H23(a), J4(n), N23(a), N58(a), P6(b), S29(a), U3(40a), W6(a).
Unpublished: **Z**1(a).

c. Sandy Spring
U3(47b).

17. MASSACHUSETTS

a. State Generally
M19(a), N80(a).

b Boston
D2(a), D2(b), K10(a), K13(a), R19(a).

c. Springfield
S37(a).

d Worcester
J16(c).
Unpublished: Z35(z).

18. MICHIGAN

a. State Generally
B1(b), L18(a), L18(b).

b. Calvin
W49(e).

Detroit
D8(a), D9(a), D23(a), H19(n), H29(a), J4(c), L15(a), L22(a), R5(a), S36(a), W9(e), W9(f), W20(f).

d. Grand Rapids
J16(c), M55(a).
Unpublished: Z35(t).

19. MINNESOTA

a. State Generally (none)

b Minneapolis
B27(a), H10(e).

St. Paul
R30(a).

20. MISSISSIPPI

a. State Generally
A15(e), G3(a), H38(a), L31(a), M44(a), N15(a), N96(a), U3(5a), W1(a), W20(a).

b Coahoma County
F3(b).

21. MISSOURI

a. State Generally
M45(a), M45(b), M46(a-e), W33(a).

b. Columbia
E14(a).

c. Kansas City
C30(a), M17(a), N22(a), W4(b).

d St. Louis
B33(b), B51(a), B52(a), C35(a), E23(a), S56(a), U6(a), W4(b), W18(a).

22. NEBRASKA

a. State Generally (none)

b Omaha
S60(a).

23. NEW ENGLAND

a. Region Generally
M39(a), N76(a).

24. NEW JERSEY

a. State Generally
F20(a), G16(a), M59(a), N86(a), N87(a), P6(a), P13(b), S4(a), W49(d).
Unpublished: Z35(o).

b Elizabeth
Unpublished: Z35 (j).

c. Morristown
Unpublished: Z35 (u).

d. Newark
P36(a), W9(f).

e. Paterson
Unpublished: Z4(a).

f Plainfield
Unpublished: Z35(w).

g. Princeton
Unpublished: Z57(a).

h. Toms River
S16(a).

i. Trenton
Unpublished: Z35(y).

NEW YORK

a. State Generally
J16(f), N3(a), N75(a).

b. Albany
A4(a), J16(c), R12(a).
Unpublished: Z35(g).

c. Buffalo
B53(a), B54(a), C3(b), C4(a), H43(a), N24(a), N63(a), N91(a).
Unpublished: Z35(e).

d. Nassau and Suffolk Counties
Unpublished: Z35(v).

e. New York City
B5(a), B19(a), B24(a), B26(a), B38(a), B49(a), B49(b), B49(c), B55(a), C16(a), C27(a), D18(n), E6(a), E15(a), E15(b), F11(a), F19(a), F21(i), G18(a), H8(a), H19(b), H19(h), H20(a), H21(a), H54(a), J4(c), J9(a), J9(d), J15(a), K10(a), K12(b), L4(a), L28(a), N8(c), N11(a), N82(a), N84(a), N90(a), N92(a), N92(b), N92(c), O6(a), O6(b), O6(c), P12(a), P29(a), R11(a), R12(b), R12(d), S30(a), S50(a), T26(a), T28(a), W4(b), W9(h), W16(a), W17(a).
Unpublished: Z2(a), Z7(a), Z10(a), Z12(a), Z13(a), Z15(a), Z16(a), Z19(b), Z20(b), Z21(a), Z23(a), Z26(a), Z29(a), Z30(a), Z32(a), Z35(f), Z37(a), Z37(b), Z38(a), Z39(a), Z44(a), Z48(a), Z59(a).

f. Troy
Unpublished: Z35(aa).

g. Westchester County
Unpublished: Z34(a).

h. White Plains
Unpublished: Z35(q).

NORTH CAROLINA

a. State Generally
A10(b), C31(a), C31(b), F5(a), G24(a), H31(a), N16(a),

N93(b), N97(a), N97(b), N97(c), O7(a), O7(c), O7(d), W30(a).
Unpublished: Z23(a).

b. Cleveland County
D4(a).

c. New Hanover County
R28(a).

d. Wilmington
R28(a).

e. Winston-Salem
H37(a).

27. OHIO

a. State Generally
J14(a), M59(a), Q1 (a).

b Cincinnati
A8(a), A8(b), B16(a), H29(1), H43(a), L11(b), M14(a), M14(b), Q1(b), R21(a), R21(b), S9(a), S14(a).
Unpublished: Z3(a), Z9(a).

c. Cleveland
A1(b), C21(a), I2(a), P16(a), Q1(c), R22(a), U3(18a), W12(a).
Unpublished: Z6(a).

d. Columbus
A9(a), M12(a), N17(a), S57(a).

e. Dayton
H29(c).

f Middletown
W41(j).

g. Springfield
R3(a).

h. Syracuse
Q1(d).

i. Toledo
J6(a), T21 (a).
Unpublished: Z35(p).

j Warren
Unpublished: Z35(l).

k Xenia
U3(50a).

28. OKLAHOMA

a. State Generally
B29(a).

b Tulsa
J16(c), T10(a).
Unpublished: Z35(a).

29. PENNSYLVANIA

a. State Generally
E18(a), F23(a), I3(a), N94(a), P7(a), P9(a), P11(a), P13(b), R12(i), R24(a), W49(g).
Unpublished: Z35(o).

b. Carlisle
L12(a).

c. Johnstown
J13(a), N78(a).

d. Philadelphia
D18(a), D18(i), E17(a), E17(b), K10(a), L3(b), L30(a), M11(a), M37(a), M56(a), M56(c), N51(a), N94(b), O2(a), P7(a), P8(a), P13(a), P14(a), P15(a), T6(a), T13(a), T18(a), W20(c), W22(a), W43(a), W49(b).

e. Pittsburgh
C18(a), E19(a), F16(a), H29(a), L18(c), N64(a), P7(a), P21(a), P22(a), R12(g), T28(b), T28(c), W49(n).
Unpublished: Z5(a), Z8(a), Z11(a), Z19(a), Z44(b).

30. RHODE ISLAND

a. State Generally (none)

b. Newport
Unpublished: Z42(a).

31. SOUTH CAROLINA

a. State Generally
A15(d), H33(a), N19(a), P4(a), R17(a), S41(a), T2(a).
Unpublished: Z17(a).

b. Charleston
K10(a).

c. Greenville
A21(a), P1(a).
Unpublished: Z58(a).

d. St. Helena Island
K10(a), W41(b).

32. TENNESSEE

a. State Generally
A10(b), F8(a), M43(b), M52(a), S26(a).

b. Knoxville
D3(a), S2(a).

c. Memphis
A21(a).

d. Nashville
C7(a), J4(o), P12(a).

33. TEXAS

a. State Generally
M15(a), P19(a), R6(a), T5(a), T7(a), W2(a).

b. Austin
Unpublished: Z35(i).

c. Houston
N8(h).

34. VIRGINIA

a. State Generally
A10(b), B20(a), B47(a), B48(a), D1(b), E1(a), E13(a), F5(a), G4(a), M2(a), M53(a), P20(a), S7(b), T2(b).
Unpublished: Z39(a).

b. Albemarle County
B20(a), I6(a).

c. Charlottesville
I6(a), K15(a).

d. Farmville
U3(12c).

e. Fredericksburg
F7(a).

f Litwalton
U3(47a).

g. Lynchburg
A18(a), C13(a), K15(a).

h. Newport News
F7(a).

i. Richmond
A15(a), A21(a), F7(a), H29(l), K15(a), R18(a), S23(a).
Unpublished: Z38(a).

J. Southampton
U3(43a).

35. WASHINGTON D C

a. District and City
D12(a), I5(a), J19(a), J19(b), O5(a), R4(a), S17(b), S22(a), W35(a).

36. WEST VIRGINIA

a. State Generally
H10(b), N56(a), P30(a), W14(a-d).

37. WISCONSIN

a. State Generally (none)

b Milwaukee
Unpublished: Z35(r).

LATE LIST

1. "Chicago Election," *Opportunity*, V, 127-28 (May, 1927).
2. Daniel, Robert P.
   Psychological Study of Delinquent and Non-delinquent Negro Boys. New York, Columbia University, Teachers College (1932), 59 pp. Teachers College Contributions to Education No. 546.
3. Edwards, Paul K.
   The Southern Urban Negro as a Consumer. New York, Prentice-Hall, Inc. (1932), 323 pp.
4. Embree, Edwin R.
   Brown America, the Story of a New Race. New York, The Viking Press (1931), 311 pp.
5. Frazier, E. Franklin
   The Negro Family in Chicago. Chicago, University of Chicago Press (1932), 294 pp.
6. Garvin, Charles H.
   "Negro Health," *Opportunity*, II, 341-42 (November, 1924).
7. Gillard, John T
   The Catholic Church and the American Negro. Baltimore, St. Joseph's Society Press (1929), 324 pp.
8. Gray, Gladys Carrion
   "A Social Worker Looks at St. Louis," *Opportunity*, V, 112-13 (April, 1927).
9. Herbst, Alma
   The Negro in the Slaughtering and Meat-Packing Industry in Chicago. New York, Houghton Mifflin Co. (1932), 182 pp.
10. Hill, T. Arnold
    "Economic Status of the Negro," *Opportunity*, XI, 185 (June, 1933).
11. Hill, T. Arnold
    "Migration Again," *Opportunity*, X, 255 (August, 1932).

LATE LIST

12. Hoffman, Frederick L.
"Present Day Trends of the Negro Population," *Opportunity*, IX 332-36 (November, 1931).

13. "Housing for Negro Wage Earners: An Experiment," *Opportunity*, I, 208-10 (July, 1923).

Johnson, Charles S.
"The New Frontier of Negro Labor," *Opportunity*, X, 168-73 (June, 1932).

15. Jones, Eugene Kinckle
"Interracial Frontiers," *Opportunity*, IX, 75-78 (March, 1931).

16. Jones, Eugene Kinckle
"The Negro's Struggle for Health," *Opportunity*, I, 4-8 (June, 1923).

17. Kelly, William V
"Where St. Louis Negroes Work" *Opportunity*, V, 116 (April, 1927).

18. Kerns, J. H.
"Social Service Needs in the North," *Opportunity*, V, 176 (June, 1927).

19. LeCount, Louis K.
"Party Affiliation in Negro Harlem" *Opportunity*, XI, 116-19 (April, 1933).

20. Lewinson, Paul
Race, Class, and Party: A History of Negro Suffrage and White Politics in the South. London and New York, Ox ord University Press (1932), 302 pp.

21. Lewis, Edward E.
"Economic Factors in Negro Migration," *American Statistical Association Journal*, XXVII, 45-53 (March, 1932).

22. Lewis, Edward E.
"Southern Negro and the American Labor Supply," *Political Science Quarterly*, XLVIII, 172-83 June, 1933).

23. Lovejoy, Owen R.
The Negro Children of New York. New York, Children's Aid Society (1932), 49 pp.

24. Mays, Benjamin E., and Joseph W. Nicholson
The Negro's Church. New York, Institute of Social and Religious Research (1933), 321 pp.

25. Myers, Beatrice A., and Ira de A. Reid
"The Toll of Tuberculosis among Negroes in New Jersey," *Opportunity*, X, 279-82 (September, 1932).

26. Neff, Lawrence W.
Race Relations at Close Range. Emory University, Georgia, Banner Press (1931), 35 pp.

27. "Negro Mortality in Baltimore," *Opportunity*, IV, 303-4 (October, 1926).

28. New Jersey Conference of Social Work, Interracial Committee, and New Jersey Department of Institutions and Agencies
New Jersey's Twentieth Citizen, the Negro. Bordentown, New Jersey Manual Training School for Colored Youth (1932), 18 pp.

29. New Jersey Conference of Social Work, Interracial Committee, and New Jersey Department of Institutions and Agencies
Survey of Negro Life in New Jersey. New Jersey Conference of Social Work (1932), 3 vols., mimeographed.

30. Nowlin, William F.
The Negro in American National Politics. Boston, The Stratford Co. (1931), 148 pp.

31. Peake, C. L.
"Negro Workers in Buffalo," *Opportunity*, II, 240-41 (August, 1924).

32. Reid, Ira de A.
"Some Aspects of the Negro Community," *Opportunity*, X, 18-20 (January, 1932).

33. Rhoades, Lillian
"One of the Groups Middletown Left Out," *Opportunity*, XI 75-77 (March, 1933).

34. Rutledge, Archibald
"The Negro in the North," *South Atlantic Quarterly*, XXXI, 61-69 (1932).

35. United States. President's Conference on Home Building and Home Ownership

Negro Housing: Report prepared by C. S Johnson and edited by J. M. Gries and James Ford. Government Printing Office, Final Reports, Vol. VI (1932).

36. Webster, Thomas A.
"The Negro in Wilmington, Delaware," *Opportunity*, X, 49-52 (February, 1932).

37. Willits, Joseph H.
"Some Impacts of the Depression upon the Negro in Philadelphia," *Opportunity*, XI, 200-4 (July, 1933).

38. Winston, S
"Migration and Distribution of Negro Leaders in the United States," *Social Forces*, X, 243-55 (December, 1931).

39. Young, Donald R.
America's Minority Peoples: A Study in Racial and Cultural Conflicts in the United States. New York, Harper and Brothers (1932), 621 pp.

40. Young Men's Christian Association, Graduate School
Survey of the Negro Boy in Nashville, Tennessee. Edited by W. D. Weatherford and directed by J. P. McConnell and others. New York, Association Press (1932), 157 pp.

INDEX

The numbers in the Index refer to pages, not to symbols.

www.ingramcontent.com/pod-product-compliance
Lightning Source LLC
Chambersburg PA
CBHW040140270326
41928CB00022B/3269

* 9 7 8 1 6 3 9 2 3 7 9 0 6 *